The Editors   At the University of Mississippi Doreen
Fowler is a professor of English, and Ann J. Abadie
is Associate Director of the Center for the Study of
Southern Culture.

Faulkner and Religion

FAULKNER AND YOKNAPATAWPHA

1989

Faulkner and Religion

FAULKNER AND YOKNAPATAWPHA, 1989

EDITED BY
DOREEN FOWLER
AND
ANN J. ABADIE

UNIVERSITY PRESS OF MISSISSIPPI
Jackson and London

94 93 92 91   4 3 2 1

The paper in this book meets the guidelines for permanence and durability
of the Committee on Production Guidelines for Book Longevity of the Council
on Library Resources.

Library of Congress Cataloging-in-Publication Data

Faulkner and religion : Faulkner and Yoknapatawpha, 1989 / edited by
    Doreen Fowler and Ann J. Abadie.
        p.   cm.
    Includes index.
    ISBN 0-87805-509-6 (alk. paper)
    1. Faulkner, William, 1897-1962—Religion—Congresses.
    2. Religion in literature—Congresses.   I. Fowler, Doreen.
    II. Abadie, Ann J.
PS3511.A86Z78321126   1991
813'.52—dc20   91-17626
                                                                CIP

British Library Cataloging-in-Publication data available

IN MEMORIAM,
Sister Thea Bowman
1937-1990

Contents

Introduction

Does a coherent system of religious values and thought inform Faulkner's novels? An answer, especially an affirmative one, is not immediately apparent. In fact, in Faulkner's fiction the very existence of God sometimes seems doubtful. What is never doubted, however, is humankind's consuming yearning for God. And perhaps this may be the key to religious meaning in Faulkner, that his texts focus not so much on God, but on a human aspiration to the divine. This aspiration is possibly nowhere more poignantly evoked than at the close of Faulkner's first novel, *Soldiers' Pay,* as two white men stand outside a Negro church listening to the voices of black men and women, singing. This "crooning," the "submerged passion of the dark race," which "swell[s] to an ecstasy," expresses "all the longing of mankind for a Oneness with Something, Somewhere." Of this longing Faulkner writes, "It was nothing, it was everything" (221).[1]

Throughout his fictional career, Faulkner relentlessly explores this human quest for God, and finds that sometimes, most notably in the Easter service in *The Sound and the Fury,* this quest elevates and transforms human beings: "And the congregation seemed to watch with its eyes while the voice consumed him, until he was nothing and they were nothing and there was not even a voice but instead their hearts were speaking to one another in chanting measures beyond the need for words" (367). But Faulkner's novels also expose a darker side to mankind's immortal longings. In *Light in August,* for example, the human desire to exalt the spirit often incites men and women to deny the flesh, to crucify one another and themselves in the name of spiritual transcendence. Thus, the Reverend Hightower listens in the gathering dark as the organ strains of the Protestant church service drift toward him, and he thinks: "even . . . the music has . . . a quality stern and implacable, pleading, asking, for not love, not life, forbidding it to others, demanding in sonorous tones death as though death were the boon, like all Protestant music" (347).

In Faulkner's later fiction, the search for God seems to take an inward turn. For example, in his 1954 novel, *A Fable*, which, with its extended parallel to the life of Christ, seems of all Faulkner's novels most directly to address the subject of religion, a black minister professes to bear witness not so much to God as to mankind: "God dont need me. I bear witness to Him of course, but my main witness is to man" (180). Ultimately, then, Faulkner seems to advocate that religion should be human- rather than God-centered, that religion should serve humanity.

These and other religious issues in Faulkner's fiction are explored in the essays in this volume which were originally presented by Faulkner scholars at the 1989 Faulkner and Yoknapatawpha Conference, the sixteenth in a series of conferences held on the Oxford campus of the University of Mississippi.

The volume opens with two essays that attempt to place Faulkner within the religious culture of the South. In "William Faulkner and Religion: Determinism, Compassion, and the God of Defeat," Alfred Kazin argues that the loss of the Civil War was for Southerners a religious crisis and that Faulkner, who was raised in a period of regional and familial decline, writes out of a deep sense of failure, guilt, and dark determinism, qualities that contrast starkly with the competitive, unforgiving religious heritage of the nation as whole. "America's religion," writes Kazin, "is success." Like Kazin, Charles Wilson also maintains that the Civil War took on religious significance for Southerners and that a Southern civil religion, a form of ancestor worship, flourished in the South especially in the years from 1890 to 1920, Faulkner's formative years. Wilson points to the Reverend Gail Hightower in *Light in August*, who makes a religion of a legend about his Confederate grandfather, as a fictional representation of this Southern civil religion.

A son of the South, Faulkner was undeniably influenced not only by the South's heritage of defeat, but also by the South's predominantly Christian culture. Faulkner himself acknowledged this religious background, maintaining that while he had never accepted as true the dogmas of any particular Christian sect, having grown up in what Mencken labelled "the Bible Belt," he had unconsciously absorbed a Judaeo-Christian tradition: "My life was passed, my childhood, in a very small Mississippi town, and that was part of my background. I grew up with that. I assimilated that, took that in without even knowing it. It's just there. It has nothing to do with how much of it I might believe or disbelieve—it's just there."[2] Several essayists attempt to examine the various ways in which this cultural/religious heritage is inscribed in Faulkner's texts. For example, citing David Reynolds's study of nineteenth-century Christian narratives, Giles Gunn attempts to place Faulkner within this tradition and finds that, like this writing, Faulkner's religious imagination is most brought into play in response to questions about the family as a source of spiritual renewal. However, Gunn questions whether Faulkner, like these religious writers, idealizes the Christian virtues of self-abnegation and acceptance which, as Gunn points out, have been used to maintain a social system predicated on racial inequality. While Gunn examines the inscription of Christian humility in *The Sound and the Fury*, Richard King seeks to identify in Faulkner's works another strain of Christianity—world-rejection. Drawing on Peter Brown's study, *The Body and Society: Men, Women, and Sexual Renunciation in Early Christianity*, which explores an inclination in early Christianity toward a rejection of the material world and material existence, King traces this Christian impulse to a number of Faulknerian couples, among them, Joe Christmas and Joanna Burden and Charlotte Rittenmeyer and Harry Wilbourne, who manifest a desire to crucify the flesh.

Other essayists who consider how a Christian frame of reference informs Faulkner's fiction include William Lindsey, Glenn Meeter, and Virginia Hlavsa. Lindsey, for example, focuses on Faulkner's use in *Absalom, Absalom!* of a central myth of the Judaeo-Christian tradition, the creation myth. According to Lindsey, Faulkner parallels the Sutpen story with the Genesis account to expose and to explain the failure of Sutpen's design: Sutpen fails to create order because he is blind to his own complicity in the disorder and irrationality he seeks to eradicate. Also examining *Absalom, Absalom!* in relation to the Bible, Glenn Meeter makes a convincing case for a Biblical analogy for the telling of the Sutpen story. More specifically, the Sutpen story is pieced together, told and retold, interpreted and reinterpreted, expanded and condensed in the same way that, according to modern Biblical scholarship, the Bible was transmitted. The relationship between Faulkner's texts and Sacred Scripture also figures importantly in Virginia Hlavsa's paper. In "The Crucifixion in *Light in August:* Suspending Rules at the Post," Hlavsa attempts to demonstrate that the nineteenth chapter of *Light in August*, which recounts the death and castration of Joe Christmas, thematically and verbally echoes John 19, which relates the crucifixion of Christ. In addition, according to Hlavsa, Faulkner expands on this counterpoint with material from Frazer's *The Golden Bough*, a work that describes primitive rituals, in particular the ritual slaying of the priest-king.

In her comparison of Frazer and Faulkner, Hlavsa introduces a new consideration in a discussion of Faulkner and religion—that Faulkner's fictional creations are influenced not only by Christian thought but also by an older primitive cosmogony. This topic is pursued by Doreen Fowler, who maintains that Faulkner informs his narratives with the myth of Demeter and Persephone, a more recent incarnation of an older pagan fertility rite that deifies nature's cycle of death and rebirth. Central to Faulkner's fiction, Fowler continues, is a tension between primitive and modern religious thinking, between a god in nature and a god that transcends nature, between a regenerative mother-goddess and an almighty father-god.

After considering the influences of Southern history, Christianity, and primitive cosmogony on Faulkner's encoding of religion in his novels, the volume closes with a discussion of the relationship between art and religion. Above all, Faulkner was an artist, a creator, who claimed he could move his characters around in time and space "like God."[3] Did Faulkner, like the Romantics, conceive of the artist as divinely inspired? Evans Harrington and Alexander Marshall propose that, for Faulkner, art, like religion, is a form of spiritual transcendence. In "'A Passion Week of the Heart': Religion and Faulkner's Art," Evans Harrington examines a definition of genius which appears in Faulkner's second novel and which seems to link artistic expression to a beatific vision. In *Mosquitoes* an artist, Dawson Fairchild, exclaims, "That's what it is. Genius. It's that Passion Week of the heart, that instant of timeless beatitude which some never know, . . . that passive state of the heart with which the mind, the brain, has nothing to do at all, in which the hackneyed accidents which make up this world—love and life and death and sex and sorrow—brought together by chance in perfect proportions, take on a kind of splendid and timeless beauty" (339). Citing Bergson's theory that mankind continues God's initial creation by responding to the vital impulse and creating new works, Harrington concludes that Faulkner saw himself, as artist, as possessed of visions of the ineffable. Alexander Marshall's essay, "The Dream Deferred: William Faulkner's Metaphysics of Absence," begins where Harrington leaves off. While agreeing that Faulkner was possessed of a vision of perfection, Marshall adds that Faulkner was always frustrated by the limitations of language adequately to signify that dream. The writer, Faulkner said, was "doomed" to use words, "about the damndest clumsiest frailest awkwardest tool he could have been given."[4] All his career, Faulkner kept "trying to say," trying to overcome the limitations of verbal discourse, trying to make the signifier, words, realize the "eternal verities" that existed in the silence of Faulkner's creative imagination.

Doreen Fowler
The University of Mississippi
Oxford, Mississippi

NOTES

1. I cite from the following editions of Faulkner's texts: *Soldiers' Pay* (New York: New American Library, 1968); *Mosquitoes* (New York: Liveright, 1927); *The Sound and the Fury* (New York: Vintage, 1956); *A Fable* (New York: Modern Library, 1966).

2. Malcolm Cowley, ed., *Writers at Work: The Paris Review Interviews* (New York: Viking, 1958), 136.

3. "William Faulkner: An Interview," in *William Faulkner: Three Decades of Criticism*, ed. Frederick J. Hoffman and Olga Vickery (New York: Harcourt, Brace, 1963), 82.

4. Joseph Blotner, *Faulkner: A Biography*, 1-vol. ed. (New York: Random House, 1984), 1305.

A Note on the Conference

The Sixteenth Annual Faulkner and Yoknapatawpha Conference sponsored by the University of Mississippi in Oxford took place from July 30 through August 4, 1989, with nearly three hundred persons from thirty-three states and seven foreign countries in attendance. The six-day program on the theme "Faulkner and Religion" was focused on the delivery of lectures contained in this volume. The literary scholars and cultural historians who lectured at the conference also led discussions of "Faulkner's Representation of the Divine" and "Faulkner, Religion, and Culture" during sessions for small groups. Evans Harrington, director of the conference since its founding in 1974, presented a lecture and selected and arranged Faulkner passages on religion for a program entitled *Voices from Yoknapatawpha*.

Sister Thea Bowman, whose presentations on Faulkner and black culture had been a regular part of Faulkner and Yoknapatawpha programs since 1980, made her last conference appearance in 1989. The granddaughter of a slave, she grew up in Canton, Mississippi. After joining the Franciscan Sisters of Perpetual Adoration at age fifteen, she earned a B.A. in English at Viterbo College and M.A. and Ph.D. degrees from Catholic University of America. As director of a program on intercultural awareness for the Catholic Diocese of Jackson, Mississippi, and as a member of the faculty of the Institute of Black Studies at Xavier University in New Orleans, she earned national recognition as an educator, evangelist, gospel singer, and writer on spirituality. Even after being stricken with cancer in 1985, Sister Thea kept up a rigorous schedule of lectures, workshops, performances, and meetings throughout the United States. She always managed to be in Oxford every summer to help Faulkner admirers deepen their understanding and appreciation of his work. Joining her in her last presentation, "Faulkner and That Ole Time Religion," a moving program of commentary and song, were friends from two Mississippi communities—Sameerah Muhammad, Billie Jean Young, and others from Jackson and the gospel group Privilege from Itta Bena.

Willie Morris, writer-in-residence and director of the Visiting Writers' Program at the University of Mississippi, presided over a session that explored the religious dimensions of Faulkner's work and recent Southern fiction. Featured speaker for that session was author William Styron, who read "As He Lay Dead, a Bitter Grief," his 1962 *Life* magazine article about attending Faulkner's funeral, and a passage from *Sophie's Choice*.

Two other Southern authors made presentations at the conference. Clyde Edgerton of Durham, North Carolina, read selections from his first two novels, *Raney* and *Walking Across Egypt*, both best sellers, and his third novel, *The Floatplane Notebooks*, which has been hailed as "a new American classic." He also discussed his reactions to Faulkner's writings. Oxford's own Larry Brown, who read from his first collection of stories, *Facing the Music*, at the 1988 conference, read from his first novel, *Dirty Work*, in 1989.

"Oxford Women Remember Faulkner," a panel discussion moderated by Chester A. McLarty, featured Mary McClain Hall, Lulu Law, Minnie Ruth Little, and Bessie Sumners. Howard Duvall and John Ramey served as panelists and M. C. Falkner as moderator for sessions on "William Faulkner of Oxford." Other conference activities included a slide lecture by J. M. Faulkner and Jo Marshall, sessions on "Teaching Faulkner" conducted by Robert W. Hamblin, guided tours of North Mississippi, and the annual picnic at Faulkner's home, Rowan Oak.

Faulkner books, manuscripts, photographs, and memorabilia were displayed at the University's John Davis Williams Library, and the University Press of Mississippi exhibited Faulkner books published by university presses throughout the United States.

Mississippi artist Marshall Bouldin's portrait of Sister Thea Bowman was on display at the University Museums, and the campus television station aired Faulkner films throughout the week.

The conference planners are grateful to all the individuals and organizations who support the Faulkner and Yoknapatawpha Conference annually. We offer special thanks to Dr. and Mrs. M. B. Howorth, Jr., Mr. Robert Townsend Jones, Dr. and Mrs. C. E. Noyes, Mr. Glennray Tutor, Mr. Richard Howorth of Square Books, the Yoknapatawpha Arts Council, St. Peter's Episcopal Church, and the City of Oxford.

Faulkner and Religion
FAULKNER AND YOKNAPATAWPHA
1989

William Faulkner and Religion: Determinism, Compassion, and the God of Defeat

ALFRED KAZIN

William Faulkner is the greatest writer the South has produced. In twentieth-century American fiction, in capturing the rich variety and disorder of American life, no one else has come anywhere close to the depth of intensity and comprehensiveness of Faulkner's imagination. But if ever an American writer took on a subject filled to overflowing with war, violence, pain, cruelty, exclusion, servitude, impoverishment, racial pride, hatred and resentment of the rest of the country, defeat, deceit, and delusions of everlasting power over others, it was Faulkner. A great writer and, as Estelle Faulkner said, in their many troubles, a man of grace, he was also a deeply suffering man who was born at a low point in the history of his region, into a family whose memories of glory in its sadly reduced state he mocked in the self-pity and self-hatred of the Compsons of *The Sound and the Fury.* His own attitude toward Oxford, long after he was derided as "Count No 'Count," took the form of defiance not by boasting of his world fame but by building up his mansion on an ever grander scale.

Nor did his genius have a kinder reception here than his early poverty and lifelong drinking. When Faulkner finally came into his own after the war and *Life Magazine* actually sent a reporter down here for what it viewed as the highest honor in American life, a cover story, the reporter was told by a school official, "You can tell from his writing that Mr. Faulkner never had a proper education."

So when we think of religion as the most intimate expression of

the human heart, as the most secret of personal confessions, there
where we admit to ourselves alone our fears and losses, our sense
of holy dread and our awe before the hidden power of a universe
that plainly regards all of us as indeed of "no account," I for one
find it hard to think of Faulkner as confiding his troubles to a
personal God. He was by no means as hardbitten as Joe Christmas, Jason Compson, Mrs. Armstid, Popeye, Percy Grimm, Doc
Hines, McEachern, Lucas Burch, the Snopeses, or the many
others in his great kingdom of characters who all remind me of
what D. H. Lawrence said of the American character—"hard,
isolate, stoic, *a killer.*" But neither did he look upon his fellow
critters as did Lena Grove, seduced, pregnant, and deserted, who
expects the best of everything—and will yet get it; or Byron
Bunch, who jolted all Saturday night on a mule so as to help
Sunday morning with the services in a backwoods church. Or Joe
Christmas's eager-loving, ever-grieving grandmother Mrs. Hines,
who sees in Lena's newborn baby little Joey himself, who never
had a chance. Or Ike McCaslin, who in love of the wilderness and
weariness of killing, deliberately sets aside his gun and compass,
comes to argue against the very concept of land ownership because of the curse that slavery had put upon the land and by his
grandfather's sins.

In the everlasting war against evil by the small amount of good
in the world, Faulkner chose not religion but art. And such is the
shallowness, not to mention the expediency, of so much public
religion in America, one is tempted to thank God that he did not
choose religion. This was an independent soul even in his most
tormented moments who said that the theme of *The Wild Palms* is
"Between grief and nothing I will take grief." He wrote to his
admirer Malcolm Cowley when Cowley helped to make him
acceptable at last with the Viking *Portable Faulkner,* "Life is the
same frantic steeplechase toward nothing everywhere and man
stinks the same stink no matter where in time."

No, I don't think it can be said of Faulkner what Tolstoy said of
himself to Maxim Gorky: "God is the name of my desire." That is

not the way the best American writers think or talk about religion, if they ever do. On the other hand religion, especially in the South Faulkner grew up in, in the form of churches and doctrine was a dominating institution and form of social and sectional culture. It was a way of life, the most traditional and lasting form of Southern community. And unlike Christian churches elsewhere in the country, it was up against issues of race, slavery, poverty, and violence in which the sense of sin and redemption, far from being pale, abstract words distantly heard only on Sunday, were issues of life and death, meaning real sin and redemption truly needed, that burned in Southern hearts and made human existence seem fraught, as it always is, with the most terrible possible consequences.

All this gave a heightened drama to the daily life of war and peace—a war that never quite ended for many Southerners after April 1865, and a peace that saw in defeat all the more exasperation with the ex-slaves and their supposed protectors in Washington. The agony of being nationally in the wrong, natural as it was to despise the North for its hypocrisy, its absentee moralism, helped to feed the religious crisis after Appomattox in which Southerners of Faulkner's class grew up between 1890–1920. The key fact here is that the Civil War saw an upsurge of religious emotion, the most intense since the Great Awakening before and after the Revolution, that had very morbid consequences in the South. The traces are all over Faulkner's work. And one of his greatest novels, *Light in August*, is essentially a study in religious pathology, with good and evil vying with each other in a context of such violence that the only healing touch is the birth of a baby as far removed from wedlock as possible, and mistaken by Mrs. Hines for another baby, her grandson Joe Christmas, who was to grow up into the most desperate soul that ever lived—and a murderer.

On 4 March 1865, Lincoln's Second Inaugural, the Southern-born president of the Federal Union, the child of two Virginians, said of both *North* and *South:* "Each looked for an easier triumph, and a result less fundamental and astounding. Both read the same Bible, and pray to the same God; and each invokes His aid against the other. It may seem strange that any men should dare to ask a just God's assistance in wringing their bread from the sweat of other men's faces; but let us judge not, that we be not judged. The prayers of both could not be answered—that of neither has been answered fully."

Lincoln added that "the Almighty has His own purposes." But what E. E. Cummings in 1917 used to call the "Gott-mit-uns boys," mocking Kaiser Wilhelm's assurances that God was pro-German, on both sides drowned out Lincoln's peculiar views.

Northern troops were fond of singing "Stand up, stand up for Jesus/The trumpet call obey/Forth to the mighty conflict/In this *his* glorious day." What an appeal the President's Biblical name had for the volunteers who in 1862 sang "We are coming, Father Abraham, three hundred thousand more."

When Julia Ward Howe was asked to provide the tune of "John Brown's Body," itself originally a Sunday school hymn composed in South Carolina, with a more dignified set of words, her words burst forth uncontrollably in the night as powerfully as when Harriet Beecher Stowe, while sitting in church, first conceived of *Uncle Tom's Cabin* in a vision of the slave beaten to death by Simon Legree. Mrs. Howe's last stanza for the *Battle Hymn of the Republic* (1861):

> He has sounded forth the trumpet that shall never call retreat
> He is sifting out the hearts of men before the judgment seat
> Oh! be swift, my soul, to answer Him! be jubilant, my feet!
> *Our* God is marching on.

The exaltation of this did not survive victory in the North. A few abolitionists determined to carry on the struggle for wider social justice became the cranks and professional reformers Henry James satirized in *The Bostonians*. But the South never quite got over a sense of guilt—this not about the justice of slavery but about the uncertain personal transgressions—whatever these could have been—that alone explained why the devout and God-fearing Confederacy could have gone down in defeat.

President Jefferson Davis early in the conflict proclaimed days of humiliation and prayer in assurance that the Heavenly Father unquestionably supported the Confederacy. The President noted that "it hath pleased Almighty God, the Sovereign Disposer of Events, to protect and defend the Confederate States hitherto in conflict with their enemies, and to be unto them a shield." When faced with defeat, James W. Silver wrote in *Confederate Morale and Church Propaganda*, "Confederates had not far to look to discover sins that could serve as a ready explanation, including 'violation of the Sabbath,' intemperance, demagoguery, corruption, luxury, impiety, murmuring, greed and avarice, lewdness, skepticism, 'Epicurean expedience,' private immorality, ill treatment of slaves, profanity, a high and mighty spirit, speculation, bribery, boastfulness and the 'sin of all sins,' covetousness. God had smiled at First Manassas, Second Manassas, Fredericksburg, and Chancellorsville, but he had frowned at Gettysburg, Vicksburg, and Tullahoma."

Such was the influence of the Old Testament on a Southland that easily identified with another pastoral people whose wars for its own holy soil were fought in the name of the Lord whose chosen they believed themselves to be, that following Sherman's capture of Atlanta, the *Daily Lynchburg Virginian*, which had once seen in Confederate successes the work of "the hand of the great ruler of the Universe," now grieved:

> Perhaps we are suffering chastisement for the same reason that it was once visited upon the once favored people; nor can we, with a true faith in the Divine Record, and an humble trust in that gracious Being who controls our destinies, that when 'the altars of Baal' shall be thrown down, and the people turn humbly to the source of all help, deliverance will come.

For Southerners, God was not someone to discard in defeat—
and the sense of defeat lasted a very long time, became the South's
own battle cry to the Lord against the triumphant North. There
the scientific certainties of evolution, never easily accepted in the
South, went to establish through Social Darwinism the rationale
that those who survive to make the largest profits are those most
fit to survive. Nature alone was God, a pitiless rapacious Nature
that gave its highest prize, money, to those who were most ruthless, the Robber Barons. Descendants of the Puritans found
justification, if they needed any, in the old Puritan doctrine of
predestination, a tautology if ever there was one. Those who alone
have made it are those who alone deserved to make it. And shed not
a tear for the victims, since nature red in tooth and claw does *not!*

The God of defeat in those years of Faulkner's growing up
bound the South together as did apartheid, the everlasting racial
tension and violence that led to defiance of the rest of the country.
In the 1930s, the scene of some of Faulkner's greatest fiction, the
depression was worse in the South than elsewhere; economic
recovery was not really accomplished until the Second World War,
with Mississippi remaining the poorest state in the Union. No one
else made so graphic as Faulkner did in *Light in August* and the
earliest tales of the Snopes tribe the poverty and primitivism that
helped to convince Faulkner's readers that more than even the
rest of the South, Mississippi was a special case. This did not make
Faulkner popular at home, where it was not just his father who
refused to read him, but much of Oxford.

If Faulkner thus had good reasons for feeling isolated and
beleaguered, the South, always feeling itself misjudged, found
inner support in a religious culture that recognized in the Old
Testament especially tribulations very much like its own, but
endured out of belief in a divine necessity that could no more be
doubted than the creation of the world from the same hand.

This sense of necessity is what Faulkner shared with the religious culture around him, though as the historical preface or
appendix he eventually included in the Modern Library edition of

The Sound and the Fury shows, he would have put it differently: we are creatures not of God but of history, prisoners of history as surely as in the light of theology we are prisoners of sin. There is a straight line in human folly, heroism, covetousness, and lust that stretches from the Scots fleeing the final defeat of the Stuarts to the migration to America and over the mountains to the delta country to the slave system imposed by the English to the cotton kingdom to delusions of the master race to the war and so on and on to the downfall of the Compsons and Caddy actually photographed in 1940 sitting in his luxurious car next to a German general.

And that's the way things are: because once things get started, there's no turning back. For the true novelist, as for the true Calvinist, there's not even a turning away. Circumstances are our life. Circumstances are *all*.

Faulkner's acceptance of all the South as fevered and complex as Quentin Compson in *Absalom, Absalom!* saying that he doesn't hate the South, no no he doesn't, is as tragic and unrelenting a vision as anything can be. This helps to explain the spell he casts on readers astonished by so much passion, so much wildness, so much bitterness of heart, so much moodiness and intemperance in words that are as stimulating to many of us as whiskey was to Faulkner. This was no latter-day bourgeois Southern Republican out at the country club chortling about one nation under God. On the contrary, Faulkner's incomparable tension conveys a sense of being trapped, in direst trouble, forever on the very edge of existence. My favorite text of this, from chapter 10 of *Light in August*, is Joe Christmas at seventeen taking off after being beaten, not for the first or last time, and this by the associates of the waitress-prostitute, Bobbie, who was his first love.

He stepped from the dark porch, into the moonlight, and with his bloody head and his empty stomach hot, savage, and courageous with whiskey, he entered the street which was to run for fifteen years.

The whiskey died away in time and was renewed and died again, but the street ran on. From that night the thousand streets ran as one street, with imperceptible corners and changes of scene, broken by intervals of begged and stolen rides, on trains and trucks, and on country wagons with he at twenty and twentyfive and thirty sitting on the seat with his still, hard face and clothes (even when soiled and worn) of a city man and the driver of the wagon not knowing who or what the passenger was and not daring to ask. The street ran into Oklahoma and Missouri and as far south as Mexico and then back north to Chicago and Detroit and then back south again again and at last to Mississippi. It was fifteen years long: it ran between the savage and spurious board fronts of oil towns where, his inevitable serge clothing and light shoes black with bottomless mud, he ate crude food from tin dishes that cost him ten and fifteen dollars a meal and paid for them with a roll of banknotes the size of a bullfrog and stained too with the rich mud that seemed as bottomless as the gold which it excreted. It ran through yellow wheat fields waving beneath the fierce yellow days of labor and hard sleep in haystacks beneath the cold mad moon of September, and the brittle stars. . . .

In the conjoined sentences there is the line of necessity again, Joe's life rolling out in sentences that Faulkner made a specialty of for inclusiveness yet made compact by an untiring propulsion of rhythm. A single man, no one more single and alone; a single life, nothing more desperate and terrible in the race hatred starting from his own grandfather, the killer of Joe's own father and in a sense the killer of Joe's mother, the grandfather's own daughter Millie. The grandfather made him a foundling, took employment in the orphanage in order relentlessly to watch over him as an abomination of the Lord. And what is the meaning of all this, one act after another, event folding into event, but that we are imprisoned in time not just *by* our acts but *in* them. The connection, the terrible straight line of our lives, one thing after another, after another, after another. Where do we find the ultimate expression of this but in the greatest book of human history there is, a book beginning with creating, then issuing straight into family, man and woman, brothers at war, the lesser wife sent into the wilderness with her son, brothers ganging up to sell the favorite of the father, all ending up far from home with the immortal cry with which John 23 greeted the Jews of Rome after so much misery and death, "I am Joseph, your brother."

Faulkner said that the Old Testament was one of his basic influences, along with Melville, Dostoevsky, Conrad. The secret thread of the Hebrew Bible is family—the terrible love that can exist within a family, and the pain, like no other pain in the world, when the very closeness from birth, or the love in marriage, or a child cut down by death, becomes the contrary of what has been the very staff of life.

My son, God will provide himself a lamb for a burnt offering. Jacob served seven years for Rachel; and they seemed unto him but a few days, for the love he had to her. But I will lie with my fathers, and thou shalt carry me out of Egypt, and bury me in their burying place.

Faulkner said that a tentative title for the Snopes chronicle was *Father Abraham*. The original title of *The Wild Palms* was *If I Forget Thee, O Jerusalem*. And of course one of his greatest books takes off from King David's cry, *Would to God I had died for thee, Absalom my son, my son*. If many of us suspect that our own family would make a novel—if only we had the temerity to write it—it is because, to adapt Tolstoy's famous opening to *Anna Karenina*, each family story is emotionally unique because it is this family and not some other. And to nothing do we owe our natural sense of determinism so much as we do to family. The Compsons in *The Sound and the Fury* become unbearably real through the repetition—"Stomp, Benjy, stomp!" said over and again of things that make up daily life in any family.

This was said perfectly by another great American writer born into Calvinism, Nathaniel Hawthorne. In *The Scarlet Letter* Roger Chillingworth, alone at last with the wife who has betrayed him with the local minister, wearily turns aside her plea that he let her old lover off.

It is not granted me to pardon. I have no such power as thou tellest me of. My old faith, long forgotten, comes back to me, and explains all that we do, and all we suffer. By thy first step awry, thou didst plant the germ of evil; but, since that moment, it has all been a dark necessity. Ye that have wronged me are not sinful, save in a kind of typical illusion; neither am I fiend-like, who have snatched a fiend's office from his hands. It is our fate. Let the black flower blossom as it may!

But Hester knows that Chillingworth in the total aloneness he has created for himself through his sin of pride suffers more than she does, outcast with little Pearl. Or Dimmesdale in the forest when she can at last tell him: "What we did had a consecration of its own. We felt it so! We said so to each other! Hast thou forgotten it?"

There is no suffering in Faulkner like that of Joe Christmas, open to everybody's contempt, hatred, and worse because he doesn't know who he is, has been left entirely to himself by his mad grandfather, and has no ties to anyone, especially not when he makes love to the New England patroness of blacks who cries "Negro! Negro!" in her sexual transports and is murdered when she attempts to pray over him.

To talk to Joe Christmas is to enter into a maze of determinism from which there is no escape—and not just for him. But why is he in any sense to be identified with the Christ story, as the idiot Benjy Compson is? *Because he, like Benjy, is the man things are done to,* the ultimate stranger to others who can wreak their horror of him by murdering and castrating him—this on a Friday. Why are Faulkner's "religious" titles not troubling to the faithful? *Sanctuary* for the story of the terrible Popeye; *Requiem for a Nun* the story of the pretty, terrible Temple Drake. But these are literary projections, in Faulkner's profoundly associative style, between the inoperative world of formal religion and the operation of our destiny, our fate, the dark thread of necessity, the end logic of our lives, as we are pulled round and round by forces that I and you may call God, but which Faulkner himself calls "Opponent," the "Player."

We are being played upon by an Opponent we cannot see or truly know. Lena Grove's miserable seducer Lucas Burch, now calling himself Brown, has the sense even as he runs away that he is being moved about by "an Opponent who could read his moves before he made them and who created spontaneous rules which he and not the Opponent must follow." So Percy Grimm in pursuit of Joe Christmas is described as moving "with that lean, swift, blind obedience to whatever Player moved him on the board." As he nears the doomed Christmas, "It was as though he had been merely waiting for the Player to move him again."

"Opponent" and "Player" are both capitalized. Man is on a track he cannot get off and there is nothing he can do to save himself if, like Joe Christmas, it seems that his *so-called* "black blood" finally did him in. Why did Faulkner throw *that* in when the whole point of Joe's fate is that he never knew whether he was partly black or not? Ironic or not, that thrust is another shovel of dirt on Joe's coffin.

We are dealing with a writer whose grimness about the human situation in his early masterpieces snaps back at the reader in every sneer, growl, and bark from his characters—and from Faulkner's own baleful vew of them. Faulkner's scorn for human folly, pettiness, daily meanness, and self-delusion can be positively funny in its snarling doggedness. Especially when he has to overlook grammar in order to get in a weary stoic bitterness about the human critter that occupies one side of his mouth like a wad of tobacco. *Everybody* gets it in Faulkner's South, even in decent society before we get to the Snopeses, who are so mad, greedy, careless, conspiratorial, preoccupied with being mean, but so endlessly inventive in their badness that they become just lunatic. But (himself so long a butt of town gossip) what does Faulkner not do with the townspeople as chorus, especially the women in *Light in August* after the Reverend Hightower's wife has jumped to her death!

It might even be said that they forgave her. No crime or transgression had been actually named and no penance had set. But the town
did not believe that the ladies had forgot those previous mysterious
trips, with Memphis as their destination and for that purpose regarding which all had the same conviction, though none ever put it into
words, spoke it aloud, since the town believed that good women dont
forget things easily, good or bad, lest the taste and savor of forgiveness
die from the palate of conscience. Because the town believed that the
ladies knew the truth, since it believed that bad women can be fooled
by badness, since they have to spend some of their time not being
suspicious. But that no good woman can be fooled by it because, by
being good herself, she does not need to worry anymore about hers or
anybody else's goodness; hence she has plenty of time to smell out
sin. That was why, they believed, that good can fool her almost any
time into believing that it is evil, but that evil itself can never fool her.

But how much more stirringly the plight of the damned human
race, as Mark Twain used to call us, is resolved by Faulkner than it
is by his fellow-Mississippian Richard Wright. Faulkner praised
Wright but with reservations, complaining that Wright seemed to
be stuck with the Negro as subject. Imagine that! In "The Man
Who Went to Chicago," Wright wrote: "What could I dream of
that had the barest possibility of coming true? I could think of
nothing. And slowly, it was exactly upon that nothingness that my
mind began to dwell."

Faulkner had no need to say anything so despairing. He was a
much tormented and self-tormenting human being whose greatest relief and happiness seems to have come from his ability to
forget everything in the act of writing, which for him became
almost mystical in his ability to reach easily and unhindered into
the uniqueness of imagination. He said about writing the first
Snopes chronicle in the teeth of great physical pain: "To me it was
written just as if I had sat on the one side of a wall and the paper
was on the other and my hand with the pen thrust through the
wall and writing not only on invisible paper but in pitch darkness
too." And of course he had more to write about than any other
American writer of his time, a veritable historical kingdom over

almost four centuries yet confined to what he liked to call his own little postage stamp of native soil.

Faulkner as a *writer* was not crushed by the frequent bouts of despair that led him to the bottle. The main reason, I believe, is that when he wrote he was positively swept away by his ability to situate his characters in an infinite present. This did not elude his determinism, the sense of dark necessity in all things that went with Scots religious heritage. But before I come to this, the heart of my paper, Faulkner's merciful and healing power to express all the grimness of a Southern situation he regarded as the epitome of human fate, I must say something about a church definitely not Faulkner's own in a setting he enjoyed rather too well and that regularly overstimulated him, New York City.

On 22 October 1989 Faulkner will be included among other American immortals now in the Poet's Corner, an attempt to reproduce a famous feature of Westminister Abbey, in the great Cathedral of St. John the Divine on the upper West Side of New York. I with other American writers will read passages from Faulkner as I face the altar. The Cathedral, really two churches in one, is the largest in the world, since St. Peter's in Rome is technically a basilica. It is very very grand, very beautiful in its Gothic style. It was designed by an architect who was mad about the Middle Ages and despised the modern industrial world. Little did the lordly bishops of the Episcopalian Church, once who practically owned New York, guess that their unfinished and perhaps unfinishable cathedral, so grand in its conception, would end up in a sea of multiracial poverty and Third World misery that deeply concerns the church.

So perhaps I will not be utterly out of place in this awesome situation when I read one of my favorite passages from *The Sound and the Fury*, the opening of part 4, where Dilsey emerges directly as she gets up to service the Compsons, as usual, before going off with *her* family to hear a visiting preacher on Easter Sunday.

This, where Faulkner takes over the narrative after we have been listening so long to the voices of Benjy, Mr. and Mrs.

Compson, Quentin, Jason, Caddy, Roskus, Luster, and most of watchful Jefferson, is one of the most beautiful pieces of writing I know. I have often, in teaching the book, been dangerously affected before a class because of the exactitude of detail, the serene gravity of tone. But the essence is Dilsey herself, in effect still the bondswoman to the Compsons, but a human being presented to us in her decline as entirely made up by a lifetime of toil and sacrifice.

> The day dawned bleak and chill. A moving wall of grey light out of the northeast which, instead of dissolving into moisture, seemed to disintegrate into minute and venomous particles, like dust that, when Dilsey opened the door of the cabin and emerged, needled laterally into her flesh, precipitating not so much a moisture as a substance partaking of the quality of thin, not quite congealed oil. She wore a stiff black straw hat perched upon her turban, and a maroon velvet cape with a border of mangy and anonymous fur above a dress of purple silk, and she stood in the doorway for a while with her myriad and sunken face lifted to the weather, and one gaunt hand flac-soled as the belly of a fish, then she moved the cape aside and examined the bosom of her gown.
>
> The gown fell gauntly from her shoulders, across her fallen breasts, then tightened upon her paunch and fell again, ballooning a little above the nether garments which she would remove layer by layer as the spring accomplished and the warm days, in colour regal and moribund. She had been a big woman once but now her skeleton rose, draped loosely in unpadded skin that tightened again upon a paunch almost dropsical, as though muscle and tissue had been courage or fortitude which the days or the years had consumed until only the indomitable skeleton was left rising like a ruin or a landmark above the somnolent and impervious guts, and above that the collapsed face that gave the impression of the bones themselves being outside the flesh, lifted into the driving day with an expression at once fatalistic and of a child's astonished disappointment, until she turned and entered the house again and closed the door.

Throughout *The Sound and the Fury* we are in a time period absolutely present, so concentrated upon the immediate moment and even hypnotized by it, that nothing counts beside the figure

Dilsey makes in the doorway, disappointed in the weather this morning of Easter Sunday, yet in Faulkner's eyes transcending everything around her as he concentrates on the ruin time has made of her body and the picturesqueness, oddity, so much part of the picture, as she prepared with hat on her head, over the turban she wears all the time, to get breakfast ready and minister to whining, awful, finally pitiful members of the once almighty Compson family.

As the great architect said, God is in the details. None of us in contemporary American writing is now looked at so directly, so fiercely, with an attention so intense that the language of it becomes feverish and even a shade brutal. Dilsey is all there—at least so far as another human being of another race and class can *see* her—and *we* are all there with *her*. This is the kind of attention devout people used to expect about themselves, their smallest acts, their secret thoughts, from a God who cared, terrible as he could be in judgment, who was an everlasting father. God was obviously a novelist when we were all His concern. Just as He is no longer there for many people who would love to believe that they are not everlasting orphans on the earth, so we are aware in Faulkner's very rhythms that he is excited about Dilsey in a way that contemporary American novelists are not excited by or about their characters, are not entirely sure who the characters are, though they exist nowhere but in the author's brain.

Now this concentration upon the minutest fabric of Dilsey's being, our being entirely here, now after being similarly involved second by second, with Benjy and Quentin and Jason, Caddy, and Mr. and Mrs. Compson, is what we associate with Andrei Bolkonsky and Emma Bovary—great characters who came out of a time when realistic fiction came for the first time, the nineteenth century, to think itself just as supreme as epic poetry and classical tragedy. Where God was dead or at least doubtful, it was up to the great novelist to *play* God by doing justice to the human creature as God alone had ever done. Tolstoy as a supreme story-teller even admitted that he sometimes felt sorry for one of his characters, endowed him with superior traits belonging to another.

Now the interesting thing about Faulkner in the context of religion is that as a Southerner brought up in a period of decline, family and sectional, all too aware of everyone as a child not of God but of history—and *what* a history—he thinks as a determinist, traces the degradation of the Compsons in particular back to their migration first here over the mountains, their land grabbing, their violence, and pride. But by locating all action and feeling entirely in the present, the deepening and widening of consciousness this brings, Faulkner gives an extraordinary human sympathy to everything—Benjy's inability to speak except to his own mind, Quentin's mad hopeless love for his sister Caddy, Jason's rages against everything and everyone, ending up in his cursing God as he runs after his niece and the money she has stolen back from him, who stole it from her.

"Don't trust the artist," said D. H. Lawrence, "trust the tale." When it comes to religion and the writer remember that any writer, no matter how religious in his/her own mind, is necessarily independent and heretical when he leaves the pieties, abstractions, and prohibitions of the church for that abyss, a piece of white paper, in which he has to grapple with things he may not have thought of before the dread moment in which he has to write.

More than that, the South as the most churchly region in the country, one historically obsessed with the elements of blood, pain, and sacrifice in the Christian story, (where New England turned everything into a cult of bland benevolence), is as much a disturbing ever present fact in the life of the Compsons as the silent anguish of Benjy and the incestuous passion of Quentin. The church is always there as an institution, as a historic culture, though we cannot miss the significance of Christ's resurrection in a service conducted in a black church by a visiting preacher said to resemble a monkey but whose hysterical eloquence in supposedly funny grotesque language does by its conviction bring peace to those within. For the Compsons the day of Christ's resurrection ends in Benjy's hoarse bellows of agony because Luster has taken the wrong turn around the monument on his way home. There is no final gift of peace for Benjy, for he, not the church, is the castrated and crucified in life, and this by his own brother, just as the murderer Joe Christmas in *Light in August* is castrated and crucified by a white supremacist who flings the bloody knife away glorying "now you will leave white women alone even in hell."

In Dostoevsky's *Brothers Karamazov* the saintly Father Zossima, meeting Dimitry Karamazov for the first time, bows low to him in homage to the suffering he knows in advance Dimitry will have to endure. That is the religious touch that Dostoevsky came to, despite his own terrible character, because of his crucial recognition, as Russians always do, of the *victim*. Where else in American writing will you find the feeling for a supposed idiot, such a shame to his patrician family that they changed his name, that Faulkner extends to Benjy because the schoolgirls stop to look at him as a possibly dangerous freak—but "he can't get out" one of the girls assures the others.

> They came on. I opened the gate and they stopped, turning. I was trying to say, and I caught her, trying to say, and she screamed and I was trying to say and trying and the bright shapes began to stop and I tried to get out. I tried to get if off my face, but the bright shapes were going again. They were going up the hill to where it fell away and I tried to cry. But when I breathed in, I couldn't breathe out again to cry, and I tried to keep from falling off the hill and I fell off the hill into the bright, whirling shapes.

There is nothing like that quality of attention even in Joyce's *Ulysses,* so clearly behind *The Sound and the Fury.* Joyce became all too specialized spreading his great network of inner language and establishing mythic structures to write a novel. He was in fact too much the egotist. But where in American fiction, in Faulkner's day and after, do you find anything like the spun out intensity of Quentin's longing and recrimination the day of his death, the maddened unwearied litany of Jason's complaints against everything and everyone in his world? These are the equivalents of tragedy, ancient and Shakespearean, in Faulkner's ability to sustain a human soliloquy until it becomes the entire measure of a person's soul, his total predicament, individual existence at last finding the voice it did not hear in life.

The purest example of this is Mrs. Hines, still grieving over her grandson Joey.

> I am not saying that he never did what they say he did. Ought not to suffer for it like he made them that loved and lost suffer. But if folks could maybe just let him for one day. Like it hadn't happened yet. Like the world never had anything against him yet. Then it could be like he had just went on a trip and grew man grown and come back. If it could be like that for just one day.

That "second chance," the imagination of it, used to be what religion is all about. It is what keeps the world from being entirely secular, determined, implacable—and worst of all, morose. There is very little of it in modern literature, especially not in American literature, which on the whole fairly presents a condition of competition in all things, even in the marriage bed, harshly unforgiving of others and ourselves for failing. America's religion—success. But Faulkner, certainly in this book, was on the side of failures, which the South in 1932 was full of. And perhaps it was this, a sense of his own tough going in everything, that in such writing gave Faulkner a grace, a power over us so unique.

William Faulkner
and the Southern Religious Culture

CHARLES REAGAN WILSON

H. L. Mencken would probably snicker if he knew we were going
to discuss the "Southern religious culture." Mencken, of course,
was the premier critic of the South in the early twentieth century,
and few have had more fun with that position than he. He took a
special glee in lampooning Southern religion. The root of the
problem with the South, as Mencken had it, was the tyranny of
the "Baptist and Methodist barbarism" below the Mason-Dixon
line. He described the South as a "cesspool of Baptists, a miasma
of Methodists, snake charmers, phony real estate operators, and
syphilitic evangelists." "No bolder attempt to set up a theocracy
was ever made in this world," he said of the South, with his typical
restraint and understatement, "and none ever had behind it a
more implacable fanaticism." There were no arts except "the
lower reaches of the gospel hymn." Sacred Harp singing, he said,
combined the sound of a Ukranian peasant melody with that of a
steam caliope.[1]

Mencken was amusing with his diatribes, and he did bring a
certain insight to his writing on the South. He coined the term
"Bible Belt" to refer to areas of the South and Midwest dominated
by conservative Christian concerns. William Faulkner was born
in, grew up in, and wrote about the area called the Bible Belt.
What was the relationship between the South's religious culture
and Faulkner's work?

Faulkner scholars in the past have been slow in exploring this
subject. Influential early critics, such as Malcolm Cowley and

Irving Howe, rarely even mentioned religion in Faulkner's work. Cowley's famous essay on the Faulkner legend did not include a place for religion, nor did George Marion O'Donnell's article on "The Mythology of William Faulkner." Later scholars focused on Christian themes. We have read much about the religious symbolism in *A Fable*, for example, or the Christ imagery associated with Joe Christmas in *Light in August*.[2] But this represents "generic" religion—broad themes disassociated from time and place. We know that Faulkner explored place, the particularities of a specific community, as a way to understand the human experience. When scholars examine Faulkner's portrayal of black characters they do so against the background of the South's tortured history of race relations. When trying to understand Faulkner's world, you must take into account the importance he assigns history, not just abstract "history" but the history of a specific people who experienced slavery, defeat in the Civil War, and poverty afterwards. Scholars in the field of Southern religious studies have, over the past generation, moved the study of religion in the region beyond stereotypes of the Bible Belt to a serious exploration of the religious groups and forces in the South that produced Faulkner. The Southern religious tradition has been distinctive within the United States in its religious picture. Did this not play a role in Faulkner's fiction?

One aspect of the South's religious tradition has been explored in some depth by scholars. Calvinism was indeed a burden to Faulkner's characters. Faulkner was a critic of Calvinism, saw it limiting human potential. Calvinism teaches the absolute sovereignty of God and the depravity of human beings. They are unable to fathom God's purposes, nor can they dictate their own destinies. Accompanying Calvinism historically has been a pronounced belief in the doctrine of the elect, a conviction that Calvinists are God's chosen. Faulkner surely targeted this Calvinism as a source of Southern evil. The absolutism, fatalism, and self-righteousness that exist in the world of his characters and mightily afflict them stem as much from this source as from any other.[3]

Although Calvinism has been a formative influence on Southern religion, Faulkner scholarship too often gives the impression that a rigid Calvinism has been the main characteristic of the region's religion and certainly the only trait of it that Faulkner explored in depth. Neither of these propositions is true. The Southern religious tradition, to be sure, grew out of Calvinism. Faulkner, like others in his era, often used Calvinist, Puritan, and puritanical as synonyms, but they have different historical meanings. In the 1920s and 1930s American writers used "Puritan" to stand for, among other things, sexual repression, narrow mindedness, intolerance, and especially anti-intellectualism. This was the meaning Edith Hamilton wanted when she later described Faulkner himself as "a violently twisted Puritan."[4] Historians have shown that the image of dour, sexually repressed colonial-era Puritans is a partial truth, at best; most American hangups stem from nineteenth-century Victorianism, not earlier. Perry Miller's studies of the New England colonial mind suggest convincingly that the Puritans were highly intellectual and that later New England rationalism grew out of their work.

The Calvinism that gradually seeped into the Southern soul was, in any event, only a distant relative to its New England relative. Southern Calvinism can be traced as far back as the Presbyterians who were active in the late colonial South. Scotch-Irish settlers in the South had once been Presbyterian Calvinists, although they had lost their churchgoing habits before immigrating to North America and preserved Calvinism simply as a half-remembered cultural legacy. Faulkner devotes considerable attention to the Presbyterians, but Southern Calvinism did not come primarily from them. Settlers in Mississippi, early or late, did not choose that denomination to join en masse, nor did Southerners elsewhere. Any discussion of Faulkner and the Southern religious tradition must confront the denominational issue. The South has been distinguished from other parts of the United States as the region dominated by Baptists and Methodists. Geographers divide the nation into seven religious regions, each dominated by one religious group or combination of groups. The South has been and still is that region dominated by Baptists, with widespread secondary influence from the Methodists. The Great Revival at the turn of the nineteenth century led to the appearance of camp meetings and revivals, which became the engines that drove these two churches to dominance on the frontier, in the rural areas, and even in the small towns and cities of the South. The Methodists were the largest Southern church up to the Civil War, with the Southern Baptist Convention surpassing them after the war, when membership figures in Southern churches skyrocketed. In Faulkner's time, Mississippi had one of the highest percentages of enrolled church members in the nation. In 1957 four-fifths of the population belonged to churches, and over half of Mississippians joining congregations were Baptist.[5]

The South, and especially Mississippi, has been among both blacks and whites Baptist land. There it is: the "B" word. A word that Faulkner often used but one that literary critics seem to want to avoid. "Ours was a town founded by Aryan Baptists and Methodists, for Aryan Baptists and Methodists," says Charles Mallison. In recounting the history of mythical Jefferson, Mallison notes that the Episcopal and Presbyterian churches were the oldest in the area, but "the Baptists and Methodists had heired from them, usurped and dispossessed" the others. Faulkner had special fun in sketching the Baptist influence among the Snopeses as they seek success. Ratliff speculates about Flem, for example, that since becoming an "up-and-coming feller in the Baptist church" he seemed to be depending more "on Providence" to get what he wanted, with getting what he wanted still his aim. The Baptist role in the South, in particular, has been extraordinary. The Baptists, writes Samuel S. Hill, began as "a collection of despised and disdained outgroups," who came to dominate the South. Charles

Mallison describes them as "incorrigible nonconformists, nonconformists not just to everybody else but to each other in mutual accord." They had not come to the wilderness that was the Deep South for religious freedom, but to establish a tyranny "in which to be incorrigible and unreconstructible Baptists and Methodists." This long dominance of a culture remains unique in the history of the Baptists and other Evangelical groups. Baptists historically were dissenters in Europe and in most of North America, but in the South they have been a culturally established religion, not just dominating numerically but infiltrating into every seam of the region's cultural fabric.[6]

The Baptists certainly inherited Calvinist theology, with its concern for God's omnipotence, human sinfulness, predestination, and other theological features. The Baptists, and the Methodists too, began as frontier religions in the South, and on the frontier this Calvinist legacy was combined with a central stress on free will. This is essential in understanding Southern religion. Humans had the ability to decide the all-important question: where will I spend eternity? "The preachers' appeal was to men's emotions on the route to their will," writes Samuel S. Hill, "precisely because this was the arena wherein, as they reckoned, destinies were determined." As a result, notes Hill, "the Calvinist dimension of the classical Baptist heritage receded under the stress of the frontier preachments."[7]

The religious tradition that has dominated Southern culture is Evangelicalism. Both the Baptists and the Methodists are a part of this branch of Protestantism, the distinguishing feature of which is a concern for religious experience. The central theme of Southern religion is the need for conversion in a specific experience that will lead to baptism, to a purified new person. The need is to be born again, to "get right with God." Outsiders often see Southern religion's central feature as a fundamentalism stressing orthodox theology, and this outlook has been important in the region's churches. Highly valued is the discipline of a strict adherence to Biblical teachings, rigorous morality, and community enforcement of selective religious teachings. But these are secondary, they simply reinforce the essential focus on individualism; the individual must seek the experience of God's grace and without that nothing else matters. The spirit is alive in Southern religion, the Holy Ghost a continuing vital presence. This belief is taken to extremes by holiness and Pentecostal groups, but even mainstream Baptists and Methodists believe in it.[8]

The characteristic concerns of Evangelicalism shaped day-to-day life in the South. The region's religious culture was based on the belief in the need to express your religion, to testify to the faith. The South is an oral culture and religion has reflected that. You stand up in church and recount your sinfulness and the Lord's work in saving you. The minister is judged by how he preaches and how many wayfaring strangers he saves—to the accompanying punctuation of amen from the congregation. Biblical stories and characters are well known. Sermons teach the faith through these stories. The Spirituals often sang of Biblical characters, and gospel songs later did the same thing. Sister Wynona Carr sings "The Ballgame," wherein Satan tosses curve balls to the hitter, Solomon is the umpire, and Job suffers throughout before hitting a home run. Politicians used a Biblical shorthand when speaking on the stump, relating the Old Testament's tales of human nature to current governmental struggles. Reformers wanted to throw the moneychangers out of the temple, the temple being the Legislature down in Jackson. The landscape reflected the religious culture with visual messages. "Prepare to meet thy God," "Get Right with God," or simply "Jesus Saves" reduced the Southern faith to its appropriate essence. Folk artists still produce dramatic visionary paintings and sculpture that translate the religion of the spirit into art.

Faulkner grew up in and knew the Southern religious culture. Critics have disagreed on the importance of religion to Faulkner. Some have seen him as essentially an agnostic or atheist, but his explicit statements suggest he claimed a broad Christianity. He attended St. Peter's Episcopal Church in Oxford after his marriage, read the Book of Common Prayer, and was buried with the rites of the church. If you visit his grave, you will find "Beloved, Go with God" there. His Episcopal connection was not an unusual one for Southern intellectuals. Others who grew up in Evangelical churches have sought refuge in the greater latitude of the Episcopal tradition. Faulkner enjoyed having fun with the connection, too. "Funny going's on in that house," says a character in *Soldiers' Pay.* "And a preacher of the gospel, too. Even if he is Episcopal."[9]

In the context of Faulkner's relationship to the Southern religious culture, the crucial issue is not whether he was a Christian or not. Faulkner learned early the religious culture of his time and place. He reflected the usual connection between family and church in the South. His father's family was Methodist and that denomination was his formative one. It is not a predominantly Calvinist tradition. John Wesley's stress on free will and on the need to cultivate spirituality set it off in the South from the Baptists and Presbyterians, who retained larger elements of Calvinist theology. Faulkner attended Methodist Sunday school when a boy and was baptized at the New Albany Methodist Church. He may have been like Samuel Clemens, who said he grew up learning to fear God and hate the Sunday school. Faulkner's mother took him to country revivals at the Methodist camp grounds near Oxford, where he surely absorbed the atmosphere of rural Southern revivalism. One relative taught the religious culture with special effectiveness. When young William Faulkner was at his great-grandfather's house in Ripley, he had to recite a Bible verse before the meal would be served to him. That is a powerful incentive to absorb the features of a culture, willingly or not. Faulkner, in fact, has offered one of the best descriptions of the religious culture of his raising. "My life was passed, my childhood, in a very small Mississippi town, and that was a part of my background. I grew up with that. I assimilated that, took that in without even knowing it. It's just there. It has nothing to do with how much of it I might believe or disbelieve—it's just there."[10] That is what culture—and in this case the Southern religious culture—is: "it's just there," all around. Faulkner recognized that a specific form of religion was a part of his cultural legacy with which to work.

Faulkner drew from a tradition of literary portrayal of the Southern religious culture that goes back at least as far as the Southwestern humorists and their accounts of camp meetings. Mark Twain sketched a vivid account of a revival in *Huckleberry Finn*. Faulkner grew to maturity at a time of dramatic events and trends in Southern religious history. The Scopes trial, the organized Fundamentalist movement, the growth of the holiness and Pentecostal sects—all of these made for dramatic news and delighted the pen of Mencken and other satirists. Faulkner does not deal at length with many dramatic aspects of the modern religious South. Baptism, for example, is a central ritual in this faith, but he sketched no memorable scene of a baptizing. Few itinerant preachers wander in out of Yoknapatawpha County. There are no visions nor any dancing in the aisles by those consumed by the spirit. There is no faith healing, speaking in tongues, nor snake handling.

The Georgians seemed somehow closer to that world. Faulkner's contemporary, Erskine Caldwell, dealt often with sectarian religion, but usually for comic purposes, portraying the South's religious forms and impulses as simply a colorful part of the degenerate world of the sharecropper and mill town South. Sister Bessie in *Tobacco Road*, for example, comes from the tradition where having the call to preach makes you a preacher, but Caldwell gives her little credit for any authentic spiritual purpose. Flannery O'Connor uses humor, of course, but she sees in her rural, religiously obsessed characters the raw materials of a religious message. Although a Roman Catholic with serious theological concerns, she made art from the specifics of the Evangelical faith.[11]

Both Faulkner and O'Connor deal often with the spiritually deformed. Old Doc Hines and Old Tarwater are kindred spirits of sorts. They are outsiders on the societal fringe, yet they are out-siders only because they have taken to life-and-death extremes key messages of their society. Tarwater is an old prophet obsessed with the need to baptize the young idiot child Bishop. Hines is twisted by race and religion, preaching a hellfire-and-brimstone version of white supremacy. Both are crazed prophets of spiritual power unrestrained by institutions, and the results of their efforts in both cases are violence. Violence is often a part of O'Connor's world, but in her art violence leads to moments of epiphany, of revelation for the reader, if not for her characters. Faulkner's world, especially in the novels considered his greatest, is some-times darker. Do the grisly deaths of Joe Christmas and Joanna Bur-den have a religious meaning in the same sense that violence in O'Connor leads to spiritual insight? They are related to the stories of spiritual hope embodied by Lena Grove, Byron Bunch, and Gail Hightower in *Light in August*, but the deaths in the novel are best characterized not as moments of divine revelation but as simply counterpoints to the other stories. Faulkner's religious sympathies, as with O'Connor's, are with those embodying a sim-ple folk religion, more than with those in the comfortable main-stream town churches. Both writers see mainstream Southern Protestant churches as embodying the complacency and self-centeredness of the modern world, but it is important to remem-ber that those complacent churches do not exhaust the meaning of religion in the South for either Faulkner or O'Connor.

The religious world that Faulkner sketched in his work was a rich one. The community church occupied a central place in it, and his little postage stamp of native soil had many congregations. Faulkner was not as interested in the wild emotional spirit of the newer sectarian groups that appealed to Flannery O'Connor as he was in the traditions, rituals, and behaviors of what he called "the spirit Protestant eternal" as it had existed since the early days of his county. Young Quentin Compson describes the religion of another Faulkner character as "a granite heritage," while still another character is said to inherit "old strong Campbellite blood," referring to such Restorationist, New Testament churches as the Churches of Christ.[12] Religion in Faulkner's world, at its best and worst, has contributed through tenacity and strength to the survival of these people.

Institutional religion was in Yoknapatawpha County from the beginning of settlement. Three churches were already there when only thirty homes could be found. The first white settler in Yoknapatawpha County arrived brawling "simply because of his over-revved glands." The earliest ministers came "roaring with Protestant scripture and boiled whiskey, Bible and jug in one hand" and "a native tomahawk in the other." Faulkner leaves little doubt that the taking of land from the Native Americans was a specifically Protestant act making way for capitalist civilization. Religion in Yoknapatawpha County remained a frontier religion for many years indeed. It was a place where, with many churches nearby, men insisted on taking an hour to go five miles to attend a particular denomination, and where Gail Hightower's father rode sixteen miles each Sunday morning to preach. It was a place of revivals. Old Bayard Sartoris of Carolina once pursued his foxes on the hunt through the middle of a Methodist tabernacle, revival in progress, returning later to take part in "the ensuing indignation meeting."[13] Hightower's grandfather, a bluff, hardy Episcopalian who seldom darkened the church doors, liked to attend revivals, luring the congregation away for horse races outside. Those comic scenes are more than counterbalanced by the fearful picture of Joe Christmas disrupting a black revival, killing Pappy Thompson and young Roz as well. The congregation thought he was the Devil.

The Bible possessed a near mystical attraction to these folks. Even in dissent, it was the source of all authority; or perhaps dissent was easy because it was the source of authority. The respectable Methodist deacon Coldfield in *Absalom, Absalom!* waited in his room for Confederate troops to march outside, reading from the Bible "the passages of the old violent vindictive mysticism." Evangelical religion and its Scriptures went off to the war and became a part of the New South afterwards. When Flem Snopes takes on the trappings of success, be becomes a Baptist deacon, a natural alliance. A young Baptist minister in *Soldiers' Pay* is described repeatedly as "a fiery-eyed dervish." This New South world is, sometimes, a less fearful one than before. A character described as "a Rotarian" in *Mosquitoes* proposes that his congregation can achieve 100 percent attendance "by keeping them afraid they'd miss something good by staying away." Circuit-riding fire-and-brimstone preachers were turning over in their graves at the thought of reducing the Gospel to such pragmatism in the Bible Belt.[14]

Preachers were a necessity in this world. Faulkner wrote about at least twelve ministers, but most cannot be described as fitting role models of virtue. As one scholar has classified them, there were "three heavy drinkers, three fanatics, and three slave traders, two adulterers, and two murderers." The Lord works in mysterious ways. Many of Faulkner's ministers are guilty of licentiousness and moral laxity. But this human failing was not the worst offense. A despicable tendency is symbolized by Coldfield, who takes refuge in "the impregnable citadel of his passive rectitude" and raises his daughters "in a grim mausoleum air of Puritan righteousness."[15]

In the end, Faulkner most disliked the austerity and authoritarianism associated with organized religion. Hightower sees churches filled "not with ecstasy or passion but in adjuration, threat, and doom." The professionals who now run the churches had "removed the bells from the steeples" and stood "against truth and against that peace in which to sin and be forgiven which is the life of man." Churches were human institutions and should have more respect for human nature that strives, inevitably fails, but must go on. The sin of the church in the religious legend of Faulkner's Yoknapatawpha world is its failure to come to terms with human nature, to think it is better than the people it serves. Faulkner turns to a cultural experience to convey his ultimate judgment upon the church. As Gail Hightower listens to church organ music one summer night, he fantasizes the shapes of the music "assuming the shapes and attitudes of crucifixions, ecstatic, solemn, and profound in gathering volume." The music is "stern and implacable," a Protestant music that demands not life and love, but "in sonorous tones death as though death were the boon." Hightower moves beyond this judgment on Protestantism to note a grim regional dimension. "Listening, he seems to hear within it the apotheosis of his own history, his own land, his own environed blood: that people from which he sprang and among whom he lives who can never take either pleasure or catastrophe or escape from either, without brawling over it. Pleasure, ecstasy, they cannot seem to bear: their escape from it is in violence, in drinking and fighting and praying; catastrophe too, the violence identical and apparently inescapable *And so why should not their religion drive them to crucifixion of themselves and one another?* he thinks." This emotional religion driving people to crucifixion is the same one that haunts Flannery O'Connor's characters, that confirms W. J. Cash's belief in a tribal Southern white God, and that lies on the underside of Southern Evangelicalism's call for an ethic of love. Faulkner once described being Southern Baptist as "an emotional condition" that came "from times of hardship" when people found "little or no food for the human spirit" and religion "was the only escape they had."[16] At its worst, then, the Southern church at the heart of his religious legend of Yoknapatawpha County actually promoted a wild blending of violence and spiritual striving.

Faulkner explored two other aspects of the South's Evangelical religious culture. One was the region's civil religion. Sociologist Robert Bellah argued in the late 1960s that an American civil religion existed, a body of institutions, myths, values, and rituals that combined religion and nationalism, that saw spiritual significance in the national experience. Since then, other scholars have shown that a variety of civil, or public, religions have existed in the United States. The South has had, as Samuel S. Hill argues, two cultures—a culture of Christian religion and one of Southern-ness. The tension between these two worldviews has helped to shape Southern life. In many ways, the churches of the region have been in cultural captivity to regional values.[17]

I have explored in an earlier book the existence of a Southern civil religion that saw religious significance in the Confederate experience. After the Civil War, Southerners made Robert E. Lee into a saint, Stonewall Jackson into a prophet, and the Confederacy itself into a sacred memory. It was a cult of ancestor worship, with its own rituals of Confederate memorial day, dedication of the ubiquitous Confederate monuments, and Confederate reunions. These were central cultural experiences to a generation of Southerners. The annual Confederate reunions drew tens of thousands of people, and Confederate memorial day in the typical small town was a key holiday on the ritual calendar. That the South developed a sense of history and an obsession with the past was, then, no accident. This Southern civil religion flourished especially in the years from 1890 to 1920, the years when Faulkner was growing to manhood, and his writings reflect its pervasiveness in Southern culture.[18]

Light in August explores the pathology of the Southern civil religion well after its high point. The past lives on in tangible ways in Faulkner's work. Sometimes it is harmless, as Pappy McCallum who has six middle-aged sons, all named for Confederate generals in Lee's army. Sometimes it is the romantic story of soldiers going off to war. But mostly the legacy is a stultifying one. Joanna Burden, for example, represents the sacred past. Her grandfather and brother, Yankee carpetbaggers come south to help the freedmen, were killed in Jefferson during Reconstruction, but, a generation later, "something dark and outlandish and threatening" still attaches to her and to her home. Despite the passage of time "it is there: the descendants of both in their relationship to one another ghosts, with between them the phantom of the old spilled blood and the old horror and anger and fear." Fear is an emotion often associated by Faulkner with religion in Yoknapatawpha County, and it was a prominent feature of the sacralized regional culture. Gail Hightower is the embodiment of the civil religion and its evils as Faulkner saw them. He is obsessed with the combination of religion and the Confederacy—with the civil religion. He is oriented toward the past and death itself. He sits "in the August heat, oblivious of the odor in which he lives—that smell of people who no longer live in life: that odor of overplump desiccation and stale linen as though a precursor of the tomb." When he remembers his childhood, he recalls, as phantoms, his father, his mother, and the old black woman who raised him. The formative influence on him was his grandfather, a bigger-than-life character, a Confederate cavalryman who "had killed men 'by the hundreds,'" or so the story went. Brooding on the war led Hightower to "experience a kind of hushed and triumphant terror which left him a little sick," and also left him with a confused identity. Faulkner has Hightower say his "only salvation"—note the use of that central term in Southern Evangelicalism—was "to return to the place to die where my life had already ceased before it began."[19] In a twisted logic, Hightower anticipated salvation not through the blood of the Lamb, but through the blood of the Confederate cavalry.

Hightower came to Jefferson's Presbyterian church from seminary, refusing any other assignment, to pastor in the town where his grandfather was killed during the war. The congregation cannot make sense of his preaching. Although a seminarian, he appears to his congregation as almost a sectarian preacher, using the emotionalism of a street preacher; the irony is that he is the only member of his sect. People he meets on the street could not sort out his blending of the Confederate legend and the Christian story. He was "wild too in the pulpit, using religion as though it were a dream." He was a cyclone of energy, and Faulkner mentions "his wild hands and his wild rapt eager voice" in which "God and salvation and the galloping horses and his dead grandfather thundered." He "went faster than the words in the Book," a telling judgment to a people steeped in the Bible. Hightower realizes he is blending Christian dogma with "galloping cavalry and defeat and glory." His obsession with the past leads to personal tragedy, as his wife becomes disenchanted and eventually kills herself in Memphis. The community, needless to say, does not approve of all this, believing "that what he preached in God's own house on God's own day verged on actual sacrilege." In the face of his wild preaching, the elders and the congregation were "puzzled and outraged," and his wife's death led to his dismissal from the church and ostracism from the community. Byron Bunch's evaluation of all this is that living people cannot do the damage that the dead can do. "It's the dead ones that lay quiet in one place and dont try to hold him, that he cant escape from."[20]

Old Doc Hines is also a product of the South's civil religion, the attempt to make a religion out of its culture. Whereas Hightower's obsession is the Confederate past, Hines's obsession is race. He has the certainty of one who knows God's will. "The Lord told old Doc Hines what to do and old Doc Hines done it." Hines indeed used Calvinist language in telling Joe Christmas that God "is the Lord God of wrathful hosts, His will be done . . . because you and me are both a part of His purpose and His vengeance." He would stand up in prayer meeting, go to the pulpit and preach "yelling against niggers, for the white folks to turn out and kill them all." He becomes an itinerant revivalist of a peculiar sort, wandering into the churches of black folk, seizing the pulpit, and preaching "with violent obscenity" their "humility before all skins lighter than theirs."[21] Hines is not typical of Southern religion, but is an extreme example of tendencies within the faith. He is not in a church, yet he proclaims God's words and teachings with ravings combining God language and racial epithets.

Both Hightower and Hines combine a determinism from Calvinist tradition with the emotional style of an Evangelical religion of the spirit. They are outside the community, but Faulkner shows that their beliefs are, in fact, central to the Southern culture he inherited. They are only extreme in the violence and the crazed enthusiasm with which they pursue them.

A final overlooked aspect of the religious culture of Faulkner's world is that of folk religion. Historian David Potter once suggested that the South's folk culture was its most distinguishing feature, and religion may well have been the central dimension of it. Southern religious studies has not, by and large, done an adequate job of exploring this aspect of Southern religion. It has much to learn from Faulkner in this regard. This religion is beyond theology. It concerns the beliefs and practices with religious meanings beyond the teachings of organized religion. In Faulkner, folk religion is that among the plain folk, the poor whites, and blacks.[22]

The church is a symbol of rural community in Faulkner's religious world. "Shingles for the Lord" is a marvelous evocation of the landscape and spirit of Southern rural folk religion. This story is of three men who meet to remove the old shingles from their country church. The church itself is a country church, "an old church, long dried out." The men recognize their obligation to contribute time and labor, although this represents a sacrifice from their own farm work. But, as one says, they "belonged to that church and used it to be born and marry and die from." The minister, Whitfield, whose name evokes the memory of George Whitfield, the English preacher who effectively introduced the revival to the South in the colonial era, has been pastor for over fifty years. He is a somber looking man "in his boiled shirt and his black hat and pants and necktie, holding his watch in his hand." He is a stern figure who represents the spiritual life of the few families who live nearby. In the course of the story, the church burns, but Whitfield's response is immediate, calling the men together the next morning to build a new building. As Grier says, "Of course we got to have a church." The young narrator, Grier's son, leaves the reader with the spirit of the church. "I had hated it at times and feared it at others," but "there was something that even that fire hadn't touched." Its "indestructability" and "endurability" were Faulkner's words to describe it. The preacher knew that the men could only give their labor toward a new church, but they "would be there at sunup tomorrow, and the day after that, and the day after that." So in a sense, this folk institution "hadn't gone a-tall."[23] Without describing any worship service Faulkner conveys the spiritual significance of this small institution to its people.

Folk religion in Faulkner involves more than churches. In *As I Lay Dying* it represents the reservoir of Biblical teachings, doctrines, sayings, and general folk wisdom that can be summoned. It provides, in some sense, an all-encompassing worldview. References to God are pervasive. This religion is shared among the Bundrens and others nearby. Folklorist Alan Dundes once suggested studying folk ideas as units of the worldview of a society, and *As I Lay Dying* offers an excellent example. Anse Bundren, husband of the late, lamented Addie, whose corpse holds the story together as it moves to Jefferson for burial, is fond of saying "if God wills it" and "the Lord giveth." When Tull hears the latter, he admits that "It's true. Never a truer breath was ever breathed." The Tulls and the Bundrens are in different social classes, which the Tulls see in moral terms, but the idea that "the Lord giveth" unites the people of this society. The Bundrens themselves do not give evidence of being churchgoers, but they are not outside the religious culture. They have absorbed sayings from the Bible and reflect the emotionalism and the religion of the heart typical of Southern Evangelicalism. As Cora Tull says, "Riches is nothing in the face of the Lord for He can see into the heart."[24]

Two characters stand out in analyzing the folk religion of the novel, and neither seems at first glance particularly admirable. Cora Tull appears as a self-righteous, complacent churchwoman, minding other people's business, while Anse is greedy and rapacious. Cora, I hesitantly suggest, is a more sympathetic character than critics who paint her as one-dimensional have suggested. She can be infuriating, and Faulkner lays it on thick sometimes. Her husband notes that it takes trust in the Lord to get through life, "though sometimes I think that Cora's a mite over-cautious, like she was trying to crowd the other folks away and get in closer than anybody else." Faulkner rarely created one-dimensional characters, and Cora is no exception. She is a specimen from the Southern religious culture that spans the institutional and folk religious worlds. She acknowledges that it may be God's will "that some folks have different ideas of honesty from other folks," and she even grants that "it is not my place to question His decree," painful though it is for her not to meddle.[25]

She has her doubts and dark moments, losing faith in human nature, but "always the Lord restores my faith and reveals to me His bounteous love for his creatures." When she sees young Darl watching his dying mother, she is moved by "the bounteous love of the Lord again and His mercy." She can even be compassionate. When Addie dies, Cora's advice to Anse is that it "comes to all of us" and "let the Lord comfort you." She has on her mind the central question of Southern Protestantism: Are you right with God? Cora asks it as she watches Addie on her deathbed: "the eternal and the everlasting salvation and grace is not upon her." Cora has the blessed assurance of the converted, and she is ready to meet her maker.[26]

If Cora is aggressively assured of the state of her soul, Anse explicitly says "I am not religious, I reckon." But he is judging himself by churchly standards of good behavior. His religion is not that of the respectable society perhaps, but he is within the bounds of folk religion. In his shiftless way, he relies on others, including the religious community of his neighborhood. When Addie passes on, his first response is "there is Christians enough to help you." "They will help us in our sorrow." They do indeed rally to participate in the death ceremonies and assist the family in various ways through their journey. Folk religion is by definition a shared community experience, and death was perhaps the chief occasion for the display of its rituals. Anse achieves the proper ritual dignity folk religion demands in the face of death. He is properly, respectably dressed for his journey to bury Addie. Faulkner notes "he is wearing his Sunday pants and a white shirt with the neckband buttoned." He is "dignified, his face tragic and composed." Anse talks of God as Old Marster and refers to "the Lord's earth." His social status and aggrieved position are wrapped up with his religion. He notes that "nowhere in this sinful world can a honest, hardworking man profit," but he confesses to expecting "a reward for us above." For him, heaven is the place where the well-off "cant take their autos and such. Every man will be equal there and it will be taken from them that have and give to them that have not by the Lord." He adds, "it's a long wait, seems like." After terrible experiences during part of the journey he expresses a frustrated sense of Christian destiny as it has worked its way down from the theologians to daily life: "I am the chosen of the Lord, for who He loveth, so doeth He chastiseth. But I be durn if He dont take some curious ways to show it, seems like."[27]

Faulkner portrayed the appreciation in folk religion for ritual and the collective wisdom, but he had special sympathy for simple piety. This becomes especially clear in his portrayal of black religion. Black Southerners stand especially removed from the Calvinist legacy that many critics have seen encompassing all of Faulkner's religious world. Black Protestant churches rejected the harsh Calvinist features of Protestantism in favor of celebratory worship centered on the loving Jesus. They rejected also the South's civil religion of the Confederate past and white supremacy. Slavery was the central event in their religious mythology, and one of Faulkner's most moving scenes is of the promise of freedom to newly freed slaves in *The Unvanquished*. They move collectively down a dusty road, singing of crossing the river Jordan. Black folk religion has always had a pronounced communal aspect; the characteristic Evangelical concern for individual salvation has been tempered by the need for collective expression of spirituality.[28]

Perhaps the most famous scene from Faulkner's religious culture of Yoknapatawpha County is Dilsey's attendance at Easter Sunday morning service. The Compson family she works for serves as a counterpoint to her spirituality. They show no involvement in either organized religion or the folk religion all around them. Reverend Shegog is the visiting preacher from St. Louis, and Dilsey goes to hear him, hoping for a sermon that "kin put de fear of God" into the younger generation. Dilsey takes the idiot Benjy to the weathered old church, ignoring complaints from blacks and whites about this violation of segregation. The processional to the church is important, and Faulkner sketches the sights and sounds of people moving to worship. But the social dimensions of worship do not seem as crucial this day to Dilsey as the search for a renewed sense of salvation. Dilsey is not feeling well, but someone notes that Shegog will "give her de comfort ed de unburdenin."[29]

Shegog is unprepossessing and is portrayed with racist imagery, but he is one of Faulkner's most memorable preachers. He preaches of the Egyptian bondage and the children of God. He preaches of the crucifixion of Jesus and the resurrection. He ends with an apocalyptic scene from the book of Revelation and tells of "de arisen dead whut got de blood en de ricklickshun of de Lamb!" As he preaches, he becomes more emotional, and soon the congregation "just sat swaying a little in their seats as the voice took them into itself." A voice keeps repeating "Yes, Jesus!" Benjy sits "rapt in his sweet blue gaze." Dilsey "sat bolt upright beside, crying rigidly and quietly in the annealment and the blood of the remembered Lamb." Dilsey is crying when she comes out, having undergone a renewal of her faith. "I've seed de first en de last." "I seed de beginnin, en now I sees de endin." Cleanth Brooks notes that of the characters in *The Sound and the Fury*, she is the survivor because she has gained a sense of eternity.[30] Brooks and others have not noted often enough that this knowledge of eternity was part of her heritage from Southern black religious culture.

The description in the "Appendix" for Dilsey is "They endured." Evangelical religion helped her and other Faulkner characters endure. The religion of black Southerners in Yoknapatawpha County was centered on a personal faith in Jesus, a loving counsellor and friend. Flannery O'Connor once noted, of course, that the South was Christ haunted. Faulkner's black characters surely are, but not his white characters. This seems to be the source of some of their problems. The stern Jehovah God is their obsession rather than the loving, forgiving Christ. The name "Jesus" hardly appears in his accounts of white religionists. Faulkner once noted that the faith of Southern Evangelicalism as embodied in the Southern Baptists represented "the human spirit aspiring toward something," although "it got warped and twisted in the process."[31] That religion was very much a part of the mythical Mississippi county that Faulkner invented. He converted the actual religion of the land into an apocryphal story in which Evangelicalism stood for a twisted striving toward salvation.

Judgmental though Faulkner the moralist was on this religion, he was not at all contemptuous of the search for salvation. A story about the great country music singer Hank Williams seems to sum up the way the Southern religious culture appears in Faulkner's world. Williams seems like a character from a Faulkner story. He was from Alabama, and he was the kind of plain Southern white boy that could have been the father of Lena Grove's baby in *Light in August*. He was not exactly a typical churchgoing pillar of the community, yet he was a product of the Southern religious culture. As well as writing songs about honky tonks, he wrote religious songs, including a classic called "I Saw the Light," which perfectly captures the essence of the born-again religious experience. After wandering aimlessly in a life of sin, he lets his "dear Saviour in." Conversion, redemption, salvation came suddenly, "like a stranger in the night." Praise the Lord, he says, I saw the light. Once, during a country show in El Paso, Texas, shortly before his early death at age twenty-nine, another self-destructive, burned-out Southern poor boy, Williams was drunk in his car outside the concert, trying to sober up. Another performer, Minnie Pearl, remembers that he started to sing "I Saw the Light." He stopped suddenly. "That's the trouble," he said. "It's all dark. There ain't no light."[32] Faulkner's characters seek the light, seek grace, using the materials their culture gave them. They seem to say to us: "I saw the light, in August. Or did I?"

NOTES

1. H. L. Mencken, "The Sahara of the Bozart," in *Prejudices: Second Series* (New York: A. A. Knopf, 1920), 136–37; Mencken, Editorial, *American Mercury*, 7 (1926), 32.

2. Malcolm Cowley, Introduction to *The Portable Faulkner* (New York: Viking Press, 1946); Irving Howe, *William Faulkner: A Critical Study* (Chicago: University of Chicago Press, 1951); George Marion O'Donnell, "Faulkner's Mythology," in *William Faulkner: Three Decades of Criticism*, ed. Frederick J. Hoffman and Olga W. Vickery (New York: Harcourt, Brace, 1963); Robert Barth, *Religious Perspectives in Faulkner's Fiction* (Notre Dame: Notre Dame University Press, 1972); John W. Hunt, *William Faulkner: Art in Theological Tension* (New York: Haskell House, 1973).

3. Mary Dell Fletcher, "William Faulkner and Residual Calvinism," *Southern Studies* 18 (Summer 1979): 199–216; Robert L. Johnson, "William Faulkner, Calvinism, and the Presbyterians," *Journal of Presbyterian History* 57 (1979): 66–81; William H. Nolte, "Mencken, Faulkner, and Southern Moralism," *South Carolina Review* 4 (1971); Alwyn Berland, "*Light in August:* The Calvinism of William Faulkner," *Modern Fiction Studies* 8 (Summer 1962); Harold J. Douglas and Robert Daniel, "Faulkner and the Puritanism of the South," *Tennessee Studies in Literature* 2 (1957); 1–13; Ilse Dusoir Lind, "The Calvinistic Burden of *Light in August,*" *New England Quarterly* 30 (September 1957): 307–29.

4. Edith Hamilton, "Faulkner—Sorcerer or Slave?" *Saturday Review* 35 (12 July 1952): 10.

5. See Samuel S. Hill, *Southern Churches in Crisis* (New York: Holt, Rinehart and Winston, 1966), 14; Hill, ed., *Religion and the Solid South* (Nashville: Abingdon Press, 1972); John B. Boles, *The Great Revival 1787–1805: The Origins of the Southern Evangelical Mind* (Lexington: University Press of Kentucky, 1972); Johnson, "William Faulkner, Calvinism, and the Presbyterians," 66–81. For analysis of church membership figures in Mississippi, see Harold F. Kaufman, "Mississippi Churches: A Half Century of Change," *Mississippi Quarterly* 14 (Summer 1961): 138–47.

6. William Faulkner, *The Town*, 306–7, 452; Hill, *Southern Churches in Crisis*, 18.

7. Hill, *Southern Churches in Crisis*, 14.

8. Donald G. Mathews, "Evangelicalism," in *Encyclopedia of Religion in the South*, ed. Samuel S. Hill (Macon, Ga.: Mercer University Press, 1984), 243–44; Hill, *Southern Churches in Crisis*, 25.

9. William Faulkner, *Soldiers' Pay* (New York: Boni and Liveright, 1926), 261. See also Johnson, "William Faulkner, Calvinism, and the Presbyterians," 66–81; Johnson, "William Faulkner," in *Encyclopedia of Religion in the South*, 250–52.

10. Frederick L. Gwynn and Joseph L. Blotner, *Faulkner in the University: Class Conferences at the University of Virginia, 1957–1958* (Charlottesville: University Press of Virginia, 1959), 41. See also Joseph Blotner, *Faulkner: A Biography* (New York: Random House, 1974), 1:88; Malcolm Cowley, ed., *Writers at Work: The Paris Review Interviews* (New York: Viking Press, 1958), 136. I have profited from a fine study of Samuel Clemens's ambivalent relationship to Southern Evangelicalism: Lloyd A. Hunter, "Mark Twain and the Southern Evangelical Mind," *Bulletin of the Missouri Historical Society* 33 (July 1977): 246–64.

11. James J. Thompson, Jr., "Erskine Caldwell and Southern Religion," *Southern Humanities Review* 5 (Winter 1971): 33–44; Louis D. Rubin, Jr., "Flannery O'Connor and the Bible Belt," in *The Curious Death of the Novel: Essays in American Literature* (Baton Rouge: Louisiana State University Press, 1967); Robert H. Brinkmeyer, Jr., "A Closer Walk

with Thee: Flannery O'Connor and Southern Fundamentalists," *Southern Literary Journal* 18 (Spring 1986): 3–13.

12. William Faulkner, *Mosquitoes* (New York: Liveright Publishing Company, 1927), 11; Faulkner, *Absalom, Absalom!* (New York: Vintage Books, 1972), 109; "Golden Land," in *Collected Stories* (New York: Vintage Books, 1977), 704. See also Walter Taylor, *Faulkner's Search for a South* (Urbana: University of Illinois Press, 1983), 52–64; William Van O'Connor, *The Tangled Fire of William Faulkner* (New York: Gordian Press, 1968), 72–87.

13. William Faulkner, *Requiem for a Nun* (New York: Vintage Books, 1975), 89; Faulkner, *Sartoris* (New York: New American Library, 1964), 25.

14. William Faulkner, *Absalom, Absalom!*, 82; Faulkner, *Soldiers' Pay*, 278; Faulkner, *Mosquitoes*, 36.

15. Robert N. Burrows, "Institutional Christianity as Reflected in the Works of William Faulkner," *Mississippi Quarterly* 14 (Summer 1961): 139.

16. William Faulkner, *Light in August* (New York: Vintage Books, 1972), 461, 347; Gwynn and Blotner, *Faulkner in the University*, 189.

17. Robert N. Bellah, "Civil Religion in America," *Daedalus* 96 (Winter 1967): 1–21; Hill, *Religion and the Solid South*, 24–56.

18. Charles Reagan Wilson, *Baptized in Blood: The Religion of the Lost Cause, 1865–1920* (Athens: University of Georgia Press, 1980).

19. Faulkner, *Light in August*, 42, 300, 452.

20. Ibid., 56, 80, 57, 69.

21. Ibid., 69, 361, 357, 325.

22. See David Potter, *The South and the Sectional Conflict* (Baton Rouge: Louisiana State University Press, 1968); John C. Messenger, "Folk Religion," in *Folklore and Folklife: An Introduction*, ed. Richard M. Dorson (Chicago: University of Chicago Press, 1972), 217–32; Don Yoder, "Official Religion versus Folk Religion," *Pennsylvania Folklife* 15 (Winter 1965–66): 36–52; Bruce A. Rosenberg, *Can These Bones Live? The Art of the American Folk Preacher* (Urbana: University of Illinois Press, 1970).

23. William Faulkner, "Shingles for the Lord," in *Collected Stories*, 27–43.

24. William Faulkner, *As I Lay Dying* (New York: Vintage Books, 1929), 7; Alan Dundes, "Folk Ideas as Units of World View," *Journal of American Folklore* 84 (January–March, 1971): 93–103.

25. Faulkner, *As I Lay Dying*, 67–68, 8.

26. Ibid., 23, 32, 8.

27. Ibid., 37, 49, 81, 104, 105.

28. See William H. Wiggins, Jr., "The Black Folk Church," in Richard M. Dorson, ed., *Handbook of American Folklore* (Bloomington: Indiana University Press, 1983); Newbell N. Puckett, *Folk Beliefs of the Southern Negro* (Chapel Hill: University of North Carolina Press, 1926).

29. William Faulkner, *The Sound and the Fury* (New York: Vintage Books, 1956), 362, 364.

30. Ibid., 370–71. See also Cleanth Brooks, *William Faulkner: The Yoknapatawpha County* (New Haven: Yale University Press, 1963), 345.

31. Gwynn and Blotner, *Faulkner in the University*, 190.

32. Roger M. Williams, *Sing a Sad Song: The Life of Hank Williams* (Urbana: University of Illinois Press, 1981), 195.

Faulkner's Heterodoxy: Faith and Family in *The Sound and the Fury*

GILES GUNN

In the United States the religious imagination is too often, and often too glibly, identified with the Christian imagination, and particularly with the loosely evangelical wing of its Protestant variant. Yet to judge from the way until very recently we have interpreted them, American literary classics, except in relation to its derivative, and usually dangerous, moral Manicheanism, have not been profoundly shaped by such an imagination. With the exception of Fireside poets like John Greenleaf Whittier and James Russell Lowell, and Genteel critics like Thomas Bailey Aldridge and Edmund Clarence Stedman, together with their descendants Barrett Wendell, William Crary Brownell, Paul Elmer More, and, with one side of himself, T. S. Eliot, it has generally been supposed that the American literary imagination has been much too infatuated, since the Puritan era, with the dissonances and disjunctions of experience, its conflicts and ruptures, to place any confidence in the possibility of sacred, much less sacramental, resolutions. Classic American literature, we have come to believe, thanks to the efforts of Richard Chase and many others, characteristically tends to explore extreme ranges of experience and to rest in dichotomous, even conflicting or contradictory, states of mind. Far from seeking through Christian strategies of redemptive catharsis and transfiguration to reconcile division and dissonance, the American literary imagination has concentrated its most important energies, according to conventional opinion, on exploring the aesthetic and even religious possibility of forms of alienation and disorder, and often in morally equivocal ways. Hence even in a standard work like *The Scarlet Letter*, where transgression and repentance form two poles between which much of the action oscillates, the novel resists all impulses toward thematic closure by terminating, finally, in an image of tragic separation. Hester and Dimmesdale both remain true, but their fidelity merely succeeds in condemning them to opposite or, at the very least, to apposite ways of being.

Consequently, the customary way of reading the religious meaning of American literature has gone something like this. If the representative American literary imagination displays what are undeniably Manichean characteristics, these internal divisions have not been produced by its absorption with the predicament of human iniquity and its transcendence so much as with its concern for the problem of human freedom and the impediments to its realization. Insofar as it is religious at all, the "classic" American story is not about repentance and possible regeneration by faith in Christ but about the limitations of selfhood and their heuristic value.

Tony Tanner has put the case for this view of the religious essence of the American literary imagination about as clearly and succinctly as anyone else by writing "that there is an abiding dream in American literature that an unpatterned, unconditioned life is possible in which your moments of stillness, choices and repudiations are all your own."[1] This is what, for example, Isabel Archer expresses in *The Portrait of a Lady*, when she confesses that "nothing that belongs to me is any measure of me, everything, on the contrary, is a limit and a perfectly arbitrary one." It is the same conviction that in Faulkner's *Absalom, Absalom!* solidifies Thomas Sutpen's ambition to wrest a house and a dynasty from 100 square miles of Mississippi wilderness, as though, like the central figure in *The Great Gatsby* or the protagonist of "Song of Myself," he was born of some Platonic conception in his own mind. It is the dream of an individual who, as Captain Ahab cries out at one point in *Moby-Dick*, would be "free as the air" but discovers that "he is down in all the world's books."

The corollary to this dream amounts to a correspondent dread, to quote Tanner again, "that someone else is patterning your life, that there are all sorts of invisible plots afoot to rob you of your autonomy of thought and action, that conditioning is ubiquitous."[2] Thus Hawthorne again when Chillingworth confesses to Hester, "My old faith, long forgotten, comes back to me, and explains all that we do, and all we suffer. By thy first step awry, thou didst plant the germ of evil; but, since that moment, it has all been a dark necessity." Or the narrator in Faulkner's *Light in August* who tends to view Joe Christmas and Percy Grimm as pawns on a chessboard drawn ever closer to their fated confrontation by an invisible Player.

The typical American narrative strategy for dealing with this situation and imaginatively encompassing it is to submit the dreamer to the dread to determine what he or she can learn from the experience. Sometimes, as in the case of Captain Ahab, or Thomas Sutpen, or Hawthorne's Hollingsworth in *The Blithedale Romance*, the dreamer is transformed into an image of the very evil he associates with the restrictions on his freedom and so must be doubled by another character (Ishmael, Judith Sutpen, and Coverdale, respectively) who initially shares the dreaded feeling of constraint, and possibly becomes for a time even corrupted by the selfish desires associated with attempting to resist it, before eventually being purged of such impulses either through the development of a feeling for others that eventually curbs their need for personal vindication, or because of the way other elements of experience, such as the contingencies of nature, break them free of the narcissistic self-absorption that threatens dreamer and dreader alike.

1

Now, however, we know that this view of American fiction and its relation to religion, and specifically to Christianity, isn't quite accurate, or, at any rate, doesn't comprise the whole story. Owing largely to the work of feminist critics, we now know, for example, that there has in fact been a Christian imagination actively at work in American literature at least since the end of the eighteenth century, and that this imagination has at times proved as vital a force in cultural criticism and renewal as some of the better-known writings of the so-called classic American writers. The most striking example of this phenomenon is provided by Harriet Beecher Stowe and the sentimental tradition of the novel to which her work in many ways belongs, a tradition which, as Jane Tompkins has most forcefully proposed, is devoted to the effort to reorganize culture around the needs and potential of women themselves.[3] In sentimental fiction such as *Uncle Tom's Cabin*, life is structured in terms of a traditional Christian soteriology in which the spectacle of self-sacrifice—Little Eva's no less than Uncle Tom's—becomes a mode of female empowerment that places the institutions of the family at the center of society and defines motherhood and the rituals of domesticity as its primary values.

But Stowe's novel, and the writing of other sentimental authors with whom her own religious politics of domestic culture can be compared—Susanna Rowson's *Charlotte Temple*, Hannah Foster's *The Coquette*, Catherine Sedgwick's *Hope Leslie*, Maria Cummins's *The Lamplighter*, and Susan Warner's *The Wide, Wide World*—was in fact supplemented, as David S. Reynolds has shown, by a vast library of other kinds of religious narratives, among them Oriental and visionary tales, historical fiction set in Biblical times, and novels later associated with the postbellum Social Gospel movement that are in no sense comparable with the best of Hawthorne, say, or Melville, Mark Twain, Stowe, Elizabeth Stoddard, or even Poe.[4] Written by clergy as well as lay people, by men no less than women, by Catholics, Protestants, and, indeed, believers of all stripes, from Calvinists and liberals to anti-Calvinists and visionaries, these Christian works rarely confronted the more important religious assumptions of the era, assumptions such as the need to provide a cosmic rationale for the creation of an American culture, or the emptiness of personal life without belief, or the centrality of moral standards to the social order. But when they did, they invariably wound up merely reinforcing those assumptions rather than questioning or challenging them. Thus to find any works of fiction outside the ranks of the traditional mid-nineteenth-century classics or their sentimental neighbors that seriously attempt to bring to bear an imagination theologically definable as Christian on some of the dominant religious ideologies of their time, one must almost of necessity move to the twentieth century and the work of such writers as William Faulkner, Robert Penn Warren, Katherine Anne Porter, James Baldwin, and Flannery O'Connor.

Here, however, and particularly in reference to a writer like Faulkner, one confronts something of a paradox. Like the Christian writers of nineteenth-century sentimental fiction, Faulkner's religious imagination is brought most fully into play in response to the question about the meaning of the family and its moral possibilities as a source of social and cultural renewal. Unlike them, however, he is far less optimistic that a religious revaluing of the family itself will allow the family to serve as a model for the spiritual and moral renovation of society as a whole.

Faulkner's skepticism seems to spring from two convictions, loosely theological, that differentiate him sharply from the Christian sentimentalists of the nineteenth century. The first is his belief that the idealization of the family, particularly in the South, has led historically to a betrayal of some of the central values of Christianity itself. The second is his perception that the values most central to Christianity, or at least to his somewhat unorthodox (the better term would be heterodox) version of it, possess a still recognizable but deeply problematic association with that image of the suffering but innocent Jesus that structures the moral economy of so much nineteenth-century sentimental writing and the traditions of piety that flowed from it. In Faulkner's fiction, by contrast, and particularly, as I shall argue, in *The Sound and the*

Fury, those religious feelings that the sentimental novel traditionally tries to arouse by means of the spectacle of Christ-like
suffering—feelings of repentance, tenderness, renunciation, self-
abnegation, love, gratitude, and forgiveness—find themselves
queried with Gerontion's particularly frightening, modern question: "After such knowledge, what forgiveness?"

The "knowledge" in this case derives from the collapse of the
family itself as a socially viable, much less morally credible,
institution; and with the disintegration of the family goes much
of the rest of what the antebellum, and later the Victorian,
novel associated with the metaphysics of sentimentality—the
idealization of women, the sanctity of motherhood, the veneration of moral innocence, the defense of sexual purity, and so on.
What dooms the family as a source of spiritual values, as
Faulkner depicts it, is the temptation, no doubt widespread in
all regions of America but particularly strong in the South, to
turn the institution of the family itself into an object of worship.
This is typically accomplished by privileging an abstract and
self-serving image of the family that not only discredits but
actively undermines any of the ethical practices of mutual support, of sympathetic understanding, of loving forbearance, and
of truthful candor that the family should foster among its members.

Yet at no point is the heterodox religious imagination responsible for this insight ever explicitly defined in *The Sound and the
Fury.* Even in Dilsey's section, Faulkner's religious imagination
makes itself known or, rather, makes itself felt, less as a set of ideas
or a coherent system of interpretation than as the source of a new
valorization of the finite, a new valuation of the ordinary. In short,
the regenerative work of the religious imagination at work in this
novel is not accomplished by redeeming the world from evil,
and hence transfiguring or transforming it, so much as by penetrating its moral darkness with the light of grace, and hence trans-
valuing it.

2

If the novel is notoriously complex, the facts around which it is built are deceptively simple. The earliest significant event is the death of the grandmother, or Damuddy, in 1898. Next comes Caddy's affair with Dalton Ames in 1909, followed by her marriage to Herbert Head in April of 1910 and the subsequent birth of her illegitimate child, Quentin, named after her brother, which in 1910 causes the annulment of her marriage. Her brother Quentin's suicide occurs in June of 1910, their father, Jason, dies in 1913, and then her child, Miss Quentin, flees with the contents of her Uncle Jason's money box on Easter Sunday in 1928.

These facts are told and retold four different times from as many perspectives. In the first three instances we are in the minds of the three Compson brothers, Benjy, Quentin, and Jason, but in the fourth we escape the Compson mind altogether to achieve a more objective perspective outside it. In each of these narrative frames or perspectives, we move back and forth in time, often, as in the case of Benjy's and Quentin's sections, without warning and without clear reason, but the frames themselves are very specifically located. All but one of them are situated between Good Friday and Easter Sunday during Holy Week, and the last is situated on a day eighteen years earlier when brother Quentin commits suicide at Harvard.

Because the movement in the book is from Benjy's highly distorted, confused perspective, where time is no longer experienced as chronologically suspended between past and future but rather as continuously present, through the semi-insane interior monologue of Quentin, to the more straightforward but highly obsessional point of view of Jason, and, finally, on to the more distanced narrative of the fourth section, one could say that the novel represents a movement from obscurity and confusion to clarity and order; yet this is not exactly the way we experience that movement. Our experience of the novel is rather more decisively influenced by the static and distorted character of its first three sections and the activities we must perform in making sense of the discrepancies and confusions among them. What we become aware of as we move from section to section, only slowly realizing that similar events are being interpreted in strikingly different ways, is how different and confining each of these perspectives seems to be, and how much of their meaning for us is a consequence of operations we must perform to compensate for what their narrators leave out or obscure. Our comprehension of the truth is dependent not only upon determining in what sense every other character, and particularly the three brothers, distort it, but also by figuring out how their distortions relate to each other and to any other larger or more inclusive view.

The key to this process is contained in Faulkner's technique. Much has been made of his use of the device of interior monologue to draw us into his stories, of his employment of temporal flashbacks, inverted narrative sequences, the repetition of key scenes or the mergence of parallel situations, and the exploitation of different as well as distinctive, often distorted, points of view, but all of these devices tend to serve a single insight. That insight could be described as Faulkner's sense of the difference, and sometimes the chasm, between event and idea, between any given act and someone's apprehension of it, between an occurrence and its interpretation. Events are notable chiefly because of the interpretations they elicit, the ideas they arouse; and the interpretations, the ideas, the apprehensions they evoke are often, and necessarily, our only mode of access to them. There is no way around these interfering interpretations to the event itself; there is only the possibility of finding one's way through them to something else, to something more nearly representing the event in its full freight of consequentiality. Hence the way through them does not lead to some truth that lies waiting in the center to be discovered deep within a thicket of meaning that surrounds it but which remains essentially secondary to it. The way through Faulkner's intervening, interfering interpretations is in part, and in substantial part, the very truth of them; or rather, the truth they seemingly enclose is the truth that only exists by their means, the truth that they, and not some essential kernel of meaning buried within them, in fact, actually constitute.

There is thus a crucial sense in which the distorting and confusing filters through which Faulkner makes us look at his subject—the four different and differing perspectives of Benjy, Quentin, Jason, and the relatively omniscient narrator—represent aspects of his subject itself and not simply so many lenses by which he seeks to bring it into focus. But if this is true, then the meaning of the novel cannot be said to lie wholly in its concluding pages when, according to more traditional, often more theological expectations, all the subterfuges and interpretive glosses have been stripped away and the mystery resolved, the enigma clarified, the accounts settled, the conflicts reconciled. What is reconciled, resolved, clarified, and settled in the last pages, indeed, in the last section of *The Sound and the Fury*, is simply where, if not in some putative center or teleological culmination, the meaning in this novel has lay secreted all along, and how, more precisely, one might try to grasp it, that is, might attempt to assess its significance.

3

This fact becomes apparent when we realize that the central event, or at least the originating event, in this book is not Damuddy's death or Caddy's dirty pants, but her affair with Dalton Ames. It is Caddy's transgression, her sin, which destroys the protective self-enclosure of the family's sense of honor and brings the outside world into the Compson family pattern. Each of the first three sections of the book is an attempt to come to terms with this intrusion, really violation, from within the family circle itself, from within the distorted perspectives of this decayed domestic society. The fourth section then moves outside and re-examines this violation from a perspective that seems to transcend society altogether, though the perspective is no less culture-bound and socially specific for all that. Faulkner gives us both inner and outer views of the stain that brings on the collapse of the Compson tradition, a tradition that could be defined as the reconstructed but self-serving sense of Southern dignity that members of the Compson family variously serve and are at the same time served by. These contrasting perspectives leave us feeling less that truth is relative than that it is complex and evanescent, and that the complexity and evanesence of the truth can only be grasped in its fullness from a point of view that acknowledges all its local and partial versions.

This is the perspective that section four provides, or rather that Dilsey's religious faith provides, but one must take care not to overinterpret the significance of her Christianity, much less confuse hers with Faulkner's. Many critics have supposed that because clarity and resolution are achieved only in section four, where Dilsey's faith is triumphant, Faulkner is making a religious statement not just *in* the novel but *with* the novel, that he is here taking up all the discordant and destructive views of the book and integrating them, indeed, reordering them, in a holistic vision of religious transcendence. The fact that all but Quentin's section fall within Easter Week, that Benjy is thirty-three, that Reverend Shegog's sermon is obviously a call to repentance and new life, and that Dilsey comes through to us in our experience of the book itself, just as she does in the Sunday morning Easter service, as one who has seen "de beginnin and de en"—all of these factors have led many critics to conclude that the book not only culminates in a Christian perspective but can be understood only by means of it; in short, that the book demands a theological reading because it is ultimately making an apologetic point.

But Faulkner himself (who, to be sure, is not always to be trusted in such circumstances) put a different construction on the religious trappings of his novels as a whole, and particularly on section four of this novel, when he spoke to students at the University of Virginia. In response to a question about the symbolic meaning he intended by the dates of *The Sound and the Fury,* Faulkner spoke of hunting around in the carpenter's shop to find a tool that would make a better chicken house. Though he was prepared to concede that there was something instinctive about selecting the Easter season for the setting of his novel, he declared that he wasn't intending any special symbolism of the Passion Week at all. It was simply that the imagery and events of Easter Week were "a tool that was good for the particular corner I was going to turn in my chicken-house and so I used it."[5] Faulkner's "chickenhouse" required, as it were, a four-part structure, but it wasn't until he had composed a fifth version of the novel, nearly twenty years after the story was first written, as the appendix for Malcolm Cowley's edition of *The Viking Portable Faulkner,* that he felt the edifice was finally complete.

The story began with an image, as Faulkner told the interviewer for *The Paris Review,* "the picture . . . of the muddy seat of a little girl's drawers."[6] This image refers to an incident that took place in 1898 at the time of Damuddy's funeral when Caddy was playing with her brothers, in what they referred to as the "branch," and fell into the mud, staining her underwear. Later that same evening, Dilsey tried without success to rub the stain out, only to discover that it had soaked clear through Caddy's pants onto her skin. This initial experience of staining proceeds by a process that most of the Compsons think of as fated, even predestined, to merge with the sin of Caddy's promiscuity, and the sin of her sexual license produces Miss Quentin, the illegitimate child in whom the image of the muddy pants seen from below by Benjy is replaced "by the one of the fatherless and motherless girl climbing down the drainpipe to escape from the only home she had, where she had never been offered love or affection or understanding." The first three sections of the novel are concerned with three distinct and almost contradictory views of Caddy's stain. The last establishes a new perspective beyond the family's deeply divergent interpretations that give them all a similar coloring.

Each of the Compson perspectives is abnormally, almost psychotically, self-absorbed, but within that single scale there is a moral spectrum that runs from the innocence of the idiot Benjy to the utterly callous calculation of Jason. The moral measure in this case is the amount of self-pity involved, which is wholly unconscious in Benjy, fully deliberated, acknowledged, and rationalized in Jason. The other Compsons range themselves somewhere between these extremes. Caddy is more like Benjy because, though generous with her feelings, she is unable to control all of her impulses. Caddy's mother, Caroline, is more like Jason, her son, since she is miserly with her affection and compulsive in her search for pity. Quentin and his father occupy the ground in the middle. Both men are deluded, and by nothing so much as the need to compensate for a sense of failure and impotence that they think has been visited upon them from outside. But Quentin's father's delusion is more self-regarding than his son's, in its cynicism more sodden with sympathy for himself and in its Stoicism less sensitive to the suffering his irresolution produces in others. By contrast, Quentin's self-regard feeds on his imagination of the plight of others, but his imagination is so solipsistic that it only tightens the circle of self the more it is aroused, and thus in the end suffocates him. Faulkner's delicate but also devastating moral calculus becomes the more evident if we examine each of the brothers's sections in turn and then compare them all with Dilsey's.

4

Benjy's world like Dilsey's, though for different reasons, is a world that transcends time. A better way to put this is to say that time in Benjy's world is an undifferentiated continuum. Events occur in succession but they all strike him as continuously immediate, and can therefore only be distinguished in terms of the specific, sensory conditions that trigger his memory of them. Thus when Benjy hears the word "caddie" on a golf course, he makes the transfer to his beloved sister whom he associates with the "smell of trees" and immediately begins to bellow his remorse at her absence. That Benjy's is the world of a very small child is no accident, since the thirty-three-year old man has the mentality of a three-year-old toddler. Though Benjy loves his sister, his memory of Caddy is as fixed and unchanging as are his instinctive responses. Benjy's Caddy is the Caddy of her childhood and his, when Caddy functioned as his protectress from a world whose threatened danger often took the form of his brother Jason's aggression, his father's indifference, or his mother's rejection. Though Benjy is incapable of abstraction of the sort that destroys his two brothers and his father, he is nonetheless as locked within his own world—in his case a world of undifferentiated sensuous impressions—as they are within theirs.

Quentin's world is no less fixed than Benjy's. But if Benjy is locked outside of time and wouldn't know how to move within it, Quentin is locked within time but anxious always to arrest its effects if not escape it altogether. Though time keeps intruding upon Quentin's fantasies and his fantasies keep trying to stay time's action, Quentin has inherited his father's sense of defeat, which simply construes clocks as "the mausoleum of all hope and desire." His father's advice to try to forget time now and then so that you don't spend all of your life trying to conquer it is advice that Quentin will be obliged to accept, but not for the reasons that his father gives. Quentin's father recommends a defeatist attitude because, as he says, no battle is ever won; they are not even fought. It is this attitude which has left the field of family relations almost wholly in the control of Caroline, Quentin's mother, who has been, as Quentin can only barely acknowledge later on, no mother at all. And it is this cynical acquiescence on the part of his father—"the field only reveals to man his own folly and despair, and victory is an illusion of philosophers and fools"—that compels Quentin, so to speak, to take up arms.

But Quentin makes the fatal mistake of taking up arms on the wrong ground, or at least on ground that too closely serves his own and his family's injured sense of pride. It is the ground of the Compson, and by extension of the Southern, conception of honor, a conception of honor which his sister's illicit affairs have dirtied, Quentin believes, by not only fouling the purity of his remembered childhood world but by staining the image of his family's and, indeed, of his region's, and even of his tradition's, store of virtue. To salvage what he can of that image of virtue, Quentin attempts to take the responsibility of Caddy's promiscuity upon himself by implying that it was caused by an initial, and initiating, act of incest. This is Quentin's way of trying to lend meaning to the degeneracy in which he finds himself by containing it within a morally stable, even honorable universe. If he can displace responsibility for Caddy's sin upon himself and then accept that responsibility by admitting his own role in her corruption, he can preserve the family's sense of honor in the act of confessing his role in defiling it, even in the process of linking the defilement of incest to some historical theory of the South's predestined collapse.

That Quentin is temperamentally incapable of committing incest with his sister and, as his father reminds him in a brilliant passage near the end of his section, never does anyway, is nothing to the point. Quentin's idealistic plan to redeem Caddy's sin by taking the stain of it, so to speak, upon himself represents a futile attempt to save his family's reputation by linking it romantically to a nostalgic and inaccurate reading of the evil that has always overhung Southern history and doomed it from the start. In effect, his fantasy is also an attempt to flee the world of ripeness and decay that Caddy's promiscuity reminds him of, and this ambition is as deluded as his attempt to escape time itself.

Jason's world is as fixed as Benjy's or Quentin's, but fixed neither because he is mentally retarded, nor because he has fallen victim to a flawed view of history, but only because he is so self-centered. Jason's is a world that is totally, almost maniacally, egotistical. He regards all others in light of the impositions they make upon him, and views all supposed impositions as an attempt to cheat him out of what is rightfully his. Possession is not just an obsession of Jason's but determines, even constitutes, his whole mode of being. He even lays tenacious claim to his own words by concluding every reported utterance with "I says" in order to differentiate his own speech from anyone else's. Yet what Jason finally wants to lay claim to is an abstraction that, like Quentin's exaggerated notion of family honor, only serves to soothe an injured, or in Jason's case, an outraged sense of self. Jason is always trying to get even for the slight he suffered when the annulment of Caddy's marriage to Herbert Head cheated him out of the job at the bank. His subsequent stealing of the money Caddy sends him for the support of her daughter is therefore merely recompense for what he defines as a "breach of contract."

But Jason's venality cannot be accounted for simply by detailing the perceived injustice which prompted it. The malice buried within him can only be brought into full view by placing it in relation to the self-excusing, childish vanity of his mother which permitted, coddled, and even inspired it. As we see in the discussions between them, Jason's resentment has been warmly encouraged and even endorsed by his mother whose feelings of self-pity are but the other side of it. Indeed, not only are Caroline Compson's feelings of self-pity the obverse of Jason's spiteful anger; all along she has nourished Jason's feeling of resentment in order to create in her son someone she assumes will protect her through a kind of grudging acknowledgment of her whining sense of Bascomb honor. Caroline's hypochondria and Jason's brutal cold-heartedness belong to the same moral continuum: both are the result of a specious sense of self that is interpreted within the moral economy of the novel as an offense not only against the other members of their family but against human decency itself.

The first glimpse we have of Jason's cruelty is when Caddy reports him to Dilsey for cutting up Benjy's dolls just for spite. One of the last is when we watch him trying to convince the suspicious sheriff about the robbery, with Jason's "sense of injury and impotence feeding upon its own sound, so that after a time he forgot his host in the violent cumulation of his self-justification and his outrage." But his self-justification and outrage are curiously, not to say, grotesquely, abstract. Even though Jason can refer to Quentin as "the bitch that cost me a job, the one chance I ever had to get ahead, that killed my father and is shortening my mother's life every day and made my name a laughing stock in the town," he is oddly indifferent to her fate and even tells the sheriff (though we may not believe him) that he doesn't intend to lay a hand on her because what matters to him is neither the girl, nor the money she stole, but the image he has of himself as someone deserving of the job in the bank, "of which he had been deprived before he ever got it."

Just because Jason is so obsessed with the money he keeps under his bed, it is tempting to think of him as a kind of a materialist. But Jason is utterly indifferent to things other than money, and money means something to him only insofar as it serves an abstract—and, we might add, absurd—conception of himself. The triumph is that Faulkner can give such vivid, comic expression to an individual he finds so unremittingly fraudulent, hard-hearted, and misanthropic.

5

In the final section of the book, the narrative opens onto a world that is seen not from within but from above. The perspective is not flattering so much as realistic, and the careful rehearsal of details gives an almost heroic aspect to the actuality they render. Dilsey's world is not a comfortable or a comforting world but she bears its lacerations, like needles of rain, without complaint. They simply constitute part of the weather, whether physical or emotional, that must be endured; and while the weather will inevitably take its toll, as time always does, its marks can ennoble, as they do to the wizened figure of Dilsey herself, those who prevail in the face of it.

Dilsey's gesture, in the opening paragraphs of this section, standing in the doorway of the cabin with the mist against her uplifted face and her hand opened out like the belly of a fish to feel the moisture before she moves her worn cape aside to inspect the front of her dress, conveys an immemorial impression just because it is so ordinary, so prosaic, so absolutely unaffected. Her breasts are fallen, her face sunken, her skeleton collapsing, and her stomach distended, but she nonetheless seems to rise indomitable above these examples of the remorselessness of time to meet "the driving day," as Faulkner calls it, "with an expression at once fatalistic and of a child's astonished disappointment, until she turned and entered the house again and closed the door."

This is the day on which Dilsey will not only hear but experience "the recollection and the blood of the Lamb," or what Reverend Shegog will call, once he moves into the language of salvation, "de ricklicksun en de blood of de Lamb," a language which brings with it "de resurrection en de light" because it allows the sinner to see "de meek Jesus saying Dey kilt Me dat ye shall live again; I died dat dem whut sees en believes shall never die." When Dilsey hears this message she knows she as seen "de first en de last"; and when her daughter Frony asks "First en last whut?" Dilsey says "Never you mind, I seed de beginin, en now I sees de endin." Dilsey's revelation is one that gives her a perspective beyond time from which to view with equanimity what occurs within time. As with Shegog's appearance as he preaches, her revelation not only absorbs the temporal but "transcend[s] its shabbiness and insignificance and make[s] it of no moment." Under the spell of Shegog's voice, Dilsey, like the other members of the congregation and even Shegog himself, loses her identity in the communion of suffering humanity for which Jesus died and thereby finds new life. More important, her perspective outside of time, or at least her perspective that encompasses time—the beginning and the end, the alpha and omega—enables her, almost alone among the characters of the novel, not only to care *about* but to care *for* those who suffer the effects of time.

As the keystone of the arch of the Compson family, then, Dilsey's strength seemingly comes from some transhuman source from which all the other characters of the book are cut off. Yet the transcendence that Dilsey's perspective seems to derive from this source is convincing less because of the authority of the source itself than because of the actions Dilsey performs, so to speak, in its name. In other words, Faulkner seems to put far less credence in the postulates of Chistianity, or even in their associated sentiments, than in certain of its practices, and these practices bear the marks not only of divine mercy but even more significantly of simple human kindness.

As important as it is to her, then, Dilsey's religion gives us, as presumably it did to Faulkner, more insight into the composition of her moral character than into where it comes from. And hers is a moral character, Faulkner suggests, that has more to do with a way of seeing and being than with a set of creedal assertions. Her religion informs us that Dilsey's capacity to perceive realistically, and without resentment or remorse, derives from the fact that she has never been caught in the vicious and suffocating cycle of self-absorption that, except for Benjy and Caddy, imprison all the other Compsons. Like her honesty, her strength springs from an unspoken, indeed unconceptualized, conviction about the meaning of family—and not just one's own personal family but the whole human family—that the Compsons' practice of it so deeply betrays. This is the conviction, no less Hebraic than Christian, that if we do not hold our tenure in life on the basis of our own moral merits, neither can we survive the continual challenges to which it is susceptible because of our common mortality and corruption without learning what it means both to recognize the other as our neighbor and also to conceive of ourselves as our neighbor's keeper. What gives this conviction its cultural resonance, and a resonance particularly strong in the South, is that it describes the belief that was so disastrously forgotten by the South itself when it acceded initially to the establishment of slavery in its midst and then, in the cruelest of ironies, subsequently proceeded to rationalize the beneficence of slavery by building a distinctive system of culture centered on the sacrality of the family.

6

It could be objected, however, and in fact it has been, that the collapse of the Compson family has less to do with the disintegration of the South than with the fall of a particular family, and one whose special vulnerability to collapse can be traced largely to the ineffectuality of a mother who is defensively obsessive about her own family's former social status, who deeply resents the existence of her idiot son, and who withholds love and affection not only from her husband but from all but one of her children. On this accounting, which has been best expressed by Cleanth Brooks, Caroline Compson is not "actively wicked" so much as selfish and petty because she prevents family relationships from flowing in normal, healthy channels, and the only significance to be accorded the Southern setting "resides in the fact that the breakdown of a family can be exhibited more poignantly and significantly in a society which is old-fashioned and which is still committed to old-fashioned [Southern] ideals—close family loyalty, home care for defective children, and the virginity of unmarried daughters."[7]

While Brooks is no doubt correct in surmising that the breakdown of the family has gone further in the suburban areas of California and Connecticut than it has in the small towns of Mississippi and Georgia, Faulkner seems to suggest that it may have proceeded in the North for reasons quite different than it has proceeded in the South. Insofar as one can generalize at all about the cultural representativeness of the Compsons' experience, the institution of the family has been jeopardized in the South because of the way people do, or can, use the notion of family itself to protect and flatter an injured and also inflated sense of self, and usually at the expense of all the other selves to whom, as Southerners are particularly aware, one is socially bonded. Committing themselves variously to an abstract image of the family that is intended to soothe their own sense of personal vanity or betrayal, the Compsons deny to each other—and even more to the Lusters and Dilseys who serve them so loyally—the love and support they give to the abstraction itself. And this love, this veneration, essentially this idolization of the abstraction itself, in turn deadens them to—or at least dissociates them from—all the concrete, sensuous resources of which the institution of the family, at least in its fully human sense, is a repository, and that might otherwise continue to hold them together—from the childlike possibility of delighting in the materialities of the natural world, or the innocent pleasures of sibling rivalry and companionship, to the adult capacity for fidelity to one's own kinfolk and beyond them to the community of life, both black and white, both human and unhuman, as a whole.

Nonetheless, if the institution of the family should—and in Dilsey's practice of it does—teach us of our damaged but undiminished solidarity with the rest of creation, this lesson is purchased at a price. It is the price of accepting as "natural," as Irving Howe once pointed out, that one race shall possess a relationship of servitude with respect to another; that black people can, and will—because for so long they have—bear the burden of white peoples' suffering and silliness and savagery.[8] This is not to say that Faulkner saw this racial economy as just but only that he could appreciate the moral and spiritual beauty that it produced in the religious virtues of Dilsey's long-suffering and forbearance and charity. But this inevitably links to the historical conditions in which they were developed as a response, if not these same "Christian" virtues, then the feelings of admiration they elicit in us as readers. And while this in no way diminishes our respect for such values, much less our respect for the extraordinary black woman who epitomizes them, it does problematize our relationship to them. While to Dilsey her Christian endurance, loving-kindness, and acceptance are, and should be, regarded as modes of empowerment and marks of her triumph, to us, Faulkner's readers—particularly if we embrace them too uncritically, as Howe suggested, or apotheosize them too com-

pletely—they risk becoming tokens of our complicity in the
maintenance of a social system predicated on racial inequality that
Faulkner knew to be doomed and believed to be damned.

NOTES

1. Tony Tanner, *City of Words: American Fiction, 1950–1970* (New York: Harper and
Row, 1971),15.

2. Ibid.

3. Jane Tompkins, *Sensational Designs: The Cultural Work of American Fiction* (New
York: Oxford University Press, 1985).

4. David S. Reynolds, *Faith in Fiction: The Emergence of Religious Literature in
America* (Cambridge: Harvard University Press, 1981).

5. William Faulkner, "Faulkner in the University," *Twentieth-Century Interpretations
of "The Sound and the Fury,"* ed. Michael Cowan (Englewood Cliffs: Prentice-Hall, Inc.,
1968), 21.

6. William Faulkner, *Writers at Work: The Paris Review Interviews,* lst Series (New
York: The Viking Press, 1959), 130.

7. Cleanth Brooks, *William Faulkner: The Yoknapatawpha County* (New Haven: Yale
University Press, 1963), 341.

8. Irving Howe, *William Faulkner, A Critical Study,* 2nd ed. (New York: Vintage Books,
1952), 123.

World-Rejection in Faulkner's Fiction

RICHARD H. KING

In considering the theme of this conference—Faulkner and religion—I was driven back to the Faulkner novel, *Light in August*, which I had most recently taught. For what had struck me most forcibly upon rereading it was its unsettling effect. Though the term is inadequate, the only adjective I can think of to describe its overall effect was "creepy."

Light in August is a veritable repository of misogynist and racist views and it contains perhaps Faulkner's most bitter denunciation of Southern Protestantism as life-denying and hostile to the human spirit. Joe Christmas is presented as a lethal combination of victim and executioner, a soul brother of Richard Wright's Bigger Thomas, though denied the prospect of regeneration through violence, and a precursor of Norman Mailer's Gary Gilmore, without the flashes of charm and intelligence that Mailer attributes to Gilmore. Christmas is a steely-eyed killer, an "Isolato," the victim as sociopath, who exemplifies less the banality than the seediness of evil.

As I tried to sort out my reactions to *Light in August* and related them to the religious issue, I discovered that the undertow of disquiet I had experienced in reading the novel had something to do with two closely related religious/philosophical questions. First was one sometime attributed to Martin Heidegger: "why is there something rather than nothing?"—a variant on the Greek idea that philosophy begins in "wonder." The second follows closely upon, but asks more pointedly, what attitude should we adopt toward the "world" in general? These are two fundamental questions that any religious vision or any coherent culture, for that matter, must try to answer.

Seen in this light, there is a fundamentally hostile attitude toward the world at work in *Light in August*. And this in turn reminds us that up to the mid-1940s, when Faulkner's reputation was rehabilitated by Malcolm Cowley and Robert Penn Warren, many critics read Faulkner as a kind of protofascist and cotton-patch nihilist. They were disturbed that the sheer force of Faulkner's rhetoric overwhelmed whatever substantive vision he wanted to impart, which itself was obsessed with the horrific and atavistic. Maxwell Geismar, for instance, noted the "perverse and pathological; and the denial of humanity" in Faulkner's work, while Bernard DeVoto spoke of a dimension of Faulkner's vision he called "The Great Hatred" and an "anti-civilizational revolt." Another critic referred more pointedly to Faulkner's "reptilian art." There would be no problem in extending the list of such critical reactions to Faulkner in the 1930s and early 1940s.[1]

From our vantage point, it is easy to smile condescendingly at such panicky (mis)readings of Faulkner, operating as we are even now in the wake of what Lawrence Schwartz has referred to as the transformation of Faulkner from "prewar nihilist to postwar moralist." Put another way, Faulkner has by now been domesticated, made safe for democracy, morality, sectional pride, racial tolerance, and even religion. But the strong reactions against Faulkner, or against something in Faulkner's work, did have the merit of acknowledging what can be called the nihilistic register in Faulkner's work. What I understand terms like "perverse" and labels like "Great Hatred" to refer to and what I hear in Faulknerian evocations of "outrage" and "fury" is a fundamental attitude toward the nature of things which might be named radical world-rejection.

In what follows I want to identify the cultural sources of world-rejection in Faulkner's work, particularly in early Christian and Gnostic theology and point to some examples of it in his work. Then I will consider an opposing claim that Faulkner neutralizes or counteracts the impulse toward rejection of the world by thematic and structural oppositions; for instance, the Lena Grove/ Byron Bunch story contains and trumps the story of Joe Christmas and Joanna Burden. Then I will end by trying to assess how we should understand this theme of world-rejection in Faulkner's work.

Before that I want to emphasize what I am not claiming here. I am not saying that Faulkner was a theologian or philosopher who consciously clothed philosophical and theological ideas in fictional garb. Rather I want to explore the way the impulse toward world-rejection pervades his work, how it "still crowds in upon us as pale forbidding presences." Nor am I interested in the personal provenance of this fictional theme or whether the ideas in Faulkner's fiction are "his." Like most of us, Faulkner had his own devils to combat and he did not always emerge victorious or unscathed.[2]

1. World-Rejection in Western Culture

From its inception Christianity has contained contradictory attitudes toward God's creation. The first chapter of Genesis records that "God saw every thing that he made and, behold, it was very good." But, as we know, it was all downhill from there, to the point that God took on human form and died to redeem the world from the sin of Adam and Eve. Following from the incarnation idea was the belief that Jesus had been literally, that is, physically, resurrected from the dead. Thus though the original creation was good, human disobedience had corrupted it. God cared enough about his creation to redeem it; yet his promise is deliverance from rather than recommitment to it. We are not to be conformed to the world but transformed. All this is a way of reiterating what Christian thinkers from St. Paul to Kierkegaard have emphasized: the doctrine of incarnation was a scandal to the Greeks, an offense to the Jews, and a paradox to believers.

Despite—or because of—the problematic relationship between celebration and renunciation of the world implied by the incarnation, during the first two centuries of the Christian era Christians fought amongst themselves, as well as with the rival Gnostics and the Roman authorities, over the issue of the status of the world.[3] Though the story is incredibly complicated, Peter Brown's monumental *The Body and Society: Men, Women, and Sexual Renunciation in Early Christianity* (1988) points out several crucial developments in Christian thinking about the world. First, though asceticism was not unknown in classical antiquity or in the Jewish cultural ethos, both pre- and non-Christian religious cultures acknowledged, sometimes enthusiastically but generally with a kind of wary acceptance, the needs of the body and, in the case of the Jews, the centrality of sexuality and reproduction in maintaining God's chosen people in the world.

But though Christianity eventually had to make its peace with the body (having taken it to stand for the world), early Christianity strongly inclined toward world-rejection. In the second century sexuality and the body replaced death as the "privileged symptom of humanity's fall into bondage." Abjuring sexuality and procreation would thus be a blow against the "present age." Once sexuality became emblematic of the fallen state of the human race, the next century saw a new celebration of celibacy in men and virginity in women. "The absence of sexuality in the chosen few," writes Brown, "provided the human race with new mediators." In particular Christian men "used women . . . in order to verbalize their own nagging concern with the stance that the Church should take to the world." Women's bodies, in particular, were the site of the sacred *and* the embodiment of the profane and worldly.[4]

Contemporaneous with the rise of Christianity was a more extreme form of spirituality called Gnosticism, whose influence upon early Christianity was profound. Briefly and oversimply, Gnosticism held to the belief that there was a true God, the "Other" or "Unknown" God, who had distanced himself from the world which had been created by lesser gods, sometimes called "Archons" or the "Demiurge." The world was the "innermost dungeon," ruled by the laws of nature and necessity. Some Gnostics felt that the Jewish God was an Archon, not the high God, and that Satan was also an Archon who vied with Yawheh for control of the world. For others the serpent was the deliverer of true and secret wisdom ("gnosis") and God had punished Adam and Eve for trying to escape his control. Not only was Gnosticism profoundly dualistic, it also attributed alienation from the true God not to human action but to the rebellion of the lesser gods. Gnostic morality was based, according to Hans Jonas, on "hostility toward and contempt for mundane ties." Further, a savior or messenger was necessary to lead the "spirit" (not the body or the soul) back to the true God and to restore the original oneness of creation. Though this savior would appear in bodily form, this incarnation was illusory rather than actual.[5]

The crucial difference between Christianity and Gnosticism lay, then, in the latter's total metaphysical and theological renunciation of the world, especially the doctrine of incarnation, and its contempt for the norms established by worldly institutions of all sorts. This Gnostic rejection of the authority of worldly institutions and laws, its antinomian dimension, was potentially subversive. Indeed, some Gnostics drew the conclusion that a libertine rather than an ascetic way of life was required. They felt the necessity of "rendering to nature its own and thereby exhausting its powers." Thus paradoxically a person earned or proved his or her salvation through "excess" rather than "absention." Moreover, Elaine Pagels has called attention to the fact that the hostility to the body and ipso facto to women in some Gnostic theology was balanced by an emphasis upon the female principle in understanding the nature of the true God. In fact, spiritual equality, even close socializing of men and women in Gnostic groups, was quite common, once it was thought they had transcended worldly concerns and desires.[6]

Interesting though these developments in and early tensions between Christianity and Gnosticism are, the question remains: what is the relevance to Faulkner's fictional world? Is there any direct or indirect causal connection? Hans Jonas has suggested that there are strong affinities between the ancient Gnostic and modern Existentialist world views. Both, he claims, view humanity as alone in and estranged from a cosmos lacking a purpose or goal: "Dread as the soul's response to its being-in-the-world is a recurrent theme in gnostic literature." More generally, the modernist ethos, the cultural context of Faulkner's emergence as a writer, was the final stage of the culture which early Christianity and Gnosticism had shaped so profoundly and which had itself been obsessed with spiritual homelessness, with a world bereft of meaning or tradition. Thus the modern ethos of what Philip Rieff has called a "waning ascetic culture" echoed the initial stages of that same culture.[7]

Though usually expressing this pervasive sense of loss and displacement in terms of Southern cultural decline, Faulkner's work was an expression of modernism's quest to make sense of a world grown opaque. Thus we might see Faulkner's fictional obsessions with violence, sexuality, and rage as explorations of those facets of existence, the access to which a stable culture normally controls through prohibitions and taboos. In their minds, and sometimes their actions, characters such as Emily Grierson, Popeye, Quentin Compson, Addie Bundren, and Joe Christmas exemplify the transgressive mode, edging up to and sometimes breaking through the boundaries of the "sacred" which Georges Bataille has defined as "whatever is the subject of a prohibition." As mentioned, the revelation of the nature of the forbidden in Faulkner's work often produces a reaction of horror not fascination, a revulsion against existence rather than a celebration of it in his characters and his readers.[8]

There is yet another parallel between the world of modernity and the early centuries of the Christian era—the breakdown of a consensus about what the dominant language of "world-description" should be. In the modern South, religious discourse was still the dominant discourse; yet the growing power of the language of modern science to describe and explain the world was at issue in the sometimes farcical controversy over the teaching of Darwinism that neither began nor ended at Dayton, Tennessee, in 1925. We can also detect a plurality of competing discourses or language games in Faulkner's work itself. The ethos is of course Protestant Christian, but Faulkner the narrator and/or his characters often deploy pre- or non-Christian vocabularies. Besides the obvious Biblical parallels evoked by the title *Absalom, Absalom!*, the parallels between Sutpen's fate and that of the Greek tragic hero are explicitly drawn; indeed, Mr. Compson is enamored of a quite un-Christian age of heroism that has disappeared. Moreover, Sutpen is even described as a "Demiurge," a familiar term, as already noted, in Gnostic discourse.

Light in August itself offers a plethora of competing discourses. Though characters in the text make reference to God's will, the narrative voice adverts more frequently to explanations of events shaped by the arbitrary decisions of the "Player" and the "dark diceman." Readers have always been tempted to see Christmas as a Christ-figure, crucified by the community; but also as an Oedipus-figure who is brought low, not only by what he does but also by what he thinks he knows. In addition, Gavin Stevens's crackpot racial metaphysics reminds us of the discourse of racism which was and still is such a powerful force in Southern and American culture. Thus various vocabularies of description and explanation vie for supremacy and symbolic referents are highly unstable in Faulkner's fictional world, a reflection in part of the "in-betweenness" of the modern condition.

But if Faulkner's response to modernity was reflected in the theme of world-rejection, the most notorious force for weaning humans from the pleasures of the world in his work is the practical Calvinism of Southern Protestantism. Calvinism, its Puritan versions and in turn their Southern variations, are complicated phenomena. Though the Scotch-Irish provenance of some versions of Southern Calvinism is clear, Southern Protestantism was less theologically Calvinist than it was ethically puritanical. What most people mean when they refer to Calvinism and Puritanism in the Southern context is less a theology than a deep suspicion of worldly pleasure, that is, sex, drinking, and dancing, combined with a canting hypocrisy and a love of worldly gain. However illogically these characteristics fit together, something which Max Weber tried to work out in his *The Protestant Ethic and the Spirit of Capitalism,* Faulkner created a prototypical Puritan in Rosa Coldfield's father in *Absalom, Absalom!* and earlier an even more adamantine Puritan in the form of Joe Christmas' foster-father, Simon McEachern.

Faulkner pinpointed what he saw as the essence of Southern Protestantism in a frequently cited passage from *Light in August*:

> Yet even then the music has still a quality stern and implacable, deliberate and without passion so much as immolation, pleading, asking, for not love, not life, forbidding it to others, demanding in sonorous tones death as though death were the boon, like all Protestant music. . . . *And so why should not their religion drive them to crucifixion of themselves and one another?*[9]

This is not the whole story of Southern Protestantism, just as modernity encompasses more than world-rejection. Still, there is no doubt that Protestantism in general and some of the frontier denominations in particular cultivated the image of themselves as revivals of the pure and primitive communities of early Christianity and, like the early Christians and Gnostics, feared the temptations of the world, the flesh, and the devil more than they welcomed the pleasures of earthly existence.

But the most interesting exemplification of world-rejection in Faulkner's fiction can be found in his obsession with the fate of the "doomed couple," for several of Faulkner's most important works cohere around the great romantic love and death theme, the *Liebestod*. Indeed, that is where the Gnostic theme returns in a fairly direct way. On one influential account, the ideal of romantic love derived, at least in part, from the influence of Gnostic sects in the Provencal in the twelfth and thirteenth centuries. As explained by Denis de Rougement, this ideal was originally posited on the "inescapable conflict in the West between passion and marriage."[10] Marriage involves the love of two people for each other and a commitment to perpetuate the world through having children; indeed, marriage is the worldly institution par excellence. But romantic love, dominated by Eros not Agape, passion not care, is suffused with "obsession by the love that breaks the law." Ultimately, and this is the Gnostic element, romantic lovers reject and withdraw from the world, while becoming absorbed by and in one another and ultimately death. Romantic love is finally a narcissistic, death-obsessed state, since "each loves the other from the standpoint of self and not from the other's standpoint." Put less cryptically, romantic lovers are in love with love rather than with each other, in love with rejection of the world rather than making a common life within it. Abandoning oneself to passion is not an affirmation of the body but an attempt to transcend it. Thus, romantic love is, says Rougement, "a Christian heresy," the outgrowth of an infusion of Gnostic elements into medieval Christianity.[11]

Whether Rougement's historical account is correct, his exploration of the opposition between marriage and passion, between the family and the couple, is powerfully suggestive. The crucial elements, he points out, in the genre of the romantic love story are the presence of obstacles to fulfillment of passion, withdrawal from and hatred of the world, the doom brought on by sexual consummation, and the ultimate fusion beyond life and death. When combined with Georges Bataille's analysis of the conflict between sexuality and eroticism, a discussion which roughly maps the same territory as Rougement explores, then another generic theme can be added: the problem of having children, or refusing to do so. For Bataille, eroticism involves a "psychological quest independent of the natural goal [of sexuality]: reproduction and the desire for children. . . . Reproduction implies the existence of discontinuous beings" while eroticism, like death, involves the desire for "lost continuity."[12] Our fear of erotic passion, like our fear of death, arises from a fear of loss of boundaries.

I have made this detour through the realms of sexuality and eroticism, marriage and passion, love and death, because, following David Minter, the tension between them constitutes one of the major preoccupations of Faulkner's fiction. Indeed, it is in Faulkner's fictional treatment of the inevitably "doomed couple" that his religious impulses are most fully articulated, particularly his highly ambivalent attitude toward the world. There are of course any number of passionate, doomed couples willing to crucify themselves in the name of the religion of love in Faulkner's fictional world. Here I would like to focus on four of them.[13]

Quentin and his imaginary love, Caddy, are perhaps Faulkner's most famous doomed couple. The obstacle to their love—the incest taboo—is the most fundamental obstacle to union with the obscure object of original desire. Quentin indicates the religious provenance of his passion to have already committed incest and to be consigned to perdition when he speaks of his desire to "isolate her out of the loud world" and imagine "[N]obody else there but her and me." By this time he hopes to undo Caddy's loss of virginity, a concept Mr. Compson acutely recognizes as a male invention. For all his cynicism, the father realizes not only that Quentin has not committed incest, but that he is highly ambivalent regarding his own and his sister's physicality: "you are contemplating an apotheosis in which a temporary state of mind will become symmetrical above the flesh and aware both of itself and of the flesh it will not quite discard."[14]

Indeed Quentin's rejection of the world expresses itself in revulsion against women's—and the world's—body, which has been fed by his father's (or perhaps his own) imaginings: "they [women] have an affinity for evil for supplying whatever the evil lacks in itself"; and more horrifically: "Liquid putrefaction like drowned things floating like pale rubber flabbily filled getting the odor of honeysuckle all mixed up." Women engulf and stifle. They embody, quite literally, the temptations of the world and loss of clear, hard and fast distinctions between self and other, male and female. Yet the temptation to succumb is there too; part of Quentin desires the fusion and eradication of difference. When Quentin finally realizes that Caddy is doomed to choose the world by getting married, he commits suicide, which, if we follow Rougement, has been his goal all along. The author of the 1946 appendix to *The Sound and the Fury* confirms this when he writes of Quentin: "Who loved not the idea of incest, which he would not commit, but some presbyterian concept of its eternal punishment . . . who loved death above all."[15]

Addie Bundren is perhaps the most secret lover of all Faulkner's characters. Though she has had an affair with the minister, Whitfield, the son of that union, Jewel, becomes the object of her desire long after the affair has terminated. Addie's doomed love is also important just because Jewel embodies the fury and hatred we learn Addie harbors. As a teacher she would "go down the hill to the spring where I could be quiet and hate them" after her pupils had left school in the afternoon. She is largely indifferent to the children she has had with Anse. Her passionate feelings are reserved for Jewel, who expresses his hate and love for his mother via the passion and hatred he shows for his horse. "Jewel's mother," realizes Darl, "is a horse." Like Quentin, Jewel yearns for isolation from the world and a way to express his hatred for it: "It would just be me and her on a high hill and me rolling the rocks down the hill at their faces."[16]

Addie's agony is also similar to Quentin's in that neither can bring together the word and the world, concept and experience. In other words "incarnation" seems foreclosed in their worlds. But where Quentin is besotted by abstractions like "virginity" and "honor," even to the point of transforming incest into an abstraction, Addie refuses the temptation of grand rhetoric and large concepts; rather, she celebrates illicit sexuality:

> And so when Cora Tull would tell me I was not true mother, I would think how words go straight up in a thin line, quick and harmless, and how terribly doing goes along the earth, clinging to it, so that after a while the two lines are too far apart . . . and that sin and love and fear are just sounds.

Addie's memory of meeting Whitfield involves a kind of trans-valuation of values, a move beyond good and evil; even an affirma-tion of what she has been taught is sinful:

> the sin the more utter and terrible since he was the instrument
> ordained by God who created sin . . . I would think of him dressed in
> sin. I would think of him as thinking of me dressed also in sin, he the
> more beautiful since the garment which he had exchanged for sin was
> sanctified.[17]

And though Addie's sin does not lead her to her literal death, she is already dead and speaks, as it were, beyond the world.

If the stories of doomed lovers in *The Sound and the Fury* and *As I Lay Dying* indicate the religious origins of the romantic love story, Faulkner wrote two other, more secular love stories in which world-rejection is central. One is the story of Harry Wil-bourne and Charlotte Rittenmeyer in *The Wild Palms*, which smacks more of *The Postman Rings Twice* than of *Tristan and Iseult*. Still, most of the central obsessions of the classic love story are there. Though Charlotte's husband is willing to let her go, or at least seems to be willing to do so, the couple are constantly on the run, fleeing from the South to Chicago, then out west to Colorado and back to Louisiana. They are clearly not fleeing him but the world of bourgeois convention and respectability which they see as the main threat to their relationship. "Love and suffering are the same thing," says Charlotte, while Harry later confesses to a friend that to his horror: "I had turned into a husband . . . blind to all passion and dead to all hope . . . unaware in the face of all darkness, all unknown, the underlying All-Derisive biding to blast him." It is to escape that fate that they reject roots or community.[18]

But Charlotte is ultimately the tougher of the two, the more resolute in her rejection of the world. Their story descends toward the doom always implicit in it, when she discovers that she is pregnant and insists that Harry perform an abortion on her: "I want it to be us again, quick." To bring another person into their world would be to bring the world into their private passion and make it "worldly." When the old doctor first meets Charlotte, he sees in her face "hatred of the whole human race . . . no . . . at the race of men, the masculine." She is described at various times as full of fury and as doing things "savagely." But Harry cannot bring himself to perform the abortion; then when he does, he makes a mess of it and kills both her and the baby. "But you return," he has told their friend McCord, presumably to the world, from the ecstasies of the orgasm and escape from temporality. And he does; but Charlotte is dead and he is in prison. His acceptance of "grief" rather than "nothing" is a kind of qualified acceptance of the world, but only in order to preserve the memory of their attempt to transcend it.[19]

Finally, there is the quite literally "awful" relationship of Joe Christmas and Joanna Burden, both an example and kind of grotesque parody of the romantic love ideal. If there is an account of love in hell, hell in love, it is this one. Joanna is already isolated from the world around her due to her inheritance and her politics; and her relationship with Christmas only heightens her estrangement. Similarly Joe has been condemned to estrangement from the world and from himself by almost everyone and everything in his world. Of this failure of incarnation, Arnold Weinstein has written: "In him, the rift between mind and body is well-nigh absolute."[20] Like Mr. McEachern, Joe has contempt for and is repulsed by softness and identifies it with women. He is pushed over the brink when Joanna begins to pray for him: "she ought not to have begun praying over me," which echoes his earlier rejection of Mrs. McEachern: "she was trying to make me cry." Analogously, his initial reaction to the "fecundmellow voices of Negro women . . . the lightless hot wet primogenitive Female" is to flee: "he began to run." As with Quentin, then, women embody that which threatens to engulf and to overflow boundaries. The male world in general, not just Joe, seems in a state of permanent revulsion against the flesh. Joe's real grandfather, Doc Hines, talks of "woman filth" and rants against "this world's sluttishness and bitchery."[21]

And yet, as the genre dictates, the passion of Joe and Joanna feeds on obstacles in order to transgress them out of the world's sight, that being the romantic love story's way of representing its profound ambivalence regarding physicality. The two come from different classes and backgrounds; they may be of different races, which would mean that their relationship is, even more than an incestuous one, taboo in the Southern context. Also, as in the paradigmatic romantic passion, there is a certain impersonality, a detached, almost solipsistic quality about the whole thing. "It was," intones the narrator, "as if he struggled physically with another man for an object of no actual value to either, and for which they struggled on principle alone."[22]

After the initial stage of their relationship, they move on or down to the regions of the obscene: "It was as though he had fallen into the sewer" with Joanna condemning herself by "living not alone in sin but in filth." And then surprisingly, but most fatefully and even predictably in terms of generic conventions, this phase give way to a third when "She began to talk about a child. . . . He was thinking fast, thinking *She wants to be married. That's it. She wants a child no more than I do.*"[23] Thus the stage is set for the ultimate end to their doomed passion. Joe murders Joanna, once she begins to want to make a life in the world and to include him in it. Christmas resumes his life on the run but inexorably returns—in a world controlled by fate not choice—to the place of his birth where he allows himself to be arrested. Then he escapes, only to be run to earth again and there to meet the fate he has been running from and pursuing all his life. His end is a gruesome parody of sexual orgasm, the one form of transcendence left to him. As Joseph Urgo comprehensively sums it up: "The Christians in the novel reject the flesh, reject the incarnation, and embrace the death of the body as its primary definition. If *Light in August* rages, it rages against the denial of the physical body."[24]

2. Counterclaims

If the critics of the 1930s were right to be shocked by Faulkner, as I suggested earlier, the question remains as to whether world-rejection is the most important dimension of his work, at least up to *Absalom, Absalom!* where history—the totality of past actions—begins to be explicitly thematized. The grounds of Quentin's horror at the Sutpen story and Ike McCaslin's rejection of his patrimony in *Go Down, Moses* are less religious or metaphysical than moral and psychological. To be unable to come to terms with these phenomena is not to reject the human world as such but only a particular version of it. To "hate" the South or want to change it fundamentally is not to hate the world, though latter-day Southern conservatives sometime seem to argue otherwise.[25]

But though I am strongly inclined to say that world-rejection is central in these early texts (along with *The Wild Palms*), such a claim runs up against an important thematic and structural objection. In each of the four texts where doomed lovers reject the world, their revulsion against the world, of men against women, of women against children, is bracketed or contained or counterbalanced by a story of acceptance of the world, or something approaching affirmation or at least willingness to come to terms with it. For instance the Quentin/Caddy story (as well as Jason's bitter but less exalted hatred of reality) is answered, as it were, by the focus on Dilsey in the novel's fourth section. That section suggests that Dilsey's black family and the black community in general hold the Compsons together quite literally; otherwise, the Compson family would completely disintegrate. The famous "they endured" of the appendix confirms and affirms the spirit which accepts this world, if for no other reason than that there is another world to hope for.

Similarly, though more ambiguously, Addie's utterly bleak rejection of Anse, of the children of their marriage, and of love in general is balanced by Anse's remarriage at the end of the novel. However limited and foolish Anse may be, *As I Lay Dying* comes close to fulfilling the generic requirements of the comedy in which marriage (or remarriage) closes the action and represents a kind of affirmation of the given order. "Meet Mrs. Bundren," he says. We know the world will go on somehow.[26]

In some ways, *The Wild Palms* is the most difficult case to sort out in the light of my concerns here, since the story of Harry and Charlotte is interspersed with "The Old Man." There are many parallels, as well as important differences, between the two stories. But I would suggest that, although Harry finally chooses "grief" and the convict allows himself to be reimprisoned, the latter's rueful, comic, and obscene last comment ("Women . . . t!") represents a sort of bemused acceptance of things as they are, a recognition of reality rather than a rejection of it.

Finally, the most obvious bracketing story is of Lena Grove and Byron Bunch in *Light in August*. It provides the comic counterpoint to the horrific interior story of Joe and Joanna and is a kind of pastoral emollient to the lacerations of the negative sublime, the unconsciously pagan as opposed to the perverted Christianity that pervades the main story. Lena has had her baby, in itself an affirmation of the created world and its possibilities. And we leave Lena and Byron, not yet united in the flesh but with the promise of that to come, their story being related in comic terms by the furniture dealer to his wife in their marital bed.

It is difficult to know what to make of these thematic and structural counterpairings, since what we take away from one story stands at odds with what we take away from its other. In terms of chronological and positional finality, the comic resolution, the closure and completion, the reaffirmation not so much of the social order as of the world as such, would seem to demand priority. The end of the story would designate the meaning or point of the story. And yet, the emotional and even philosophical heart of each of these four works, I would claim, is the story of world-rejection. In particular, Dilsey's section in *The Sound and the Fury* and Lena's story in *Light in August* are too obviously formulaic, even tacked-on. In other words, thematic resolution, particularly in these two novels, undermines aesthetic or formal closure and vice versa.

Finally, I vaccillate between two related but somewhat different readings of the texts in which world-rejection and affirmation of the world vie for the last or fullest word. Most harshly, I would follow James Snead's claim in reference to *As I Lay Dying*: "Without Darl's voice, the novel funnels out into an uncertain ending—is it tragic or comic?" Snead goes on to observe more generally that there is "a pattern of artificial redemption not uncommon elsewhere in Faulkner," a judgment he extends when he wonders in reference to *Light in August* "to what extent Faulkner himself hides from a truth he has uncovered, mainly by encasing it in an overcomplex, even dual, narrative structure?"[27]

Less harshly—though not by a whole lot—we might read the "truth" Faulkner has illuminated to be similar to the drift of Auden's "Musee des Beaux Arts." There Auden observes:

> About suffering they were never wrong,
> The Old Masters, how well they understood
> Its human position; how it takes place
> While someone is eating or opening a window or just walking
> dully along;

But the low-key Audenesque voice should not beguile us into overlooking the bleakness of this vision—the world is one in which death, torture, and suffering are part of its very fabric. All that can be done is to live on through it, not taking too much notice either way. Cosmic indifference is matched by a necessary human blindness and forgetfulness, punctuated by occasional outcries of protest and the will to survive. I'm not sure Faulkner's Nobel Prize Address amounts to much more than that.

In other words, there is very little "good news" in Faulkner's world. He disposes less over a positive religious vision than an ethical one, by no means exclusively Christian and almost desperately adopted in the face of the bleakness of the world. Where the early critics, then, made their mistake was in arguing for the emptiness and nihilism of Faulkner's work, when they might better have concerned themselves with the pervasive scene of emptiness, loss, and nothingness in his work. Thus his powerful rhetoric can be seen as a response to that lack or absence at the heart of human existence, sometimes powerfully effective in evoking that absence but sometimes merely substituting its own sonority for the absence.

Coda:

Though I think the Gnostic theme—as much a fascinating parallel as an influence—is important, it may seem an obscure and pretentious way to generalize about what are, as most of us see these things, very disturbed individual characters whom Faulkner has created and set loose in his world. If we use the discourse of modern depth psychology, then clearly world-rejection and revulsion against creation, particularly against the physicality of women, are pathological attitudes. From this point of view, we might say, provisionally, that the fundamental Gnostic attitude of world-rejection comes to us in pathological symptoms, as a rage at absence and lack and loss, as a sense of hopeless estrangement between self and world, body and mind, and as an inordinate fear of engulfment and loss of boundaries.

But there are other Gnostic motifs in Faulkner's fiction. The dialogue between the Corporal and the General in A Fable has powerful Gnostic resonances, as does Christ's temptations in the Wilderness by Satan from which the former clearly derives. Two principles—worldy power and spiritual power—seem irreconcilably set against one another. But in line with Snead's observation, we can say that Faulkner fudged the strong opposition by asserting that the two principles were ultimately, somehow, reconcilable, though the final scene of the novel suggests the persistence of rage against injustice in the world.

More crucially, it could be argued that the vocation of the modern or post-Romantic artist is to challenge the created world and to create another cosmos, one which doesn't merely stand in mimetic relation to the "real" world but rivals and seeks to transform it. The distinction is perhaps drawn too finely between mimesis and metamorphosis; but the point is that the world somehow needs reparation. Metaphysically, it is less than it could be; historically, it has become less than it was. Whatever the case, the psychology of creation, at least in Faulkner's case, seemed to involve making good an experienced inadequacy in self and/or world: "Those who can, do, those who cannot and suffer enough because they can't, write about it."[28]

More defiantly, Faulkner celebrates the titanic, amoral, willful, rebellious world-creators such as Sutpen and Carothers McCaslin. Here finally we must remember the map that accompanies *Absalom, Absalom!* The "owner and sole proprietor" of that world is William Faulkner, one of our modern Demiurges, a rival creator, and one who, as he himself asserted, "improves on God."[29]

NOTES

1. Lawrence Schwartz, *Creating Faulkner's Reputation: The Politics of Modern Literary Criticism* (Knoxville: University of Tennessee Press, 1988), 12–14.

2. Peter Brown, *The Body and Society: Men, Women, and Sexual Reproduction in Early Christianity* (London: Faber and Faber, 1988), 47. David Minter's *William Faulkner: His Life and Work* (Baltimore: Johns Hopkins University Press, 1980) takes the interactions of Faulkner's life and work as its central focus and provides considerable detail on Faulkner's own attitudes toward sexuality and women.

3. Besides Brown's recent work, Hans Jonas, *The Gnostic Religion*, 2nd ed., revised (Boston: Beacon Press, 1962) is a masterpiece of intellectual history, while Elaine Pagels, *The Gnostic Gospel* (London: Weidenfeld and Nicolson, 1979) tries, unconvincingly, to turn the Gnostics into "progressives" in the setting of early Church politics and theology.

4. Brown, *The Body and Society*, 86, 187, 153.

5. Jonas, *The Gnostic Religion*, 43, 46.

6. Ibid., 175, 274.

7. Ibid., 239. Jonas was a student of Martin Heidegger in the late 1920s. Rieff develops his sociology of a waning ascetic culture in *The Triumph of the Therapeutic* (New York: Harper and Row, 1966).

8. George Bataille, *Death and Sensuality: A Study of Eroticism and the Taboo* (New York: Ballantine Books, 1969), 62.

9. William Faulkner, *Light in August* (New York: Modern Library, 1950), 322.

10. Denis de Rougement, *Love in the Western World*, revised and augmented (New York: Harper Torchbooks, 1974), 8. Cleanth Brooks discussess the Rougement thesis and relates it to *The Town* in *William Faulkner: The Yoknapatawpha County* (New Haven: Yale University Press, 1963), 192–218; and also links it with *The Wild Palms* in *Toward Yoknapatawpha and Beyond* (New Haven: Yale University Press, 1978).

11. Rougement, *Love*, 17, 52, 137.

12. Bataille, *Death and Sensuality*, 5, 9.

13. Minter, *William Faulkner*, especially chapter 3.

14. Faulkner, *The Sound and the Fury* (New York: Vintage Books, 1954), 220, 97, 220.

15. Ibid., 119, 159, 411. Much the same attitudes toward flesh and corporeality pervade Jean-Paul Sartre's *Nausea*.

16. Faulkner, *As I Lay Dying* (Harmondsworth, U.K.: Penguin Books, 1963), 134, 75, 15.

17. Ibid., 137–38, 138.

18. Faulkner, *The Wild Palms* (New York: Vintage Books, 1939), 48, 132.

19. Ibid., 210, 11, 138.

20. Arnold Weinstein, "Fusion and Confusion in *Light in August*," *The Faulkner Journal* 1 (Spring 1986): 4.

21. Faulkner, *Light*, 147, 100, 115, 325. Joseph Urgo writes further that "at the heart of Joe Christmas's inability to accept a definition of himself as black or white is self-hatred and alienation from his physical, male body." ("Menstrual Blood and 'Nigger' Blood: Joe Christmas and the Ideology of Sex and Race," *Mississippi Quarterly* 41 [Summer 1988]: 395.)

22. *Light*, 205.

23. Ibid., 226, 230, 231.

24. Urgo, "Menstrual Blood," 397.

25. I am referring here to latter-day Southern conservatives who, under the influence of Eric Voegelin, attribute all desire to change society and all utopian impulses to Gnosticism which they see as the impulse to respiritualize a fallen reality. This metaphysical conservatism essentializes and spiritualizes the existing order and thus makes it practically impossible to distinguish world-rejection from rejection of this or that particular social arrangement. Thus my use of Gnosticism has little to do with the world view (and, by extension, politics) associated with Southern conservatism.

26. *As I Lay Dying*, 204.

27. James A. Snead, *Figures of Division* (New York: Methuen, 1986), 62, 95.

28. Faulkner, *The Unvanquished* (New York: Oxford University Press, 1980), 139–45.

29. See my *A Southern Renaissance* (New York: Oxford University Press, 1980), 139–45 for a discussion of these matters.

Order as Disorder: *Absalom, Absalom!*'s Inversion of the Judaeo-Christian Creation Myth

William D. Lindsey

> It was order that gave beauty to this goodly fabric of the world, which before was but a confused chaos, without form and void. Therefore when Job—when he would set out the terribleness of the grave and dismal state of death—he calls it the land of darkness, and the shadow of death without any order (Job 10:22).
>
> William Hubbard, *The Happiness of a People in the Wisdom of Their Rulers Directing and in the Obedience of Their Brethren Attending*

As William Hubbard's 1676 Massachusetts election sermon *The Happiness of a People* suggests, order was a significant preoccupation of colonial American Puritan divines. Persuaded as they were of the first settlers' divine commission to tame a new land, they envisaged the disorder of the wilderness as a figure of the dark satanic presence that continuously disturbs and subverts the divine order established at creation.[1] The mandate to tame the wilderness was for the Puritans a *religious* mandate: the act of wresting land from its aboriginal inhabitants, clearing and planting it, was not merely secular; it was also a means of overcoming satanic disorder by imposing divine order. In their sermons, poems, journals, and political addresses, early American Puritans expressed their conviction of the divine commission to subdue the continent and their trepidation about carrying out this task. To order the wilderness required a submissive spirit, a willingness to remain in covenantal relationship with the Lord who had charged his peculiar people with this work. As studies of American civil religion have demonstrated, these mythic themes of Puritan thought continue profoundly to inform the American psyche: Americans persist in seeing themselves as a people who have a divine errand into the wilderness, a mission to quell disorder and establish divine order.

From seventeenth-century Massachusetts to twentieth-century Mississippi is a far stretch geographically, temporally, and culturally. Yet the fiction of William Faulkner suggests that the two regions and cultures—those of colonial New England and of post-Reconstruction Mississippi—are intimately linked. In probing the myths that undergird modern Southern culture, Faulkner is probing *American* myths.[2] This is perhaps nowhere so evident as in the novel widely regarded as his masterpiece, *Absalom, Absalom!* In *Absalom, Absalom!* Faulkner recounts the story of an American type, a self-made man. Using the mythic language of the Judaeo-Christian creation narratives, Faulkner depicts Thomas Sutpen's settling of a plantation in the wilderness of early nineteenth-century Mississippi as an act of *hybris* that engenders a series of tragic consequences spanning generations. In Faulkner's telling, the story of this self-made man becomes a story about how attempts to create order tend to go tragically awry, when they derive from a facile assumption of human innocence and of the unambiguous power of human rationality to calculate what is good. Sutpen's story is the story of the nation: in critiquing Sutpen's achievements, Faulkner is implicitly questioning the myths by which the American people live.[3]

The Judaeo-Christian Creation Myth and *Absalom, Absalom!*

In *Absalom, Absalom!* Faulkner makes deliberate use of the imagery and rhetoric of the Biblical account of the Judaeo-Christian creation myth.[4] The creation theme is not incidental to the statement made by the novel. Rather, the inverted creation

myth with which the novel begins is central to the Sutpen narrative around which all other narratives in the novel revolve.[5]
Faulkner employs creation imagery to comment on Sutpen's pretentious self-creation and his ironically destructive creation of the
domain of Sutpen's Hundred.

The notion of creation is fundamental to the Judaeo-Christian
scriptures. Though the mythic account of the original creation
occurs in Genesis, the first book of the Hebrew canon,[6] both
creation imagery and theological reflection on the theme of creation are to be found throughout the Hebrew and Christian canons.
Just as the former canon opens with the story of the original
creation, the latter closes with a mythic description of an es-
chatological renewal of creation (Revelations 21:1f). In the view of
exegete Gerhard von Rad, the creation motif is so fundamental to
the Hebrew scriptures that it is the single unifying thread of the
disparate literary pieces collected in the book of Psalms.[7]

Recent scholarly discussions of the Biblical creation narrative
argue that the creation account is precisely mythic.[8] That is, far
from purporting to be scientific reportorial descriptions of an
historical event, the creation stories are literary reflections on the
creative presence of the divine that, in the view of the Biblical
authors, continuously underlies the natural world.[9] Scholars of
religion use the term *myth* to refer to a sacred story that seeks to
depict abstract religious doctrines in literary narrative.[10] This
scholarly use of the term avoids the value judgments carried by
common usage (as in the phrase "only a myth").

As myths, the creation narratives of Genesis have an important
function throughout the Judaeo-Christian scriptures. This is that
of providing a reference point for human attempts to achieve
order. A significant motif of the Genesis creation myth is the
notion that humanity is endowed by the Creator with the task of
exercising dominion over the natural world (Genesis 1:26, 28). As
Biblical authors reflected on the meaning of this dominion imperative, they saw the task of dominion as that of co-creation, of
sharing in the creative responsibility of God for creation and of

continuing an unfinished creation. The author of that portion of the book of Isaiah that exegetes call second Isaiah (Isaiah 40–55) particularly accents this theme. For scriptural authors such as second Isaiah, the Genesis creation myth points primarily not to some originating event of the past, but to an unfinished task that will culminate in the future—the edenic story is a mythic description of the world made perfect through divine-human cooperation.[11]

In *Absalom, Absalom!* Faulkner uses Biblical creation images to parallel and at the same time invert the mythic function they demonstrate in Biblical books such as Isaiah. That Faulkner's fiction exhibits a strong mythopoeic intent is well-nigh a byword of Faulkner criticism.[12] That in weaving his mythic narratives Faulkner often employs both Biblical and classical myths has also been recognized.[13] What critics less commonly note (and this deserves more analysis) is the way in which Faulkner sometimes transmutes myths in the process of adapting them. His use of the creation myth in *Absalom, Absalom!* evidences such transmutation. Where the Biblical account uses the story of creation as a reference point for attempts to achieve order, Faulkner uses it in *Absalom, Absalom!* as a vantage point for critiquing Sutpen's pretensions and for explaining their inevitable destructiveness.

The creation allusions of *Absalom, Absalom!* have received insufficient scholarly attention. Though H. L. Weatherby recognizes that Sutpen's garden has mythic Biblical overtones, he thinks that Faulkner failed to make these overtones explicit in *Absalom, Absalom!*[14] Maxine Rose notes that the novel demonstrates a "unity of tone . . . which is clearly biblical."[15] Rose also discerns in *Absalom, Absalom!* a structure which parallels that of the Bible.[16] In her view, the entire Bible, and not merely the Davidic parallels suggested by the novel's title, is relevant to understanding the design and theme of *Absalom, Absalom!*[17]

Though Rose analyzes the creation imagery of *Absalom, Absalom!*, she does not seek to examine the function of this imagery, and in particular its function in the Sutpen narrative. As I have argued, there is an intrinsic thematic connection between the creation imagery of the novel and the Sutpen narrative. In the subsequent sections of this essay, I want to isolate the creation allusions in *Absalom, Absalom!* and to show how these function to provide a critical perspective on Sutpen's self-creation and his creation of Sutpen's Hundred. The link between Sutpen and the Judaeo-Christian creation myth is established in the opening pages of the novel; these pages provide a perspective fundamental to interpretation of the Sutpen narrative and thus of the novel itself. Faulkner clearly intends that the reader view Sutpen as a creator whose very act of creation engenders disorder rather than order.

Creation Imagery in *Absalom, Absalom!*

From his initial appearance in *Absalom, Absalom!*, Sutpen is associated with the Biblical theme of creation. As Quentin Compson listens to Miss Rosa Coldfield recount the Sutpen story, Sutpen "abrupts" in Quentin's imagination onto the peaceful wilderness of frontier Mississippi.[18] The word *abrupt* has Biblical resonance: it is epiphanic. It recalls those Biblical passages in which the divine presence manifests itself to humanity (Exodus 19:18f, Psalm 18:7, 29:3f, 77:16f, 97:2f, Isaiah 6:1f). In Biblical passages describing divine epiphanies, God "abrupts" suddenly into human history through thunder, fire, smoke—in ways that break through human expectation and shatter human illusion. Significantly, in Quentin's imaginative reconstruction of the scene, Sutpen abrupts on the Mississippi frontier with a thunderclap (ibid.).

The word *abrupt* has another connotation that casts important light on Sutpen's creation of a plantation. As the root of the word suggests, acts of abruption are acts of *rupture*. Sutpen abrupts violently into "a scene peaceful and decorous as a schoolprize water color" (ibid.). From the beginning Sutpen's epiphany is inherently destructive; he sets into motion a series of events that destroy rather than build up. In view of the fact that Sutpen comes to Mississippi precisely as a planter of the wilderness, one who wrests out of the frontier a fertile plantation, such destruction is ironic. Throughout the novel Sutpen's appearances jar against the domesticity of the town of Jefferson. When Sutpen comes into Jefferson to ask for Ellen Coldfield's hand in marriage, for example, a lynch mob which assumes that his wealth is ill-gotten arrests him (47). As the mob parades him through the town, the ladies, children, and house servants of Jefferson watch from behind curtains and shrubs. These images of domestic order are in marked contrast to the maelstrom of destructive energy and violence that follow Sutpen wherever he goes. Sutpen is a *demonic* creator. The novel continually applies the term "demon" to him (e.g., 8, 11, 13). The Greek word *daimon* means "energy." The term enfolds a double sense, that of simultaneous creative activity and destruction: the demonic energy that drives Sutpen as he creates his plantation is one that also subverts his act of creation.

Another aspect of Sutpen's appearance scene is pertinent. As I have noted, Quentin imagines the scene as he listens to Miss Rosa drone on about Sutpen. Throughout *Absalom, Absalom!* Quentin struggles with the recognition that the past is inescapable; it continues to unfold in the present, and in the case of the Sutpen family and those associated with the family, it does so in destructive ways. The theme of the past-as-present is, of course, a favorite Faulknerian motif. In Faulkner's view,

> No man is himself, he is the sum of his past. There is no such thing as was because the past is. It is a part of every man, every woman, and every moment. All of his or her ancestry, background, is all a part of himself and herself at any moment.[19]

As Quentin recognizes, the disorder that Sutpen causes reaches into generations after him. Quentin's meditation on Sutpen's story leads him to see that "nothing ever happens once and is finished" (261): through Sutpen, the past deconstructs the present.

Throughout, *Absalom, Absalom!* employs a viewpoint that is a syzygy of past and present. As Quentin listens to Miss Rosa's story, he is both the Quentin Compson preparing for Harvard in 1909 and the Quentin Compson of the antebellum South, who knows the Southern past because he is himself the South: "His very body was an empty hall echoing with sonorous defeated names; he was not a being, an entity, he was a commonwealth" (12; cf. 9). In 1909 he still breathes the air in which the church bells rang at Sutpen's appearance in Jefferson in 1833 (31). Quentin cannot escape the burden of Southern history: though his personal history is only tangentially related to that of Sutpen and his descendants, Miss Rosa chooses him because his grandfather had befriended Sutpen, and he is thus "partly responsible through heredity" for what has happened to her family (13). It is this burden that Quentin's Canadian friend at Harvard, Shreve McCannon, cannot understand: for him as for many North Americans, the past is a closed book that has no bearing on the present (361).

The violent rupture of Sutpen's epiphany in Mississippi is a prelude to the inverted creation scene that follows. In his imagination Quentin watches Sutpen overrun the tranquil earth and drag house and gardens "out of the soundless Nothing" (8). The appeal to the Genesis creation narrative is explicit: in the Genesis account, God surveys the trackless void and shapes it through a creative word (Genesis 1:1–2). Drawing on these Biblical notions, Christian theology has developed the doctrine of *creatio ex nihilo*—that is, the affirmation that the Creator God preceded all matter, and that all else has its origin in God. Like the God of Genesis, Sutpen is one who creates "out of the soundless Nothing." This is a recurrent image in *Absalom, Absalom!* Later in the novel, Sutpen builds his house "apparently out of nothing" (11), and, after Sutpen's Hundred has been set up, Sutpen and his horse appear in Jefferson "as though they had been created out of thin air" (32).

The creation theme is made even more explicit in the passage following Sutpen's *creatio ex nihilo*. As Quentin looks back, he sees Sutpen "creating" his plantation by speaking an efficacious word akin to the divine *fiat* of Genesis: "*Be Sutpen's Hundred* like the oldentime *Be Light*" (9).[20] Later, the creation theme is further underscored as Sutpen, like some new Adam, names all his offspring and the offspring of his slaves (61).[21]

Sutpen's creation is, however, in ironic contrast to the divine creation in Genesis. Whereas the God of Genesis establishes order and harmony, in the very act of creating Sutpen engenders a disorder that is to span generations following. The paradoxical nature of Sutpen's creation is suggested by the oxymoronic words and phrases that the novel associates with it. These phrases— "notlanguage," "notpeople," "nothusband" (7–9)—torture language, subvert its evident sense. Similarly, Miss Rosa characterizes Sutpen's settlement of Sutpen's Hundred as a violent tearing of the land rather than a peaceful planting of it (9). The rape motif is intentional: Sutpen's establishment of a plantation ruptures the land; Sutpen begets a daughter of his wife Ellen by an act of rape akin to his rape of the land itself (9). These images point to one of the underlying preoccupations of the novel, the relationship between humanity and nature.

Absalom, Absalom! parallels Sutpen's creation of a plantation with the Genesis narrative in another respect. Sutpen appears initially in Jefferson on a Sunday morning (11), and he returns to the town after having finished his creation of Sutpen's Hundred on another Sunday morning (41). As with the divine creation of Genesis, he finishes his creation in a seven-day cycle.[22] The Genesis parallel is reinforced by the observation that Sutpen had worked to build his plantation from sunup to sundown (38); this echoes the "evening came and morning came" of the Genesis story.

Though the primary locus of creation imagery in *Absalom, Absalom!* is the opening passage of the novel, echoes of the imagery recur at various points in the novel. A scene from Sutpen's family life underscores the quasi-divine efficacy of his word. This is the passage in which Sutpen's carriage races past another as it carries his family to church. Though we soon discover that Sutpen's daughter Judith had been responsible for instructing the carriage driver to race, when the event occurs the townspeople assume that Sutpen had ordered the driver to let the horses run away. A townsman chides the driver. His response is, "Marster say: I do" (25). Sutpen is an absolute master; as with the God of Genesis, when he speaks, what he commands occurs.

Passages describing Sutpen's self-creation also employ creation imagery. Sutpen creates himself *ex nihilo* just as he creates his plantation *ex nihilo*. Not only does Sutpen seem to appear out of thin air; he is a man who has no past at all (16). As the narrative unfolds, we discover that Sutpen has come to Jefferson with the deliberate intent of making himself a planter to rival those high-toned Virginia planters who had made him feel worthless as a boy. He coldly and ruthlessly calculates to settle a plantation, marry a well-bred wife, and make himself a gentlemen (40–41). Sutpen has an overarching (and, as it turns out, overweening) trust in the power of human rationality to manipulate events and circumstances to human good:

[He had] that unsleeping care which must have known that it could permit itself but one mistake; that alertness for measuring and weighing event against eventuality, circumstance against human nature, his own fallible judgment and mortal clay against not only human but natural forces, choosing and discarding, compromising with his dream and his ambition like you must with the horse which you take across country, over timber, which you control only through your ability to keep the animal from realizing that actually you cannot, that actually it is the stronger. (53)

Absalom, Absalom! makes plain that this fatuous trust in the power of rationality to calculate and to effect what it calculates is directly responsible for Sutpen's downfall. Sutpen errs in thinking that he can create himself *ex nihilo*. Through the Sutpen narrative, Faulkner stringently critiques the fatuity of a central American myth—that of the ability of people to create themselves *de novo* and *ex nihilo*.

The Significance of the Creation Theme in *Absalom, Absalom!*

The inverted creation myth of *Absalom, Absalom!* is central to the novel. Though the telling of the myth occupies only a limited space in the narrative, the creation myth functions as a thematic center for several probing intellectual reflections around which the narrative revolves. *Absalom, Absalom!* is above all a novel of ideas. It is a penetrating commentary on several key issues of twentieth-century intellectual discourse, and, in particular, of twentieth-century *American* intellectual discourse. Modern thought has dissected perhaps no myth of the Enlightenment so savagely as the myth of innocence. Those great post-Enlightenment "masters of suspicion"[23] Freud, Marx, and Nietzsche taught us that beneath the surface of human "innocence" lie savage tendencies that we ignore at our peril. This recognition has radically altered the way twentieth-century persons look at themselves and the world around them. As studies of American life and thought—notably, Henry May's *The End of American Innocence*[24]—have shown, the Enlightenment myth of innocence has taken particularly virulent forms in American culture. One of the central problematics of twentieth-century American political thought has been to expose how this myth underlies the messianism that often informs American foreign policy. As critics of this messianic mentality have noted, American foreign policy commonly presupposes that American motives with regard to other countries are aseptic, when in fact American policy sometimes serves the interests of this country better than those of countries Americans regard themselves as charged to "save."

Absalom, Absalom!'s critique of Sutpen is a contribution to modern thought's dissection of the myth of innocence. As Cleanth Brooks observes, Sutpen's innocence is the key to his tragedy.[25] His downfall and that of his house are a direct result of his belief that he can create himself and his plantation *ex nihilo*. Sutpen believes this because he presupposes his innocence. Sutpen's downfall is implicit not in his presumption that he can create order out of the chaos of personal and natural existence, but in his assumption that he can do so as a "planner."[26] Sutpen's rationalism, his confidence that one can chart and manipulate the world via human rationality, is in the final analysis a miscalculation that rests on his erroneous belief in human innocence. What his "scientific" approach fails to take into account is the stubborn resistance of the irrational both within the mind of the "rational" planner and in those whom he seeks to manipulate.[27] In James H. Justus's view, Sutpen's activity as a planner is in the final analysis *loveless*: "The absence of love in Sutpen is demonstrated by his inability to see anyone or anything as more than object."[28] Sutpen's assumption that he can create himself and his world *ex nihilo* incorporates an assumption of human innocence that allows him to reify others, because it allows him to act without subjecting his motives to radical scrutiny.

Brooks argues that Sutpen is an innocent who "has scarcely arrived at the distinction between good and evil."[29] Such innocence is submoral; it is at the root of much of the destruction which the "innocent" individual blithely causes.[30] The innocent can wreak havoc precisely because his understanding of the potential of human beings for good and evil is dangerously limited. As critics of American culture often observe, American innocence sometimes has tragic consequences because it fails to recognize that innocence may mask impure motives. Sutpen is indeed the *American* innocent—optimistic, given to abstraction, confident that he can appropriate his *persona* in bourgeois fashion through the community rather than by situating himself in a life-giving and life-sustaining tradition.[31] Southern thought has traditionally combatted the assumption that one can appropriate one's *persona* as a commodity. For Southern thinkers, the *persona* is derived in a dialectical relationship to tradition. We are necessarily part of a

heritage that continues to shape us, and against which we form
our own individual identity.

The Southern intellectual tradition's rejection of the philosophy of atomistic individualism is thus simultanously a rejection of
the myth of innocence. Southern writers as diverse as C. Vann
Woodward and Flannery O'Connor have argued that the Southern experience of evil and guilt has provided the South with
a critical perspective on both the American myth of the self-
constituted individual and the myth of innocence.[32] For Woodward and O'Connor, American individualism and American
notions of innocence are not merely wrong; they are also *dangerous*. They are so because they fail to recognize that every attempt
to achieve what we like to call progress must work against the
backwards pull of human error and irrationality, sloth, the tendency to choose evil rather than good. In theological terms, the
myth of innocence ignores the reality of original sin.

I introduce this theological term deliberately. The notion of
original sin is clearly implicit in Faulkner's treatment of Sutpen in
Absalom, Absalom! Sutpen's fall is an echo of the primordial fall of
the Biblical creation accounts. The novel persistently applies the
Biblical term "curse" to Sutpen and his descendants.[33] His cal-
culations go awry because his rationalistic and abstract plans do
not recognize the tragically flawed situation in which postlap-
sarian human beings must achieve their humanity.

Faulkner confronts Americans who assure themselves of their
innocence and of their ability to be self-reliant with the curse on
humanity. He does so as a warning against the tendency of those
who presume themselves to be innocent and capable of self-
reliance to become "tragic and pathological figure[s] of alienation."[34] Mississippi novelist Stark Young objects to the American
myth of innocence on similar grounds. In Young's novel *So Red the
Rose*, Natchez planter Malcolm Bedford expresses misgivings
about the lessons that the New England schoolmarm who teaches
his children is presenting. In particular, he objects to the "fetid
idealism" that she seeks to inculcate:

Well, then agree with me that I could stand my children being taught transcendentalism, witch burning, even abolition, but I'm damned if I'll have 'em taught that all things work together to make life sugar-coated. . . . Sugar-coateder and sugar-coateder every day. Making fools out of helpless children.[35]

Note the basis of Bedford's objection to his tutor's idealism. He objects not only because it presents a monochromatic picture of life (and life is much more complex), but because it misleads his children into thinking that evil has less power to distort and corrupt than it actually has. Faulkner and Young concur in rejecting a philosophy of innocence that enables us to wreak havoc even as we do "good," because it allows us to overlook the complexity and ambiguity—the impurity—of our motives.

As the preceding analysis of Faulkner's critique of the myth of innocence implies, this myth underlies the American expansionist impulse and is responsible for some of its pernicious effects. *Absalom, Absalom!* explores this linkage. Sutpen is not merely an American innocent; he is an American innocent who tames the wilderness. The Sutpen story is a commentary on American expansionism.[36] The nineteenth century was *the* century of American expansion, an expansion that had as its motivating impulse American belief in the manifest destiny of an innocent messianic people to subdue and civilize. What happens to Sutpen is a warning against those who seek to conquer secure in the assumption of their innocence. Such expansionism—whether it be an expansionism that annexes more land or that subjects other peoples to a dominant culture—easily translates into exploitation of nature and domination of others.

It is interesting to compare Faulkner at this point with the nineteenth-century Southwest humorist Joseph Glover Baldwin. Baldwin's *The Flush Times of Alabama and Mississippi* (1853) tells a story akin to that of *Absalom, Absalom!* Both comment on the early nineteenth-century settlement of the Mississippi frontier. Faulkner echoes Baldwin in blasting the frontier settlers' pretensions. But where Baldwin finds material for sharp satire, Faulkner

sees tragedy: the settlement of the Alabama-Mississippi plantation country is for Faulkner a lowercase account of a larger tragedy, that of the European settlement of the continent as a whole.

The conquest of the continent raises for Faulkner profound and
troubling questions about the relationship of humanity to nature.
Sutpen's creation of a plantation is a violation of the aboriginal
harmony of the land. This point is easily misunderstood. *Absalom, Absalom!* does not present Sutpen's taming of the wilderness *per se* as a rape of the land; it is the conjunction of this act
with the myth of innocence that makes it an act of violation. As
Brooks notes, Faulkner persistently rejects the myth of the edenic
South; in none of his works do we find the Rousseauian assumption that the wilderness is a paradise in which human beings can
find peace and tranquility if they live in harmony with the primordial state of nature.[37] Indeed, Faulkner recognizes the human
obligation to order the world. For Brooks, this notion has Calvinist overtones in Faulkner: we must "work out" our salvation in
the arena of nature.[38]

What Faulkner rejects is the translation of the dominion imperative of the creation narratives into an imperative of domination. It
is the "impious violence" often exhibited by settlers of the land
that constitutes a rape of nature, and that nature itself revenges by
establishing the conditions for the downfall of those who pillage
and exploit.[39] As Uncle Ike says in the story "Delta Autumn,"
"The woods and fields [man] ravages and the game he devastates
will be the consequence of his crime and guilt, and his punishment."[40] For Southern writer Wendell Berry, the callous and
destructive exploitation of the land that has occurred on the North
American continent from its European settlement is a direct
consequence of the settlers' belief that they were innocent and
endowed with a divine mission to subdue the continent.[41]

Faulkner's perspective on the relationship of humanity and
nature is tragic. On the one hand, humanity is charged with the
obligation to tame the natural world; on the other, humanity often
carries out this charge in a way that unsettles the natural harmony

of the world. The taming of the wilderness is for Faulkner tragically ambivalent,[42] because it is in the very act of ordering the
world that human beings create disorder. This tragic perspective
places Faulkner in the tradition of such critics of the Enlightenment as the Frankfurt critical theorists Max Horkheimer and
Theodor Adorno. In their *Dialectic of Enlightenment* Horkheimer and Adorno argue that humanity's alienation from nature
originates in the very moment in which humanity becomes con-
scious of itself as an entity over against nature.[43] The breach of
humanity and nature is necessary if humanity is to fulfill its
potential and claim its destiny. At the same time, the emergence
of consciousness forever cuts humanity off from the natural world
from which it has emerged. Like Faulkner, Horkheimer and
Adorno do not propose that human beings heal this breach by
returning to the state of nature; what they reject is the "instru-
mental rationality" that causes humans to approach nature as an
object to be exploited.[44] Faulkner's understanding of the human
task as that of working within nature without callously exploiting it
is very close to that of Horkheimer and Adorno. Like the critical
theorists, Faulkner appears both to accept the Enlightenment call
for human autonomy and to reject the translation of this call into
an imperative for domination of the natural world.

Faulkner's exploration of the theme of order and disorder has a
discernible theological underpinning that draws together the
various themes of the Sutpen narrative's critique of American
innocence and gives it tragic depth. Faulkner's use of the creation
theme in *Absalom, Absalom!* is clearly Calvinist.[45] Both Luther
and Calvin emphasized the human obligation to order the world.
This emphasis arose from the reformers' insistence that every
Christian (and not just those who choose a monastic vocation) has a
particular vocation: "secular" work has a sacred dimension, because all that the believer does is an expression of his or her
commitment to Christ. Though aspects of Max Weber's classic
essay linking the rise of capitalism to the Protestant ethic continue
to be debated, one central contention of the essay has not been

refuted. This is Weber's contention that Calvin regarded the secular vocation of the believer with the utmost seriousness, and that Calvin's understanding of vocation issues in a strong work ethic. For Calvin, believers work out their salvation by working in the world—all that the believer does has religious implications.

Like Calvin, Faulkner stresses the obligation of humanity to order the world. But (again like Calvin), he sees the tragic potential for attempts at order to go awry and to spawn disorder. In the view of Robert J. Barth, Faulkner stands in the *orthodox* (as distinct from liberal) stream of Calvinist thought; orthodox Calvinists retain Calvin's somber emphasis on the Fall, the curse of Adam, and the depravity of fallen humanity.[46] A persistent theme of Calvin's *Institutes* is the obligation of human beings to be humble as they carry out their work in service to God.[47] Sutpen's act of creating a plantation is tragic and flawed not because he seeks to establish order: this is the human task. It is guilty because he creates with a hybris that assumes himself to be the center of the universe.

NOTES

1. On these themes in early American Puritan thought, see Perry Miller, *Errand into the Wilderness* (Cambridge: Harvard University Press, 1956), 2–15; and Charles M. Segal and David C. Stineback, *Puritans, Indians, and Manifest Destiny* (New York: G. P. Putnam's Sons, 1977), 32–39.

2. On Faulkner's conviction that the history of the modern South is an aspect of the broad crisis of modern Western civilization, see Lewis P. Simpson, "Isaac McCaslin and Temple Drake: The Fall of New World Man," in *Nine Essays in Modern Literature,* ed. Donald E. Stanford (Baton Rouge: Louisiana State University Press, 1965), 88.

3. On the Biblical background to American belief in the messianic role of America, and on echoes of this belief in American literature, see Carlos Baker, "The Place of the Bible in American Fiction," in *Religious Perspectives in American Culture,* ed. James Ward Smith and Leland Jamison (Princeton: Princeton University Press, 1961), 245–46. See also Simpson, "Fall of New World Man," 90, 94.

4. In her study of the Biblical allusions of Faulkner's novels, Jesse Coffee finds allusions to the Biblical creation narrative in all the novels from *Soldiers' Pay* to *A Fable: Faulkner's Un-Christlike Christians: Biblical Allusions in the Novels* (Ann Arbor: UMI Research Press, 1983). Coffee finds ninety references to Genesis in Faulkner's novels— more than to any other book of the Hebrew testament (129).

5. For Faulkner's assertion that Sutpen is the central character of *Absalom, Absalom!,* see *Faulkner in the University,* ed. Frederick L. Glynn and Joseph L. Blotner (Charlottesville: University Press of Virginia, 1959), 71, 275.

6. I am using the terms "Hebrew canon" and "Christian canon" or scriptures to refer to

what the Christian tradition has conventionally called the Old and New Testaments. The former terms avoid the supersessionist implications of the latter. My use of the terms Hebrew and Christian canons does not mean to imply that the Hebrew scriptures are noncanonical for Christian traditions.

7. See Gerhard von Rad, *Old Testament Theology* (New York: Harper and Row, 1962), 1.138.

8. A penetrating analysis is Langdon Gilkey's *Maker of Heaven and Earth* (New York: Doubleday, 1959).

9. On this, see Langdon Gilkey, *Reaping the Whirlwind: A Christian Interpretation of History* (New York: Seabury, 1976), 153–54.

10. See Mircea Eliade, *Myths, Dreams, and Mysteries* (New York: Harper & Row, 1960), 23–24.

11. The futurity of Judaeo-Christian ideas of creation is maintained by Ernst Bloch in *The Principle of Hope*, trans. Neville Plaice, Stephen Plaice, and Paul Knight (Cambridge: MIT, 1986), 3:1283–90. On creation theology in second Isaiah, see von Rad, *Old Testament*, 2.241–43.

12. On the mythic overtones of *Absalom, Absalom!*, see Ilse Dusoir Lind, "The Design and Meaning of *Absalom, Absalom!*," in *William Faulkner: Three Decades of Criticism*, ed. Frederick J. Hoffmann and Olga W. Vickery (New York: Harcourt, 1960), 281.

13. On the diverse mythic patterns in *Absalom, Absalom!*, see Richard P. Adams, *Faulkner: Myth and Motion* (Princeton University Press, 1968), 181.

14. H. L. Weatherby, "Sutpen's Garden," *Georgia Review* 21 (1967): 354–69. On Calvinist overtones in Faulkner's use of the garden image in many of his works, see Mary Dell Fletcher, "Edenic Images in *The Sound and the Fury*," *South Central Bulletin of SCMLA* 40 (1980): 142.

15. Maxine Rose, "Echoes of the Prose of the King James Bible in the Prose Style of *Absalom, Absalom!*," *Arizona Quarterly* 37 (1981): 139.

16. Maxine Rose, "From Genesis to Revelation: The Grand Design of William Faulkner's *Absalom, Absalom!*," *Studies in American Fiction* 8 (1980): 219.

17. Ibid. For studies of the Davidic allusions in *Absalom, Absalom!*, see Lennart Björk, "Ancient Myths and the Moral Framework of *Absalom, Absalom!*," *American Literature* 35 (1963): 196–204; John V. Hagopian, "The Biblical Background of Faulkner's *Absalom, Absalom!*," *CEA Critic* 36 (Jan., 1974): 22–24; and Baker, "Place of Bible," 269–70.

18. William Faulkner, *Absalom, Absalom!* (New York: Modern Library, 1936), 8. Subsequent references to this work will appear in parentheses in the text.

19. Faulkner, *Faulkner in the University*, 84.

20. Italics in original.

21. Other allusions to the creation motif in *Absalom, Absalom!* that are of incidental thematic significance are a reference to Eve and the snake (144), to the curse of Adam (200), and to creation in the divine image (282).

22. Maxine Rose draws attention to various parallels between the order of the Genesis and account and that of the Sutpen narrative: first the wilderness is tamed, then the animals appear, followed by the plants. Sutpen has a son in the sixth year, just as Adam is created on the sixth day: "Genesis to Revelation," 220.

23. David Tracy, *The Analogical Imagination* (New York: Crossroad, 1981), 53.

24. Henry F. May, *The End of American Innocence: The First Years of Our Own Time, 1912–1917* (New York: Knopf, 1959).

25. Cleanth Brooks, *William Faulkner: The Yoknapatawpha Country* (New Haven: Yale University Press, 1963), 6; and "*Absalom, Absalom!*: The Definition of Innocence," *Sewanee Review* 59 (1951): 545. See also Brooks, "Faulkner and the Theme of Innocence," *Kenyon Review* 20 (1958): 466–87; and "The American 'Innocence' in James, Fitzgerald, and Faulkner," *Shenandoah* 16 (Autumn, 1964): 21–37.

26. Ibid., 306. Ralph Behrens notes the persistent application of the term "design" to Sutpen's plans in *Absalom, Absalom!*; in Behrens's view, the "thematic import" of the novel

hinges on understanding why Sutpen's design fails: "Collapse of Dynasty: The Thematic Center of *Absalom, Absalom!*," *PMLA* 89 (1974): 24, 32, n. 1.

27. Brooks, *Yoknapatawpha Country*, 308.

28. James H. Justus, "The Epic Design of *Absalom, Absalom!*," in *William Faulkner's "Absalom, Absalom!": A Critical Case Book*, ed. Elisabeth Muhlenfeld (New York: Garland, 1984), 49. John W. Hunt also locates the significance of Sutpen's downfall in his failure to love: *William Faulkner: Art in Theological Tension* (Syracuse: Syracuse University Press, 1965), 101–36.

29. Brooks, *Yoknapatawpha Country*, 302.

30. On Faulknerian innocence as submoral, see Lawrence E. Bowling, "Faulkner and the Theme of Innocence," *Kenyon Review* 20 (1958): 467.

31. Brooks, *Yoknapatawpha Country*, 427; and "Definition of Innocence," 546–47. For a contemporary argument that such presuppositions continue strongly to inform American cultural notions, see Robert N. Bellah, *et al.*, *Habits of the Heart* (Berkeley: University of California, 1985). The authors lament the increasing development in American society of "fragile communities" that seek to define the meaning of the person without recourse to those traditional communities and traditions of discourse that have in the past defined social meaning (50).

32. C. Vann Woodward, *The Burden of Southern History*, rev. ed. (Baton Rouge: Louisiana State University Press, 1968); and Flannery O'Connor, *Habit of Being*, ed. Sally Fitzgerald (New York: Farrar, Straus, Giroux, 1979), 302.

33. Rose, "Genesis to Revelation," 255; and J. Robert Barth, "Faulkner and the Calvinist Tradition," *Thought* 39 (1964): 110.

34. David W. Noble, *The Eternal Adam and the New World Garden* (New York: George Braziller, 1968), 176.

35. Stark Young, *So Red the Rose* (New York: Scribner's, 1934), 61.

36. On Faulkner's critique of the Adamic myth of American expansionism, see Herman E. Spivey, "Faulkner and the Adamic Myth: Faulkner's Moral Vision," *Modern Fiction Studies* 19 (1973–74): 498, 503–4.

37. Brooks, *Yoknapawtapha Country*, 37.

38. Ibid., 45.

39. Ibid., 31.

40. William Faulkner, *The Portable Faulkner*, ed. Malcolm Cowley (New York: Viking, 1946), 719.

41. Wendell Berry, *The Unsettling of America* (San Francisco: Sierra, 1977).

42. Brooks, *Yoknapatawpha Country*, 31. On the ambivalence which arises from American cultural affirmation of manifest destiny and the American Romantic idealization of the wilderness, see Perry Miller, "The Romantic Dilemma in American Nationalism and the Concept of Nature," *Harvard Theological Review* 48 (1955): 239–53.

43. Max Horkheimer and Theodor W. Adorno, *Dialectic of Enlightenment* (New York: Seabury, 1972), 48, 54–57. See also Paul Connerton, *The Tragedy of Enlightenment: An Essay on the Frankfurt School* (Cambridge: Cambridge University Press, 1980), 65–71.

44. Ibid., 6, 54, 57.

45. On Faulkner's Calvinism, see Perry Westbrook, *Free Will and Determinism in American Literature* (Granbury, N.J.: Associated University Press, 1979), 177–87; Mary Dell Fletcher, "William Faulkner and Residual Calvinism," *Southern Studies* 18 (1979), 199; and Harold J. Douglas and Robert Daniel, "Faulkner and the Puritanism of the South," *Tennessee Studies in Literature* 2 (1957): 2–3.

46. Barth, "Faulkner and Calvinist Tradition," 100–20.

47. See, for example, Calvin's *Institutes*, 3:12 (John Allen ed. [Philadelphia: Presbyterian Board of Christian Education, 1936], 1:830–10.

Quentin as Redactor: Biblical Analogy in Faulkner's *Absalom, Absalom!*

Glenn Meeter

In 1974 Ralph Behrens set out the parallels between Faulkner's story of Thomas Sutpen in *Absalom, Absalom!* and the Biblical account of the house of David in Second Samuel.[1] It is these parallels, Behrens says, that provide a historical critique of the concept of dynasty that Sutpen's "design" assumes and, in so doing, provide the book with its thematic center.

Behrens's argument rests in part on Faulkner's comment at the Nagano conference that he read the Old Testament "once every ten or fifteen years" and his comment at the University of Virginia that the idea of the novel and the choice of its title (from 2 Samuel 18:37) were "simultaneous."[2] He also cites W. J. Cash's *The Mind of the South* on the importance of the Old Testament for the "average Southerner" (29). In the main, however, the evidence is internal. Aside from the Biblical title, Behrens cites a dozen or more Davidic parallels to the story of Thomas Sutpen: "David's rise to kingship in many ways parallels Sutpen's rise, and David's unhappy later days suggest many of the horrifying events that bring Sutpen's dynasty to an end" (29).

Behrens's argument seems to be conclusive; and his analogies between the house of Sutpen and the house of David—along with parallels to Greek tragedy and epic observed by other critics— help explain the timeless and universal quality of the Sutpens' story and *Absalom's* superiority to the general run of Southern Gothic. However, since 1974 studies of *Absalom* have concentrated on the novel's telling, rather than the tale—or, to put it

103

differently, have concentrated on Quentin rather than Sutpen. And these studies have found no Biblical analogy for the telling equivalent to that for the story.[3] Analogies of other sorts have been used. Cleanth Brooks, for example, compares the novel in its telling to the detective story and to the ballad (for its incremental repetition), and he compares Shreve and Quentin in their work of interpretative reconstruction to novelists and historians.[4] Among more recent studies of the way the novel is told, Robert Dale Parker's look at the "discrepancies, new and unexpected details, uncertain assertions, and outright errors" in the appended Chronology and Genealogy places Faulkner in "the Hawthornian mode" because of his "playings with probabilities."[5] Stephen M. Ross's essay on oratory and the dialogical in the novel, which argues that "a single oratorically derived overvoice" masks the other voices in Faulkner's text and thus makes it more difficult to explicate, takes its categories from Mikhail Bakhtin.[6] David Krause's essay on the letters in the novel argues that "all readers of *Absalom* must sooner or later confront methodological, ontological, and epistemological uncertainties about reading, about what is and is not in the book and thus—more radically—uncertainties about how we are and are not in the world."[7] Krause sees the novel in the light of contemporary theorists such as Barthes, de Man, Derrida, and Foucault.

Yet a Biblical analogy for the Quentin side of the novel seems a likely possibility for several reasons. We know that Faulkner's difficulties with the novel had to do not with the events but the relating and interpreting of them; we know too that although he said at the University of Virginia, "The central character is Sutpen," he wrote in 1934 to Harrison Smith that Quentin was the "protagonist": "Quentin Compson, of the Sound & Fury, tells it, or ties it together; he is the protagonist so that it is not complete apocrypha."[8] If, as Cleanth Brooks has said, the difficulty of the novel is not forced or factitious, if in fact there are "few instances in modern fiction of a more perfect adaptation of form to matter" (324), then we might expect that the detective, as well as the

Southern Gothic, aspect of the novel has been given "universal and timeless significance" (Behrens, 31). And if as Behrens says the "tone and flavor of the Old Testament continue to pervade *Absalom, Absalom!*" (28), we might expect that they pervade all aspects of the novel, that in which Quentin is "protagonist" as well as that in which Sutpen is the "central character."

Such a Biblical analogy should be consistent with Quentin's function as "protagonist"—that is, with what Quentin is (a Southern youth with ambivalent attitudes toward the South, who is beginning his first year at Harvard) and what he does (listens, sees, tells, discusses). It should be consistent with the story of the Sutpen family that is the *subject* of his listening, seeing, telling, and discussing. And it should be consistent with what criticism has already found concerning the novel's telling—as, for example, that Quentin and Shreve function like historians and novelists; that the way the novel is told involves an "overvoice" in conflict with the voices of the separate characters; and that the way the story is told involves us as readers in uncertainties about the act of reading, the relationship between text and truth.

The analogy I propose is this: the way the Sutpen story is told, in the novel—that is, the way we see it being pieced together, retold, reinterpreted—is the way in which the Bible, according to modern Biblical scholarship, was made. To demonstrate this analogy requires looking more closely at Quentin's function as protagonist and also at the Biblical process, or the making of the Bible, as modern scholarship sees it.

1

Quentin's activities in the novel may be summarized as follows: he hears stories about Sutpen from his father, who in turn has heard them from Quentin's grandparents. He hears other stories from Rosa Coldfield, who has her own "tradition" (to use a word from Biblical criticism) of the Sutpen story and has added to it certain other "material" from her sister, niece, and nephew. And, with Rosa Coldfield on his last night in Jefferson before leaving for Harvard, Quentin himself becomes a witness and even participant in the story's last events.

Quentin, that is to say, has received orally transmitted material from two main traditions, each of these dependent on several sources—one tradition taking a grimly moralistic view of events, the other a more worldly and fatalistic one—and is beginning his own "redaction" of the story. But before the Sutpen saga can be completed, Quentin must explain it to, and receive interpretation from, a member of his own generation, Shreve McCannon, his roommate at Harvard. Only then will it have attained its full meaning as a tragedy of pride, a tragedy of love and fate and sacrifice, and a tragedy of retribution in which one generation's debts are settled upon another.

Now this is the way, in the view of modern scholarship, that oral tradition became Biblical literature. In *The Making of the Old Testament*, Enid B. Mellor summarizes the process: "So Israelite history could never be relegated to the past; these and other living traditions, so well known that they could be cited without any explanation, must constantly have been *redacted*—that is, told and re-told, interpreted and reinterpreted, even expanded and contracted, to meet the needs of succeeding generations . . . and eventually the whole was edited into the literature as we know it."[9]

Involved in the Biblical side of this analogy are several elements easily seen in the novel. One of these is the presence of a traditional community as the source of oral tradition. As Hugh Kenner put it, "Faulkner's oral storytelling mode, it is commonplace to observe, is that of a provincial culture with its small towns, its agriculture, its still living religion, its implicit norms of conduct."[10] Quentin, as well as Faulkner, belongs to that world. At the opening of chapter 2 he learns "mostly about that which he already knew, since he had been born in and still breathed the same air in which the church bells had rung on that Sunday morning in 1833 and . . . heard even one of the original three bells in the same steeple where descendants of the same pigeons strutted"; and the next dozen pages are told to us as what the *town* knew, as "the stranger's name went back and forth among the places of business and of idleness and among the residences in steady strophe and antistrophe."[11] There is truth in Quentin's remark to Shreve, as well as self-protectiveness, when he says about the South, "You can't understand it. You would have to be born there" (361).

In the Biblical process the traditional stories remain "alive"; they do not become mere museum pieces. "Instead," says Mellor, "it seems as if each generation encountered these events, wrestled with their meaning . . . but above all was challenged by them in the contemporary situation" (71). Quentin's response to the "challenge" is a certain kind of resentment: "Quentin had grown up with that; the mere names were interchangeable and almost myriad. His childhood was full of them; his very body was an empty hall echoing with sonorous defeated names; he was not a being, an entity, he was a commonwealth. He was a barracks filled with stubborn back-looking ghosts" (12). And later: *"I have heard too much, I have been told too much; I have had to listen too much, too long"* (207).

But this resentment is inseparable from his sense of responsibility for what he has heard. *"It's because she wants it told,"* he thinks during his visit with Rosa Coldfield—though later he learns she wants him to *partake* of the story as well, by accompanying her to the old Sutpen place. Miss Rosa, though not a parent, knows how to charge her commission with the energizing force of guilt: "Perhaps you will even remember kindly then the old woman who made you spend a whole afternoon . . . while she talked about people and events *you were fortunate enough to escape yourself*" (10, italics mine). When Quentin resists his commissioning—"What is it to me that the land . . . got tired of him at last and turned and destroyed him?" (12)—his father adds a kind of genetic responsibility to whatever Quentin owes through chivalry, courtesy, or community membership: "if it hadn't been for your grandfather's friendship, Sutpen could never have got a foothold. . . . So maybe she considers you partly responsible through heredity for what happened to her and her family through him" (13). And by the time Quentin goes north to Harvard he bears responsibility as well for what he himself has seen and heard of Henry Sutpen.

But of course the making of the Old Testament involved not only a personal but a communal and national challenge. The process by which oral tradition became Biblical literature begins, as modern scholarship sees it, during the United Kingdom under David and Solomon, at the height of national success. It does not conclude until after the defeat and humiliation of both Israel and Judah, one by the Assyrians and the other by the Babylonians. It does not conclude, that is, until after the "challenge" of the old traditions to the "contemporary situation" has been posed to the generation of the Babylonian Exile. It is the exilic and postexilic generations above all that would have been challenged by the task of finding the old stories meaningful. In *An Introduction to the Old Testament*, published in 1917, Harlan Creelman, professor of Hebrew at Auburn University, states the matter rather drily: "The Exile was a fitting time for review and revision of past history on the part of Israel's religious teachers. The destruction of Jerusalem furnished the occasion for thoughtful interpretation of that past; and the Exile gave the leisure necessary."[12] We are given a more fully human version of these events, the fall of Jerusalem and the Exile, in some of the exilic and postexilic Psalms: "We are become a reproach to our neighbours, a scorn and derision to them that are round about us. . . . How long, Lord?" (79: 4–5). "By the rivers of Babylon . . . we wept, when we remembered Zion. . . . How shall we sing the Lord's song in a strange land?" (137:1–4).[13]

In the novel, the parallel to the destruction of Jerusalem is the defeat of the South—indeed, its ceasing to exist as an independent nation. Although the question of how representative Sutpen is of the South is a controversial one, we do know that from the book's third page, when Quentin thinks of himself as "preparing for Harvard in the South . . . dead since 1865," to its last, when he protests that he does *not* hate the South, and throughout the recounting of the story of the Sutpens, whose rise and fall parallels Southern fortunes before, during, and after the war, Quentin is aware of himself as a Southerner and of the story as concerning Southern history. Faulkner was still calling his novel "Dark House" when he wrote to Harrison Smith that "the story is an anecdote which occurred during and right after the civil war," and that he was using Quentin's "bitterness which he has projected on the South . . . to get more out of the story itself than a historical novel would" (78–79).

If the book is about the South, we can also say that it concerns a nation *in defeat.* Mr. Compson describes Coldfield's refusal to look upon "his native land in the throes of repelling an invading army" (60) and later gives us Jim Hamblett's speech in which "our country is struggling to rise from beneath the iron heel of a tyrant oppressor" (203). Though Mr. Compson himself might not admit to patriotism of this sort in 1909, Rosa Coldfield still seeks to explain history in terms of *"Why God let us lose the War"* (11); and Compson would surely agree with her summary of the war's result: *"the stable world we had been taught to know dissolved in fire and smoke until peace and security were gone, and pride and hope"* (150). Moreover, John Shelton Reed's comparison of various nationalist movements with the Southern sectionalism of the Vanderbilt Agrarians makes it plain that such feelings were very much alive in the South during the 1930s as Faulkner was writing the novel. Quoting Frank Owsley, Reed makes the point that the resentment of the Third World toward "Yankee imperialism" is much the same as the resentment felt by the twelve Southerners who wrote *I'll Take My Stand* in 1930. The book was a protest not only against industrialism but against the North's "brazen and contemptuous treatment" of the South as a "colony and as a conquered province."[14]

If Quentin, then, as a Southerner in a defeated South, can be

compared with the Hebrews after the destruction of Jerusalem—
the "occasion," we remember, for their "review and revision" of
Israelite history including the Davidic dynasty—we can see in
Quentin's experience at Harvard a parallel to the Babylonian
exile. Again, Reed's comparison of Southern sectionalism with
typical nationalist movements furnishes a link. An experience of
exile is an important factor in the production of "great literature,
as in Ireland, Russia, and the South," and also of nationalist
movements (59, 63).[15] The experience of exile produces both
"distancing" from one's native culture, a distancing necessary to
bring it to full consciousness, and an active or reactive *memory* of
that culture. Reed quotes a line from Stark Young, one of the
twelve Southerners who wrote *I'll Take My Stand*, that could
serve as a gloss for both Quentin's experience in the last chapter of
Absalom and the Biblical Psalm of Exile, Psalm 137. Stark Young
wrote from New York of the sort of experience that "brings tears to
your eyes because of its memory of some place. That place . . . is
your country" (60). And he quotes Donald Davidson, another of
the twelve, on the active, creative exercise of memory that follows
such renewed awareness of tradition: "We must recover the past,
or at least in some way realize it in order that we may bring the
most genuine and essential parts of our tradition forward in
contact with the inevitable new tradition now in the process of
formation" (62). It is clear to Reed that *I'll Take My Stand* was a
"counterattack" in a "spiritual and intellectual war" whose aim was
to produce a "countermyth" of Southern history (46, 47).

This process, which Biblical scholars note as part of the making
of the Bible and Reed notes as part of the making of both great
literature and nationalism, is in effect prescribed for Quentin by
Rosa Coldfield when he first visits her: the process of humiliation,
exile, and remembering. "So I don't imagine you will ever come
back here and settle down . . . in a little town like Jefferson, since
Northern people have already seen to it that there is little left in
the South for a young man. So maybe you will enter the literary
profession as so many Southern gentlemen and gentlewomen too

are doing now and maybe some day you will remember this and write about it" (9–10). It is the same process that has recently been seen, in a literary context, as central to the Biblical process and also as consonant with postmodern understandings of textuality: "But when we say that remembering is the condition of survival in the Bible, we cannot mean it in any naive sense. . . . Rather it is interpretation that becomes the ground of continuity, enabling a future." [16] Both remembering and interpretation, in this view, are dependent on loss and repression, which become "occasions for remembering, for interpreting, that is, for re-creation" (118). And it is this process which Faulkner portrays as operating in Quentin.

Quentin's experience at Harvard is given us in an incrementally repeated image of estrangement. The narrator's look forward sees Compson's letter coming over the "long iron New England snow" (31), first of all; later, from Quentin's perspective, we get "this strange iron New England snow" (173), "zero outside . . . above the iron quad" (217), "iron and impregnable dark" and "iron and icelike bedclothing" (360), and, finally, "the cold air, the iron New England dark" (378). The only references to Harvard *without* this image occur during the youths' excited re-creations in chapters 7 and 8.

Like that of the exiles of Psalm 137, Quentin's sense of loss is exacerbated by taunts from the people of the place: "Sing us a song of Zion!" *"Tell about the South,"* Shreve says. *"What's it like there. What do they do there. Why do they live there. Why do they live at all"* (174). Shreve in 1910 has not heard of the 1925 "Monkey Trial" of Dayton, Tennessee, which in some of the Agrarians' opinions marked the beginning of the movement owing to the bad press the South received throughout the rest of the country. But his baiting of Quentin on page 217 ("better than the theatre," "better than *Ben Hur,*" "no wonder you have to come away now and then") anticipates the cultural stereotypes the Agrarians would later resent: "a region full of little else but lynchings, shootings . . . and a few decayed patricians." [17]

But Shreve is not, finally, a member of the great Northern

empire that has conquered the continent. As a Canadian, he too is
an outlander, and one who envies Quentin precisely for his sense
of tradition and meaningful history, because "it's something my
people haven't got" (361)—or, as he goes on to say, something they
have lost. It is out of his loss, and Quentin's, that the two of them
re-create the meaning of the story of the Sutpen children. Like
the inspired reinterpretation that marks the Biblical redactors,
theirs develops from an *identification* of themselves with the
story: Faulkner speaks of their *existing in* the character whom
they create (316). As Donald M. Kartiganer's reading of this
section of the novel makes especially clear, Shreve comes to share
with Quentin both the experience of exile and the re-creative
communion which that experience makes possible.[18] That experience produces nothing closer to "nationalism," finally, than Quentin's insistence that he does not hate the South; but, in Faulkner's
representation, it does produce "great literature."

2

If the analogy of the Biblical process as seen by modern scholarship does inform *Absalom*, there are a number of implications
for our reading of the novel. But before exploring these, it would
be well to ask what Faulkner might have known and did in fact
know about modern Biblical scholarship.

Faulkner would have heard of the modernist view of Scripture if
only in news of its condemnation by Pope Pius X in 1907, or in
news of the Dayton trial in 1925; he would have been interested if
only because of the kind of fiction he was writing. A Southern
intellectual growing up in the "Bible Belt" during the time the
phrase was coined would be aware of the "higher criticism," and
one producing his own literature would have been interested in
what that criticism had to say about the formation of the Biblical
literature. It can be argued that in Protestant countries, where the
function of the Bible as a foundation document has been especially marked, the work of modern Biblical scholars was more

unsettling to conventional faith, more important an ingredient in the modernist crisis of authority, than the work of Darwin or Marx or Freud. For that reason I would add the name of Thomas Mann, and strongly underline it, to the list of those modern writers against the background of whose work Faulkner is increasingly seen. Mann also came of age in Protestant and Bible-believing territory; he too wrote twentieth-century fiction influenced by the Bible—including perhaps the greatest of modern attempts at the epic, *Joseph and His Brothers.* Faulkner admired Mann; and the first two volumes of the Joseph tetralogy, where Mann's familiarity with Biblical scholarship is very evident, were available in English, published by Knopf, as Faulkner was writing *Absalom.*[19]

Modern Biblical scholarship emphasized the process by which the text came into being—in contrast to traditional views, in which the Bible stood as Sacred Text or foundation document. "If men have hitherto been content to contemplate the counsel of the Most High only in its final state—laid out before them, as it were, in a map—hereafter it seems that they are to consider it by preference in its stages, in its vital processes of growth and development."[20] Warfield's metaphor tells why the modern view was controversial: a map gives directions and demands following; but a record of the "processes of growth and maturing," like a fossil-laden hillside, demands questioning, analysis, and criticism. The two fruits of modern scholarship mentioned as controversial in *The Making of the Old Testament* are the documentary theory of the origin of the Penteteuch, which "set aside the traditional view of Moses as the author," and the progressive or evolutionary theory of Biblical theology, in which a "clearly stated monotheism" is not reached until the Babylonian Exile (i.e., in Isaiah 45:5).[21]

Both of these ideas would have been available to Faulkner in such a book as John Crowe Ransom's unorthodox defense of orthodoxy, *God Without Thunder*—a book which Ransom calls "mere lay work, and meant for laity."[22] In it Ransom makes casual reference to three of the four Penteteuch sources usually posited by the documentary hypothesis ("the authors of the Hebrew Scriptures—J, E, P, and however they may be named and dated"); and in his discussion of the fact that it is Jehovah, in 2 Samuel 24, who out of anger with Israel inspires David to make a census, while it is Satan who inspires the same act in 1 Chronicles 21, he cites a familiar bit of evidence for a progressive view of Biblical theology (41, 42, 110).

If Faulkner wanted to see for himself what Biblical criticism had to say about the story of David and Absalom, he might have looked at the two volumes on the books of Samuel in the *Cambridge Bible for Schools and Colleges, A Commentary*, which appeared in fifty-seven volumes 1877–1900 and in a one-volume edition 1895–1919 (NUC 91, 482–83).[23] The Samuel volumes were edited by Alexander Francis Kirkpatrick, who eventually became Old Testament editor for the series. If Faulkner did read Kirkpatrick, in the Cambridge Bible or elsewhere, he would have come across such ideas as the following, as they appeared in Kirkpatrick's collection of lectures (1891, 1909): the "Penteteuch or Hexateuch" had a composite origin in four principal documents, these based on still older materials (xv); the books of the Old Testament are the result of "processes of compilation and combination and . . . 'editing'" (11); "the Chronicler (1 Chron. xxix. 29) actually names as the original authority for the history of David's reign, *The history of Samuel the seer, and the history of Nathan the prophet, and the history of Gad the seer*" (13); the Bible is "the record of a gradual and progressive revelation which was made known to men by slow degrees as they could bear it," and "inspiration has not obliterated the steps of the progress" (107–8).

That Faulkner did know something of modern Biblical criticism is indicated by his statement at the Nagano conference that the Old Testament is "some of the finest, most robust and most amusing folklore I know," and that the New Testament is "philosophy and ideas, and something of the quality of poetry" (45–46).

The word *folklore* implies both multiple sources and an extended process of transmission, and the description of the two Testaments is itself a brief content analysis like those that form the basis of much Biblical criticism.

Among Faulkner's characters are several who illustrate his knowledge of various strands of Biblical literature. In *Light in August* McEachern's "enormous Bible with brass clasps and hinges and a brass lock" represents, to him, The Law in its most rigid form; to Hines, the Bible that he holds in his lap just before he calls the dietician "Jezebel" is a source and inspiration for Prophecy.[24] In *The Hamlet* the farmer from whom Ike steals sees the Bible as the source of the "ancient biblical edict" that "man must sweat or have not"; but to I. O. Snopes, the "proverbist," it is one of many sources of such garbled Wisdom sayings as "cast the beam outen your neighbors' eyes and out of sight is out of mind."[25]

More importantly, there are two Faulkner characters who understand the concept of "gradual and progressive revelation made known to men by slow degrees as they could bear it." In *Absalom* Mr. Compson describes the Bible passages declaimed by Coldfield against the Southern troops as "passages of the old violent vindictive mysticism" (82). And in *Go Down, Moses* Faulkner has Ike, in his dialogue with Cass on God's purposes in human history, answer Cass's challenge that "the men who transcribed His Book for Him were sometime liars" with a version of progressive revelation that amounts to a paraphrase of Kirkpatrick's. "Yes," Ike says. "Because they were human men. What they were trying to tell, what He wanted said, was too simple. Those for whom they transcribed His words could not have believed them. It had to be expounded in the everyday terms which they were familiar with and could comprehend, not only those who listened but those who told it too."[26]

All things considered, it seems likely that Faulkner did know and make use of Biblical scholarship's view of the making of the Bible.

3

Faulkner's handling of the David analogy is fluid—nothing at all like the point-for-point political allegory of Dryden's *Absalom and Achitophel* and considerably more fluid than even Hardy's use of the Saul and David parallels in *The Mayor of Casterbridge*. The theme of "collapse of dynasty" outlined by Behrens involves a foreshortening of the 400-year Davidic monarchy into three generations of Sutpens; and if at times Henry and Bon parallel Absalom and Amnon, at other times they evoke David and Jonathan, Isaac and Ishamel, Esau and Jacob. If Judith serves in the Biblical analogy as Tamar, she also reminds us of Antigone. The characters themselves, as they search for the meanings of the Sutpen story, draw analogies from Greek, Roman, and Western European history and literature. Faulkner referred to Sutpen as being destroyed by "the old Greek concept of tragedy," by "too many sons," and by "the land."[27]

The point is that the structures Faulkner sees lie very deep, below the periphery formed by many individual texts, so that the analogies we find for these structures must be broad and general.

In applying the analogy of the making of the Bible to *Absalom*, then, we should not look for such specific sources for the book's narrators as the four gospel writers; or J, E, D, and P; or Gad, Nathan, Samuel, and the Chronicler. The analogy rather suggests the general process by which, from one generation to another, oral sources become traditions and these in turn become retellings and reinterpretations. Just as the David analogy allows the Civil War in *Absalom* to resonate largely as that time of war when all these things happened to the Sutpens—and thus to evoke all of David's many wars as well as the Trojan War when all these things happened in the House of Atreus—so the analogy of the Biblical process allows the same Civil War to resonate as the background of defeat and humiliation against which the story is told, evoking the conquests of Israel and Judah by all conquerors from Assyrians and Babylonians to Greeks and Romans.

It becomes clear, then, that Faulkner draws his Biblical analogy

from the Bible as a whole, insofar as it concerns a recounting of
and meditation upon history. The text indicates the larger dimensions of its Biblical model in two sets of images. First, the creation
of Sutpen's Hundred "like the oldentime *Be Light,*" along with
other Genesis references, carries the book's allusions back into
primeval history (9). In the second half of the book, Shreve's
repeated though casual exclamation, "Jesus," as he and Quentin
"speak of love" and imagine Bon's self-sacrificing resignation to his
own murder, hints at a movement toward, or into, the New
Testament; and at the end of the novel there is an implied apocalypse in the disappearance of Sutpen's house and lineage, save
for Bond, in fire and smoke.

There is also a link between the motifs of Sutpen's "house," in
Faulkner's novel, and David's "house" in the Bible. David's palace
is built of cedar and with the aid of Hiram, king of Tyre, and a
contingent of foreign workers (2 Samuel 5:11). Sutpen's house is
built near a cedar grove (which later becomes the family burying
ground) and with the aid of a French architect and a band of "wild
blacks" (8, 126). David's "house" is linked, in 2 Samuel 7, to the
Davidic monarchy and the Jerusalem Temple, which is also built
of cedar by Hiram of Tyre and his foreign workers (1 Kings 5).
Thus, in Sutpen's attempt to restore his house after the war (both
plantation and lineage) there is an echo of the postexilic restora-
tion of the Temple by David's heir Zerubabel—who, like Sutpen,
works in much reduced circumstances (Haggai 1:14, 2:3). Finally,
the destruction of Sutpen's house echoes the motif of the Temple's
destruction (2 Kings 25:9, Jeremiah 26:7, Amos 3:15, 8:3, Mark
13:2) historically carried out by the Babylonians and, six and a half
centuries later, the Romans. As the Genesis-Revelation sequence
parallels the beginning and the ending of the novel, the building-
restoration-destruction sequence parallels the telling of the
story—for in the period from David's monarchy to the Roman
destruction of the Temple the Bible was written down and
edited.[28]

The four narrators, then, function within this larger Biblical analogy. Among them, Quentin serves as "final redactor," inasmuch as it is he who receives the two narrative traditions represented by Miss Rosa and Mr. Compson; it is he who recounts these, along with material on the early life of Sutpen from his grandfather, to Shreve, the first outsider to hear the story; and it is he who gathers textual evidence (Bon's letter, Mr. Compson's letter), archaeological evidence (his visits to the tombstones and the house), and firsthand ethnographical evidence (his meeting with Henry, his memories of Jim Bond) and presents these to Shreve and to the reader. Finally, it is he who forms with Shreve the new interpretive community of insider and outsider, Jew and Gentile, that supplies the conclusion to both stories, one of which may be called the fall of the house of Sutpen and the other the making of the Sutpen story.

Miss Rosa—a woman betrayed, bereaved, unfulfilled; a poet of lost causes; partisan, moralistic, embittered—voices the earliest stratum of material about the Sutpens. It is she who begins the novel by bringing Sutpen sulphurously back from the "victorious dust," much as the witch of Endor brings Samuel up from the dead (1 Samuel 28:7-20), and it is she whose summons, "out of another world almost," written on the "queer, archaic sheet of ancient good notepaper," begins Quentin's career as redactor (8, 10). In the Bible the barren or bereaved woman often represents the land or nation—for example, Rachel in Jeremiah 15:30 and Matthew 2:18, the virgin of Israel in Amos 5:2, and the barren woman in Isaiah 54. So Miss Rosa as "polymath love's androgynous advocate" and mourner of her wasted youth represents the Southern land in defeat. As a poet, she reminds us of the Psalms of lament (e.g., 44, 88, 94); as both woman and poet she reminds us of the warlike singers Miriam and Deborah. Modern scholarship suspects, on the basis of Micah 6:4 and Exodus 15:20, that Miriam may have rivaled her brother Moses in some early traditions, and affirms that the song of Deborah (Judges 5) is one of the oldest extant Hebrew compositions.[29] Their songs of triumph also represent the Biblical strain of "old violent vindictive

mysticism" declaimed by Miss Rosa's father and not absent from
Miss Rosa's own "demonizing." Finally, her attitude toward the
Sutpen history reminds one of the stance taken in the "Deuter-
onomist history-work" (Deuteronomy through Kings, excluding
Ruth): "All these things happened to the Israelites because they
sinned against the Lord their God who brought them up from
Egypt" (NEV, 2 Kings 17:7; Mellor, 72).

Mr. Compson, on the other hand, voices the attitudes of the
Bible's Wisdom literature. Like the speaker in the book of
Proverbs and the Preacher of Ecclesiastes, he is a father instructing a son. Wisdom was international in scope and had little to say
of national history or tradition; the practical advice of Proverbs,
including much about the nature of women, is addressed to the
young male; and the inquiring agnosticism of Job and Ecclesiastes
is concerned with the individual, not the community. Mr. Compson likewise is not partisan and indeed when telling of Henry and
Bon's relationship seems to prefer Bon's *laissez-faire* French
Catholicism and worldweary aestheticism to Henry's Anglo-
Saxon, yokel Puritanism. His love for the South is expressed
mainly in his looking askance at Coldfield; the war and many
lesser human events are mysterious, inexplicable; perhaps they
are arranged by fate, or perhaps "we are not supposed to know"
(100). But he sees, attractively, that sometimes when we "try to
reconstruct the causes which lead up to the actions of men and
women . . . with a sort of astonishment we find . . . they stem-
med from some of the old virtues," and it is he who provides our
heroic image of Judith, whose stoicism is a superior version of his
own: *"if happy I can be I will, if suffer I must I can"* (121). And like
the writer of the apocryphal Wisdom of Solomon, he allows
himself, in his letter to Quentin, at least the hope of an afterlife
(377).

To these older traditions Quentin and Shreve, as insider and
outsider forming a new community of interpretation, bring fresh
information (the burning of the house and the deaths of Clytie,
Henry, and Miss Rosa) and fresh insight. They bring to light

forgotten or repressed truths (the opposing sexual taboos, incest and miscegenation) and with them certain moral triumphs: Judith's *"hurdling of iron old traditions"* when she says to Bon's son, *"Call me Aunt Judith, Charles"* (207, 208); and Bon's decision, in the face of his father's refusal to recognize him, to let himself be murdered. " 'And he never slipped away,' Shreve said. . . . 'Jesus, maybe he even went to Henry. . . . Ain't that right? Ain't it? By God, ain't it?' " (358–59).

Frank McConnell has expressed the movement from the Old to the New Testament as a movement from "epic" to "biography," from "folk-sociology" to "existential self-discovery," and Quentin and Shreve do supply something of this movement in *Absalom*.[30] More particularly they supply, in terms of the larger Biblical analogy I have been describing, a movement from the insights of Prophetic History and Wisdom, of necessity incomplete, to those of Apocalyptic and Messianism. As insider and outsider collaboratively reworking the old stories, they may remind us of an early Christian community of redactors: Wash kills Sutpen (in Mr. Compson's narrative recalled by Quentin to Shreve) out of a disappointed political Messianism based on the rights of white insiders over black outsiders (282); but the deaths of Judith and Bon are self-sacrifices of the Suffering Servant kind of Messianism, both made in deliberate opposition to the "iron old traditions" keeping insider and outsider apart. Even Clytie and Henry may fall into this category: "me and Judith and him have paid it out" (370).

However, a Biblical analogy for the insights of Quentin and Shreve may also be found in the Old Testament. The Suffering Servant is found in Job and Second Isaiah, and the apocalypse of the apostle John was preceded by centuries of Jewish apocalpytic. Indeed, as early as the prophet Amos we have a kind of last judgment that is applicable to the house of Sutpen ("and the songs of the temple shall be howlings in that day"), and with it a view of insider-outsider relations equally appropriate: "Are ye not as children of the Ethiopians unto me, O children of Israel?" (8:3; 9:7).

The point is that if Quentin and Shreve in their acts of narration parallel an early Christian community of redactors they also parallel a Hellenized Jewish community. They produce a retelling of the old stories, not a new story or gospel—though their reinterpretation of the old provides a context in which the new story can arise.

As important as Quentin and Shreve's insights while retelling the story is the fact that they *do* retell it. Again and again *Absalom*'s last chapters remind us of their own hermeneutics—as when Quentin's correction of Shreve's facts ("Miss Rosa, I tell you") is followed by Shreve's correction of Quentin's ("there wasn't any West Virginia in 1808"), which in turn is followed by mutual agreement that the "facts" about roses blooming at Christmas "did not matter" (176, 220, 295). Miss Rosa reveals doubts about the memory as a path to truth, and Mr. Compson doubts the possibility of understanding the past; their doubts are founded in part on their lack of information which Quentin and Shreve possess (143, 100–1). But Faulkner makes it clear in the last chapters that, beyond matters of fact, it is the nature of Quentin and Shreve's interpretive community, marked by imagination and sympathy both with each other and with the characters they re-create, that produces their insights. If what the Bible bequeaths to the West is "not only a book, which can be read as a myth, but some quintessence of the act of writing," the Biblical analogy in *Absalom* refers to both.[31]

4

Seeing a Biblical analogy for Faulkner's narration is helpful in interpreting certain difficult passages in *Absalom*. For example, we do not need to see Quentin as denying the difference between generations or as having "succumbed to psychosis" in the passage in which he says, *"Or maybe Father and I are both Shreve, maybe it took Father and me both to make Shreve or Shreve and me both to make Father or maybe Thomas Sutpen to make all of us"* (262).[32]

The passage, particularly in the light of the metaphor of the ripple passing through several differing but umbilically connected pools established on page 261, rather suggests the continuity of generations, through the telling and retelling of stories—and the reciprocally creative relationships between tale and teller. Dickens creates Pickwick—but Pickwick also "created" Charles Dickens. Quentin is thinking of a *communal* creation, like the Bible and Biblical figures, which even more than the work of an individual author "makes" its maker.

Moreover, the various questions about the relationships between text and truth, between novel, chronology, and genealogy, between the voices of characters and the editorial/authorial "overvoice" that recent readings of *Absalom* have generated, may themselves take on meaning in the context of Faulkner's Biblical analogy. For it is exactly these questions that modern scholarship's view of the Bible has presented us in regard to the central document in Western culture. The quest for the fictionally historical Sutpen(s) is not more convoluted and tortuous than the quest for the historical Jesus or Moses. As we ask these epistemological questions concerning Quentin's (and Faulkner's) "final redaction," we repeat the relationship of the higher critics to the Bible, and thus extend Faulkner's Biblical analogy to include the criticism, as well as the story and the narration, of his novel. In a unique way we become a part of the work we read.

Finally, it should be noted that in seeing *Absalom* against a Biblical background we broaden our sense of the world to which it refers far beyond the borders of the South. In relating a Southern experience of "collapse of dynasty" to the paradigmatic, synecdochal experience of the Hebrews that went into the making of the Bible, Faulkner relates it to other experiences for which the loss of Zion and the Babylonian Exile stand as symbols. For many if not most modern writers the First World War was such an experience, one that challenged received and traditional notions of the meaning of Western history; and the Great Depression during which Faulkner wrote was another. The South in 1936 was not the only "defeated nation" on American soil. It was necessary for many Americans to meet the traditional stories on new ground and reinterpret them. In echoing, even in an ironic and modern way, the Biblical community's work of reinterpreting a family and national saga—a work carried out over centuries and enduring through radically changed situations—Faulkner suggests, in a before-the-fact coda to his Nobel Prize Address, that if the human community does prevail it will be owing in part to the puny human voice still telling and retelling stories.

NOTES

1. Ralph Behrens, "Collapse of Dynasty: The Thematic Center of *Absalom, Absalom!*," PMLA 89 (1974): 24–33. Further references appear in the text.

2. Robert A. Jellife, ed., *Faulkner at Nagano* (Tokyo: Kenkyusha, 1956), 42; Frederick L. Gwynn and Joseph L. Blotner, eds., *Faulkner in the University* (Charlottesville: University of Virginia Press, 1959), 76. Further references are cited in the text.

3. A partial exception is the remark by Virginia Hlavsa, in an essay concerned chiefly with *Light in August*, that if in *Light in August* each of the four main characters represents an aspect of Christ, and if each of these aspects in turn is reflected in one of the four gospels, then the "four narrators of *Absalom, Absalom!* may represent a similar fragmentation"—with Shreve as the "non-synoptic" who nevertheless "intuits the most." See "The Mirror, the Lamp, and the Bed: Faulkner and the Modernists," *American Literature* 57 (1985): 42. A New Testament parallel is also hinted at in Patrick Samway, S.J.'s discussion of the figure of Jason Richmond Compson as represented in several Faulkner texts including *Absalom.* See "Searching for Jason Richmond Compson: A Question of Echolalia and a Problem of Palimpsest," Michael Gresset and Noel Polk, eds., *Intertextuality in Faulkner* (Jackson: University Press of Mississippi, 1985), 178–210.

4. Cleanth Brooks, *William Faulkner: The Yoknapatawpha Country* (New Haven: Yale University Press, 1963), 311, 315, 322. Further references are cited in the text.

5. Robert Dale Parker, "The Chronology and Genealogy of *Absalom, Absalom!*: The Authority of Fiction and the Fiction of Authority," *Studies in American Fiction* 14 (1986): 191–98.

6. Stephen M. Ross, "Oratory and the Dialogical in *Absalom, Absalom!*," Gresset and Polk, eds., 73–86.

7. David Krause, "Reading Bon's Letter and Faulkner's *Absalom, Absalom!*," PMLA 99 (1984): 225–41.

8. Gwynn and Blotner, eds., 71; Joseph Blotner, ed., *Selected Letters of William Faulkner* (New York: Random House, 1977), 79. Further references are cited in the text.

9. Enid B. Mellor, ed., *The Making of the Old Testament* (London: Cambridge University Press, 1972). 71, 73. Further references are cited in the text.

10. Hugh Kenner, "Faulkner and the Avant-Garde," Richard H. Brodhead, ed., *Faulkner: New Perspectives* (Englewood Cliffs: Prentice Hall, 1983), 69.

11. William Faulkner, *Absalom, Absalom!* (New York: Random House, 1936, 1964), 31, 32. Further references are cited in the text. The reader following this passage with an eye to the *Biblical* quality of the developing oral tradition in Faulkner's community may be put off by his use of "strophe and antistrophe." But the point I would make about Biblical

analogy for Faulkner's narration is that we should see the Biblical process as paradigmatic or synecdochal: it *implies* other traditions rather than excludes them. Faulkner's "classical" metaphor here, then, is equivalent to his use of classical allusion elsewhere. Neither usage contradicts the central allusion of the title; both, rather, extend it.

12. Harlan Creelman, *An Introduction to the Old Testament* (New York: Macmillan, 1917), 23.

13. Scripture citations are from the Authorized Version unless otherwise indicated.

14. John Shelton Reed, "For Dixieland: The Sectionalism of *I'll Take My Stand,*" William C. Havard and Walter Sullivan, eds., *A Band of Prophets* (Baton Rouge: Louisiana State University Press, 1982), 41–64.

15. The use of exile or some other form of enforced separation as the still point from which to view a story is familiar in modern literature. Faulkner himself was to use Psalm 137 as thematic background in *The Wild Palms* (1939), whose original title, according to Thomas L. McHaney's study, was "If I Forget Thee, Jerusalem" (xiii–xiv); and François Pitavy's essay explores a number of ways in which the background of the Biblical Exile informs (and is informed by) this novel. See Thomas L. McHaney, *William Faulkner's "The Wild Palms": A Study* (Jackson: University Press of Mississippi, 1975), xiii–xiv; and François Pitavy, "Forgetting Jerusalem: An Ironical Chart for *The Wild Palms,*" in Gresset and Polk, eds., 114–27.

Absalom is unique, however, in its structural use of the theme of exile in conjunction with other major elements in the Biblical process: two or more sets of oral tradition; a community story with national and historical importance; a background of national defeat and humiliation; two or more generations of "redactors."

16. Regina M. Schwartz, "Joseph's Bones and the Resurrection of the Text: Remembering in the Bible," *PMLA* 103 (1988): 121. Further references cited in the text.

17. Reed, 45. In *The Faulkner–Cowley File* (New York: Viking, 1966), Malcolm Cowley remarks that Faulkner "hoped that the material would have more than a regional meaning, and very often . . . he thought back to archetypes not in Southern legend, but in the Bible" (15–18). (In the letter that Cowley summarizes, Faulkner compares Quentin to a young Philistine of Biblical times brooding over the ruin completed by Samson.) In the reference by Shreve to *Ben-Hur,* Quentin is by implication compared to the young scion of the Jewish race, Ben-Hur, with Shreve for the moment in the antagonistic role of the young Roman, Messala. One likes to imagine that the phrase "better than *Ben-Hur*" implies also an evaluation: Faulkner's reperformance of the Bible in *Absalom, Absalom!* is "better" than Lew Wallace's immensely popular reworking of Biblical history in his novel and drama.

18. Donald M. Kartiganer, "Toward a Supreme Fiction: *Absalom, Absalom!,*" Richard H. Brodhead, ed., 153–73.

19. In Joseph Blotner's *Faulkner: A Biography,* 2 vols. (New York: Random House, 1974), Faulkner in 1931 praises Mann's *The Magic Mountain* (741); in 1932 he cites Mann, Hemingway, Cather, Dos Passos, and himself as "the best living writers" (787); in 1942 he writes in a letter that Hitler has gained immortality by expelling from his native land the "foremost literary artist of his time" (1119–20); and in 1958 he says in an interview that Mann and Joyce "were the great writers of my time" (1693). But in 1938, when asked by Emily Stone whether he had read Thomas Mann's *Joseph and His Brothers,* he "perversely answered, 'I never heard of him,' though the previous year he had put his name in his own copy of *Stories of Three Decades*" (1012).

20. Benjamin B. Warfield, "The Century's Progress in Biblical Knowledge" (1900), John E. Meeter, ed., *Selected Shorter Works of Benjamin B. Warfield II* (Nutley, N.J.: Presbyterian and Reformed Publishing Co., 1973), 12.

21. As Mellor makes clear, the documentary theory has been considerably modified since the nineteenth century (62), and the theory of the evolution of Old Testament theology is "no longer universally popular" (64).

22. John Crowe Ransom, *God Without Thunder,* 1930 (Rptd. Hamden, Conn.: Archon, 1965) ix. Further references are cited in the text.

23. Virginia Hlavsa's footnote giving evidence that Faulkner read this particular commentary seems premature (28, *n*). The evidence is from Blotner, who quotes a Laurence Stallings column in the New York *Sun* (Saturday, 3 September 1932), 7: "He bought one book to read over his lonely nights. It was a second hand twelve-volume edition of the Cambridge edition of the Holy Bible" (1:777). Blotner's annotation, however, refers to the *fourteen*-volume Bible listed in his catalog of Faulkner's library (87), and this Bible contains no commentary, notes, or exegesis. See Joseph Blotner, *Faulkner's Library—A Catalogue* (Charlottesville: University Press of Virginia, 1964), 87.

Faulkner's Bible is an excellent reader's edition, however, and does have some features in accord with modern Biblical scholarship. It has no verse numbers; its chapter numbers appear only parenthetically at the top of each page; and it prints verse as verse, so that interpolations like the Song of Hannah (1 Samuel 2: 1–10) or the Last Words of David (2 Samuel 23: 1–7) are more readily seen as interpolations. There are no genealogical inserts such as those in the family Bible inherited by Faulkner in 1932. In other words, this Bible's character as text, rather than foundational or Sacred Text, is enhanced. (I wish to thank Howard Bahr, Curator at Rowan Oak, for his kindness in making available photostatic page-copies from Faulkner's Bible.)

But why would Stallings write "twelve-volume edition of the Cambridge edition" if Faulkner had a fourteen-volume R. H. Hinkley edition? There is in fact no twelve-volume Cambridge edition listed in the National Union Catalogue. Perhaps Stallings knew or had used a "Cambridge Bible" himself, or knew that Faulkner had. Perhaps Faulkner, having read either the one or the many-volumed commentary, *told* Stallings his twelve- or fourteen-volume set was a Cambridge Bible. Or perhaps Faulkner cited enough information from one commentary or another to make Stallings convince himself that what Faulkner owned must be a Cambridge Bible. However one explains Stallings's apparent mistake, his article furnishes two other clues to Faulkner's thinking in 1932: Faulkner spoke archaeologically of Hollywood, saying that the future's only evidence of its existence would be the horseshoe stakes left by transplanted Iowans; and he thought of his own existence there as a kind of exile, complaining of the cloudless weather and later writing Stallings of the lovely showers he was enjoying in Mississippi.

24. William Faulkner, *Light in August* (New York: Random House, 1932, 1959), 137, 118, 123.

25. William Faulkner, *The Hamlet* (New York: Random House, 1964), 191, 161, 201.

26. William Faulkner, *Go Down, Moses* (New York: Random House, 1942), 260. Faulkner in *Absalom* seems to replay the Dayton "monkey trial" by pitting an evolution-based ideology of race against an evolutionary view of Biblical revelation. Social-Darwinian racism is given a mythological beginning in Sutpen's brutal fights with his slaves, which echo the Canaanite myth of "primaeval combat between the gods and chaos . . . probably re-enacted annually . . . to ensure fertility," a myth that has echoes in the Bible; thereafter, the offensive term for "black outsider" obtrudes itself in the novel and is associated with lower forms of life (monkey, ape, bull, dog, *etc.*), and the white woman as angel or "ghost" is associated with the highest (29–30; Mellor, 46–47). Meanwhile the narration's re-enactment of the making of the Bible moves from Miss Rosa's "old violent vindictive mysticism" through Mr. Compson's resigned tolerance to Quentin and Shreve's discovery of Judith's and Bon's suffering and heroism in the face of the "iron old traditions" keeping insider and outsider apart. In other words, it is the Darwinian evolution championed by Clarence Darrow and the Northern newspapers that proves reactionary in matters of race. In *Go Down, Moses* Ike's progressive view of Biblical revelation is similarly opposed to Cass's stubborn insistence on the old vindictive mysticism of the curse against the "sons of Ham," a view echoed by Wash in *Absalom, Absalom!* (282).

27. Gwynn and Blotner, eds., 35, 71; Blotner, ed., 79–84.

28. With some rounding of numbers. The last New Testament writings are thought to have been completed by the end of the first century, thirty years after the Romans destroyed the Jerusalem Temple. The writing of the last Hebrew Scriptures had been

completed more than two centuries before; but the "main form and contents of the Hebrew canon were decided by A.D. 100" at the Council of Jamnia (Mellor, 124–26). If David's temple in its three versions lasts 1000 years, Faulkner's Chronology makes Sutpen's house endure for seventy-seven, from its building in 1833 to its burning in 1910.

29. John L. McKenzie, S.J., *Dictionary of the Bible* (New York: Macmillan, 1965), 185, 580.

30. Frank McConnell, ed., *The Bible and the Narrative Tradition* (New York: Oxford University Press, 1986), 7.

31. Herbert Schneidau, *Sacred Discontent: The Bible and Western Tradition*, 1976 (Rptd. Berkeley: University of California Press, 1977), 253.

32. Nancy Blake, "Creation and Procreation: The Voice and the Name, or Biblical Intertextuality in *Absalom, Absalom!*," Gresset and Polk, eds., 122–43.

The Crucifixion in *Light in August:*
Suspending Rules at the Post

VIRGINIA V. HLAVSA

Some five years ago, this conference discussed my findings that Faulkner paralleled the twenty-one chapters of *Light in August* with the twenty-one chapters of the St. John Gospel. To give a small example, in John's chapter 5, the halt man is cured when Jesus says, "Rise, take up thy bed and walk." Now unlike those marvelously concrete medieval representations of this scene, the "bed" would have been the simple pallet of a poor man. Thus, in Faulkner's chapter 5, we read that Joe "was in the act of reclining when he stopped, halted." If we allow the pun, it simply confirms what we know about Joe anyway, that society has made him the halt man, especially since he then takes "the single half cotton blanket which composed his bedding" and begins "walking" to the stable.[1] In a similar way, each of Faulkner's twenty-one chapters has specific thematic and dictional echoes from the corresponding chapter of John.

But there is more. Faulkner also expanded on each of John's stories with some fascinating primitive and mythic material from James Frazer's complete edition of *The Golden Bough.*[2] For example, in John's chapter 3, we find Nicodemus, the scribe, living in darkness and abiding by the letter rather than the spirit. So in Faulkner's chapter 3, we find Hightower, surrounded by books, prints, letters, and other scribal materials, living in darkness and impotently abiding by the letter rather than the spirit of human relationships. But Hightower also reflects Frazer's discussions of the Public Magician, a holy figure who was so important to

127

the well-being of the tribe and of all creation that he must stay hidden and protected from ordinary intercourse—which Faulkner has amusingly reflected in Hightower's lack of intercourse with the people of the town in general and his own wife in particular. But Hightower further reflects Frazer's account of the mythic Hippolytus, whose name means "horseloosed," both because horses were sacred to Poseidon, his grandfather,[3] and because Aphrodite had him dragged to death—by horses—because he spurned her love in favor of hunting. Again we recall that Hightower spurned his wife's sexuality because he was obsessed with horses, particularly his grandfather's horses, out hunting with grandfather for chickens.

Last time I argued that, as a modernist, Faulkner devised these elaborate designs partly for the fun of it, because even in his most serious works, he loved to out-Joyce Joyce, and no doubt it amused him to create humorous dimensions all unknown to the casual reader and especially to the critics.

Now I want to argue that Faulkner also devised such elaborate designs out of his obsession with religion, or more precisely, out of his need to place his own religion into a universal context, into cultures that exist across such vast tracts of time and space, they might indeed have been universal because they represent completely different worlds. His purpose in doing so was moral. He loved the people of his religion. In fact, he loved them so fiercely that he was profoundly angry with most of them, most of the time. Moreover, unlike Joyce or Pound or Stein, he never became a permanent exile. On the contrary, he stayed here, and he wrote to his own people, wanting them to be aware that the savage roots of Christianity go down not only into history but also into their own hearts. Because ultimately, Faulkner believed we are one. I picture him hanging around the square here in Oxford (as it was told to me by a local), "talking to Negras," or trekking the bottom lands with his cronies. In these daily encounters, he must have seen patterns in their behavior and heard tales that reminded him of the tribes he was reading about in Frazer. Like Eliot, who maintained that myth opened modernist writers to the "vanished mind" of our own past, Faulkner believed he could hold his Mississippi folk in the light of the Biblical tale as it is illuminated by mythic or primitive behavior. In fact, the one could be electrified by the other.

Light in August's chapter 19 is a fascinating case in point. Like John 19, it is the crucifixion chapter, and particulars of the Passion emerge in Faulkner's descriptions. Mrs. Hines wants Joe "decently hung by a Force" (421), while Stevens explains that Joe's "black blood . . . swept him up into that ecstasy out of a black jungle where . . . death is desire and fulfillment" (425).[4] Regarding Jesus' words on the cross, "I thirst," Joe's past "left him at last high and dry in a barred cell with the shape of an incipient executioner everywhere he looked" (424). Regarding the casting of lots by the soldiers, the many games include the poker game by Grimm's men, playing soldier. Regarding the "five wounds," Joe receives five gunshot wounds. In every other chapter, we may have trouble accepting Joe Christmas as a parallel to Jesus Christ, but not here, especially not at the end, where the "pent black blood" from his savage castration seems "to rush like a released breath . . . like the rush of sparks from a rising rocket," so that "upon that black blast the man seemed to rise soaring into their memories forever and ever" (440), as if one could only respond, "Amen."[5]

But Faulkner's chapter 19 also presents a particularly elegant counterpoint of John and Frazer, full of themes peculiar to John, the most literary of the four gospels, expanded on with rich material from Frazer. Once we know these underlying conjunctions, we can better understand just how Faulkner used religion to preach his own moral gospel.

Biblical scholars say that unlike customary representations of the road to Calvary, Jesus probably carried only the crosspiece, a post, which was then affixed to a stationary post. In fact, the various meanings of the word "post" are everywhere in John 19. Without suggesting that this was John's intention,[6] all of the events in his chapter have associations to this word: in the scourging, Jesus is fastened to a post; dressed in purple, crowned with thorns, Jesus is given the post of king; the post as a phallic symbol is suggested in Pilate's "Behold the Man"; the post as an ancient symbol of gods is suggested in the crowd's complaint that Jesus "made himself Son of God"; that the post is a doorway is appropriate to the hour, which is "the preparation of the Passover" when blood was smeared on the doorpost; to be like a "post," or unresponsive, is appropriate to Jesus' refusal to answer; a post is a fixed route or road for carriers, like the road to Calvary; as mentioned, it is the cross itself; a post is a sign or placard, like the one on which is written "KING OF THE JEWS"; a post is a station for soldiers like those posted at the cross; it is even a game, like the soldiers casting lots; to post means "to relay," and Jesus does give over his mother to the Beloved Disciple; a post is a starting or winning stand, like Jesus' last words, "It is finished"; to post is to hurry or call for haste: because of the Sabbath, the soldiers hurry to break the legs of all, only to discover that Jesus is already dead; a post is a thin lance, like the one used to pierce Jesus' side; a posting is a book entry: John repeats that these events fulfill scripture; and finally, the prefix "post," meaning "after," reflects John's words, "And after this" when Jesus' body is lain in a garden sepulchre.

Even discounting the symbolic examples, it is striking how often this word applies. The fact that Faulkner's own chapter reflects the multiple meanings of the word "post" suggests his awareness of this odd phenomenon. Indeed, the main thrust of his chapter is precisely on the symbolic elements: the position of authority, the meaning of manhood, and the inexorability of blood when the authority and manhood are relinquished. In other words, John's story is not just about the victim, Christ; it is also about the forces which destroy Christ. To personify these forces, Faulkner introduces a brand new character, Percy Grimm, whose name in Latin (Percival) means "valley-piercer" or in Greek (Perseus) "destroyer." But like "Prufrock," which can be read either

"Proof/rock" or "Pru/frock," Percy's name also reflects the Southern idiom for "sissy" or "pansy," as we shall see.

But what kind of a destroyer is this killer and castrator of Joe Christmas? He is said to represent Youth (he wishes he had been old enough to fight in World War I); Jingoism (he feels he represents "the protection of America and Americans"); Racism (he believes "the white race is superior" to all races); or Fate (he appears to be moved by the Player). What are we to make of this multiplicity of issues?

The same problem arises in John. Who or what kills Jesus Christ? The Jews, say both tradition and, heavily, John. Pilate says he finds no fault in Jesus, but the Jews continue to cry for his crucifixion. Even the scourging and the mocking may have been vain attempts to awaken the crowd's pity. Now, while anti-Semitic modernist writers such as Pound and Eliot might have seized on this issue, to his credit, Faulkner's parallel focuses instead on Pilate's surrender of authority; on the swiftness of events because Passover is at hand; and on their inexorability: everything occurs as it is written.

But then John's emphasis on Passover and the suspension of authority led Faulkner to a wealth of material in Frazer, for the same question arises out of the primitive tradition behind Passover. When the Angel of Death passed over the Israelites, killing the firstborn sons of the Egyptians, who or what was that Angel? Frazer relates the Passover story to the ancient, widespread practice of killing the king's first-born as a substitute for the king.

The sacrifice of such redeemers was widespread. Among the Semites, especially in times of danger, the king would "give his beloved son to die for the whole people, as a ransom offered to the avenging demons" to be "slain with mystic rites" (4:166). The ancient kings of Boeotia were regularly bound to sacrifice their first-born, although in time, a ram might be substituted, provided the prince kept away from the sacrificial hall (4:165).

Among the Hebrews, Passover may mark an early turn from

infanticide: after the Jews' firstlings are saved by the lamb's blood on the door posts, henceforth "God ordained that all the firstborn of man and beast among the Israelites should be sacred to him" (4:175). Even the practice of circumcision may represent a custom "to save the life of the child by giving the deity a substitute for it" (4:181).

Much of this may be understood in Freudian terms. The institution of Passover can be seen as a societal control of conflicting impulses, the father's desire to perpetuate himself in his own form versus the form of his son, the body renewed. For Frazer, these psychological questions do not arise.[7] He saw the young god's death as a primitive attempt to revive the land. But perhaps the two traditions together suggest that the king's sacrifice represents his belief that he or his most precious member (his son, his penis) is so important that God and all life depend on it being proffered.

But gradually (and not surprisingly) it came to be thought that both losses could be avoided if a deputy would take on the role of king: wearing the kingly costume and having kingly sway would give one the mantle of the divine (4:160). In Java, suicide for the Sultan's sake was witnessed by a fourteenth-century traveller, who said that although the deceased's family was given liberal pensions, apparently the act reflected his desire "to immolate himself out of affection for the sovereign" as his father and as his grandfather had done (4:53–54). Frazer "explains" this sacrificial phenomenon with his usual nineteenth-century hokum, suggesting that, unlike the English or other civilized races, many people have an "indifference or apathy" (4:136) towards death, partly because of a comfortable, pre-Christian belief in the pleasantness of afterlife, and partly because of "the less delicate nervous system of the negro" (4:138). Thus, heathens often "laid down their lives without a murmur or a struggle" (4:139). Nevertheless, with the coming of civilization (and some inkling of Christian Hell), these customs were reduced to symbols. For example, in Cambodia, the "office of temporary king was hereditary in a family distantly connected with the royal house." Briefly in power, the mock king wore special costumes and was escorted in processions around the city, until a mock execution was carried out on the third day (4:148). So also in Siam, the temporary king enjoyed royal pre- rogatives until, on the third day, he was forced to stand on one foot for three hours, but not before he had demonstrated the connec- tion to agricultural fertility by tracing nine furrows with a gaily decorated plough and oxen (4:149).

But the symbolic sacrifice of the son may be more obviously blood-on-the-post. During the Spring Festivals of Attis and Cybele, particularly on the third day, the high priest of the Galli offered blood drawn from his arm, while the lesser priests, stirred by the music "of clashing cymbals, rumbling drums, droning horns, and screaming flutes . . . gashed their bodies with pot- sherds or slashed them with knives in order to bespatter the altar and the sacred tree with their flowing blood" (5:268). Moreover, Frazer believes that

> it was on the same Day of Blood . . . that the novices sacrificed their virility. Wrought up to the highest pitch of religious excitement they dashed the severed portions of themselves against the image of the cruel goddess. These broken instruments of fertility were afterwards reverently wrapt up and buried in the earth or in subterranean chambers sacred to Cybele. (5:268)

And this mode of sacrifice is likened to the festival of the Syrian goddess, Astarte:

> While the flutes played, the drums beat, and the eunuch priests slashed themselves with knives, the religious excitement gradually spread like a wave among the crowd of onlookers, and many a one did that which he little thought to do when he came as a holiday spectator to the festival. For man after man, his veins throbbing with the music, his eyes fascinated by the sight of the streaming blood, flung his garments from him, leaped forth with a shout, and seizing one of the swords which stood ready for the purpose, castrated himself on the spot. Then he ran through the city, holding the bloody pieces in his hand, till he threw them into one of the houses which he passed in his mad career. The household thus honored had to furnish him with a

suit of female attire and female ornaments, which he wore for the rest of his life. (5:270)

If the Passover Angel of Death may be generalized to include these related traditions—the infanticides of the first-born, the suicides or executions for the sake of the king, and the priestly castrations in the worship of the mother-goddess—it can be seen as the destructive consequence of giving over authority to Caesar or other false gods, exemplified in John by the Jews' cry, "We have no king but Caesar," and in Faulkner by all the false values held by Percy Grimm. Thus, as we will discover, Faulkner's point in featuring Grimm is not so much his villainy as the absence or the suspension of rule that he—as mock king or castrated priest— represents.[8]

Reflecting these discussions in Frazer, the theme of a suicidal sacrifice of the scapegoat emerges in many forms in Faulkner's chapter 19. Centrally, Joe Christmas is said to have "made his plans to passively commit suicide" (419). But then Grimm's articles of faith include knowing "that all that would ever be required of him . . . would be his own life" (427), while during his brief ascension in the town's affairs, called a "suttee of volition's surrender," his men feel that "they might die for him, if occasion rose" (432). And noting Frazer's generations of self-sacrificing slaves, their survivors cared for by generations of grateful kings, we find Stevens, whose "ancestors owned slaves" (420), caring for the Hineses, "the voluntary slaves and sworn bondsmen of prayer" (423).

Although Faulkner's sacrificial deaths in this chapter range from the ridiculous to the sublime, Frazer himself notes that many dramas of death and resurrection "originated in a rustic mummers' play," such as "English yokels on Plough Monday" (7:33). Faulkner's Monday is a "holiday," a "parade," with a "throng of people thick as on Fair Day" (433), and some tense scenes are filled with agricultural language. Running among faces "empty and immobile as the faces of cows" (433) is Grimm, "the

black, blunt, huge automatic opening a way for him like a plow."
In the throng "was the inevitable hulking youth in the uniform of
the Western Union, leading his bicycle by the horns like a docile
cow." The bicycle Percy grabs "possessed neither horn nor bell"
(434), while Percy's men are twice called "sheepish" (431).

Notice too, all the "running," like the running Priests of Attis.
Everyone runs here, along the streets, the alley, the rutted lane,
the ditch, and the ravine. They even run metaphorically: Stevens
says, "there was too much running with [Christmas], stride for
stride with him. Not pursuers: but himself: years, acts, deeds
omitted and committed, keeping pace with him, stride for stride,
breath for breath, thud for thud of the heart, using a single heart"
(424).

The running also reflects John's rush of events and the inexorable fulfillment of scripture: Joe rushes "into the embrace of a
chimera, a blind faith in something read in a printed Book"
(425); for Mrs. Hines, the events "had already been written and
worded for her on the night when she bore his mother" (423).
But particularly Percy Grimm has "something about him irre-
sistible and prophetlike" (428), as if he is "served by certitude,
the blind and untroubled faith in the rightness and infallibility
of his actions" (434); he moves "as though under the protection
of a magic or a providence" (437) or "with the delicate swiftness
of an apparition, the implacable undeviation of Juggernaut or
Fate" (435).

Indeed, Percy Grimm and his men at the execution (four all
together, like the four soldiers in John) are like the inexorable
Angel of Death itself. Rushing into Hightower's house, they
"bring something of the savage summer sunlight. . . . Out of it
their faces seemed to glare with bodiless suspension as though
from haloes" (438). And above the automatic, Grimm's face "had
that serene, unearthly luminousness of angels in church win-
dows" (437).

Even calling the pistol an "automatic" suggests the theme of
irresistibility, as if its firing were not just easy but inevitable.

Similarly, Joe's "bolts," in all senses of the term, are responsible for his death. When he bolts, his manacled hands, which "glint" and "glare" as if "on fire," or "like the flash of a heliograph" from the sun (436), empower him "like lightning bolts, so that he resembled a vengeful and furious god pronouncing a doom" (438). Yet his "bright and glittering hands" on the edge of the overturned table also bolt him to, mark him for, death.

But the most elaborate use of Frazer to illuminate a pattern in John relates to the mock king wearing the kingly clothes. John particularizes Jesus' clothing to show that it includes the purple robe, worn by kings, the seamless coat, worn by the high priest, and the linen clothes, wound round the dead.[9]

Faulkner has made elegant use of this theme of clothing, which, invested with authority, becomes sacred—seamless—and therefore capable of winding the dead. Repeatedly we read of Percy Grimm's obsession with uniforms. Recall that he wears the scars of his battle with the exsoldier "as proudly as he was later to wear the uniform itself for which he had blindly fought" (426). Arguing with the legion commander, Percy speaks of "we, as soldiers, that have worn the uniform" (427), and when the commander refuses to "use the Post," Percy retorts, "Yet you wore the uniform once" (428).

In fact, the growing authority of Percy's "army" is evinced by the metaphor of clothing which finally becomes one—seamless:

> So quickly is man unwittingly and unpredictably moved that without knowing that they were thinking it, the town had suddenly accepted Grimm with respect and perhaps a little awe and a deal of actual faith and confidence, as though somehow his vision and patriotism and pride in the town, the occasion, had been quicker and truer than theirs. His men anyway assumed and accepted this. . . . They now moved in a grave and slightly aweinspiring reflected light which was almost as palpable as the khaki would have been which Grimm wished them to wear, wished that they wore, as though each time they returned to the orderly room they dressed themselves anew in suave and austerely splendid scraps of his dream. (432)

As their game continues, the "caution, the surreptitiousness, which had clothed it was now gone." By Monday morning, "the platoon was again intact. And they now wore uniforms. It was their faces" (432). But the theme is capped when Percy cries like a "young priest": "Jesus Christ! . . . Has every preacher and old maid in Jefferson taken their pants down to the yellowbellied son of a bitch?" (439); when he slashes Joe's "garments," making "the pent black blood . . . rush like a released breath" (440); and when his five (gunshot) wounds are later covered with one, presumably seamless, and possibly linen, handkerchief.

Appropriate to the castrating priests of Attis, Grimm has been characterized as "a mixture of a Spanish Jesuit and a primitive priest of a blood cult."[10] In fact, the language of that castrating blood cult is pervasive in this chapter,[11] with words for the operation (cut, break, detach, slashed, dropped, hacked); the thing cut (post, picket, stake, horn, plow, pistol, poker, bar, bolt); the priests "leaping" or "springing" or discarding (fling, pitch, cast, shot, thrown); and the scar left (orifice, gape, hole, rut, fault, ditch). But before he ever brings Christmas to earth, it is Percy who has "lost a point" (437). He wears the "scars" of his tussle with the exsoldier. And like the unmanned priests, often seen on the streets in costumes "with little images suspended on their breasts" (5:266), Percy is often found downtown in his uniform, displaying his marksman badge and his bars with "the self-conscious pride of a boy" (427). And boy or youth or "young priest" he remains, as when the sheriff calls, "Come here, boy," and pats him familiarly on the hip (430). With inspired irony, Faulkner's characterization of this "Percy" suggests that the Grimm castrator has himself been castrated on the altar of his phony beliefs.

Now what does all this tell us about Faulkner and religion? First, this chapter shows that Faulkner was not necessarily, as Lawrance Thompson believed, "contrasting certain pagan attitudes with certain Christian attitudes for the purposes of honoring the pagan."[12] Indeed, Faulkner has used the most poignant moment of his own religious belief system to show that adherence to false gods and false values can sabotage the good people of any religion. Moreover, if all were Black Mass, all reversed, we might expect Faulkner to have ennobled Christmas's murderer. Instead, the parallel with John and Frazer confirms what we suspected: that this Percy is no man; he has no authority other than the uniform of uniformity. He is a false prophet. And by developing John's theme of "post" in relation to the castrating priests, Faulkner universalizes the Christian tragedy, applying it to people of any time and place and reminding us that the post on which Christ was crucified as the Son of the Father stands as well for our tragically persistent yearning for a scapegoat, even—or perhaps especially—if it be our own son.

For Faulkner, the modernist, neither the Christian nor the primitive world was less powerful when the family ties between them were revealed. Of course, to present a Christ figure as a "mock king" or "typical scapegoat" means that *Light in August* cannot be a tract for the literal truth of Christianity. But then, like his contemporary, Santayana, who held that Christ was "constructed by the imagination in response to moral demands," Faulkner may have been suggesting that the value of religion depends not on its historical truth, but in its ability to generate understanding of and sympathy for the human condition.

Thus, Faulkner's message is neither anti-Christian nor pro-primitive. But, as his use of John and Frazer in *Light in August* demonstrates, particularly in this crucial chapter, Faulkner saw that the good people of this earth—Christian or not, past or present—always have the potential for savagery. Religion not only cannot save us from this savagery; religion can be the cause of it. When we allow ourselves to be clothed in flags, when our faces become seamless with fanaticism, we have indeed wound ourselves round with the linen of the dead, for we have lost our humanity. Ironically, sadly, it may only be restored by the distant mirroring memory of the Joe Christmases we have slain.

NOTES

1. William Faulkner, *Light in August* (New York: Random House, 1968), 101. All subsequent references to this edition are given in the text.

2. See Hlavsa, "The Levity of *Light in August,*" in *Faulkner and Humor: Faulkner and Yoknapatawpha, 1984,* ed. Doreen Fowler and Ann J. Abadie (Jackson: University Press of Mississippi, [1986]), 47–56.

3. Sir James George Frazer, *The Golden Bough: A Study in Magic and Religion,* 3rd ed. (New York: St. Martin's Press, 1911–15), 1:27. All subsequent references to this edition are given in the text.

4. Stevens's endless discussions of the black blood versus the white blood may also reflect the lengthy speculations by Biblical scholars on the "blood and water" which pour from Jesus' side. That Faulkner read Biblical commentary is evidenced in Laurence Stallings's 1932 report from Hollywood: "Unlike practically everyone else, he has remained cold sober. He bought one book to read over his lonely nights. It is a second-hand twelve-volume . . . Cambridge edition of the Holy Bible." See Joseph Blotner, *Faulkner: A Biography* (New York: Random House, 1974), 1:777.

5. We even find an amusing parallel to Pilate's sign over the cross, which John alone universalizes into Greek, Latin, and the local Hebrew: Stevens is a "Phi Beta Kappa"; Grimm commands a platoon "vide his active commission"; while the soldiers use the local language:

> There was something about it too assured and serenely confident to the braggadocio; tonight when they heard the marshal's feet on the stairs, one said, "Ware M.P.'s" and for an instant they glanced at one another with hard, bright, daredevil eyes; then one said, quite loud: "Throw the son of a bitch out," and another through pursed lips made the immemorial sound. (432)

6. It should be noted, however, that a distinguishing feature of John's gospel is word play.

7. Frazer's first edition was completed by 1890, some ten years before Freud's *Interpretation of Dreams.*

8. As Michael Millgate remarks, the occasion of Joe's crucifixion "permitted the worst elements in Jefferson to emerge and take command." *The Achievement of William Faulkner* (Lincoln: University of Nebraska Press, 1963), 129.

9. The Cambridge Bible: *The Gospel According to St. John,* ed. A. Plummer (Cambridge, England: At the University Press, 1923), 345. All three are combined in the description of Mrs. Hines as "beneath a nodding and soiled white plume, shapeless in a silk dress of an outmoded shape and in color regal and moribund" (420). But then Walter Brylowski remarks that Mrs. Hines's dress is "suitable to the passion." *Faulkner's Olympian Laugh: Myth in the Novels* (Detroit: Wayne State University Press, 1968), 112.

10. R. G. Collins, "*Light in August*: Faulkner's Stained Glass Triptych," *Mosaic* 7 (1973): 142.

11. Noting that in Matthew 19:12, Christ says "there be eunuchs, which have made themselves eunuchs for the kingdom of heaven's sake," John T. Irwin says that "the principle of [Christ's] sacrifice is the same as that of self-castration—the giving up of a part to save the whole, and in both sacrifice and self-castration the part is given up to save the whole from the wrath of the father." Thus, "the essence of Christ's sacrifice [is that] the subject is both the agent and the victim, at once active and passive, a conjunction of masculine and feminine." See *Doubling and Incest/Repetition and Revenge* (Baltimore: Johns Hopkins University Press, 1976), 153–54.

12. *William Faulkner: An Introduction and Interpretation* (New York: Barnes & Noble, 1963), 80.

The Ravished Daughter: Eleusinian Mysteries in *The Sound and the Fury*

Doreen Fowler

The first gods were not transcendent, but immanent; they existed not above, but in the natural world. And these first gods were female. In the beginning, what inspired worship was that there was food, and because women's bodies, like the earth, produced food and new life, the feminine principle was venerated as a source of primal power.

To ancient people, what was most holy and mysterious was the annual disappearance of the food supply in winter and its reappearance in spring. Because their lives were intimately bound up with seasonal rhythms and because they understood their own lives not as transcending these rhythms, but as an integral part of this cycle, the fundamental sacred mystery of existence was seasonal recurrence, an endless cycle of renewal, in which the individual life matters less than the continuity of life itself. All primitive myths commemorate death—the sowing of the seed— and rebirth—the harvest of the corn—the principle that life follows death, what Joseph Campbell calls the "monomyth" or what Mircea Eliade calls the myth of the eternal return. Some variation of this myth is central to all primitive cosmogony, as Frazer demonstrates in *The Golden Bough*, which lists encyclopedically hundreds of pagan forms of worship all of which celebrate the central mystery of existence: the seasonal renewal of life.

Because women, who periodically reproduce life and die, seem to recapitulate nature's cycle of renewal, when primitives translated the sacred mystery into myth, the central protagonists were women. In a latter-day, Greek formulation, seasonal recurrence is personified in Demeter, the goddess who gives life, and her daughter, Persephone, the goddess who dies. According to the myth, one day while picking flowers, Demeter's daughter was lured away from her companions by a particularly wondrous bloom, the Narcissus. Suddenly the earth opened and from a chasm erupted the god of the underworld, Hades, in a horse-drawn golden chariot. The dark god seized the weeping Persephone and carried her down to the world of the dead and made her his bride. Veiled and in mourning, Demeter searched the earth for her daughter; and, when she learned Persephone's fate, her grief was terrible, and the corn would not grow. After a time, Zeus intervened and Persephone was released from the underworld and returned to her mother. But because she had swallowed a single pomegranate seed, she periodically must return to the world of the dead.

The myth of Demeter and her daughter lyrically recasts the cosmic drama of eternal recurrence. Each action in the Greek myth stands for a stage in nature's regenerative cycle. At the fundamental level, the carrying off of Persephone to a world beneath the earth corresponds to the sowing of the seed. Hades' rape of Persephone is analogous to the fertilization of the seed. Persephone's reemergence in the upper world is the mythic expression of the sprouting of the corn. And the ingested pomegranate seed symbolically rehearses Persephone's rape: because Hades' seed has been implanted in her, periodically she will die again. The myth of Demeter and Persephone, then, is the story of the harvest. Demeter, the corn goddess, personifies the ripe corn; her daughter, the seed produced by the corn. The seed must be planted in the earth to produce the corn which, in turn, produces the seed. The Persephone of this year is the Demeter of the next. And in this endless progression, this ceaseless transformation and replacement of life, embodied in mothers and daughters—fruit and seed—is the hope of human survival.

As primitives understood the mystery of eternal recurrence,

and as they formalized it in myth and ritual, both death and sex were necessary prologues to the advent of rebirth. Death and sex, like the fertilized seed buried in the earth or Persephone raped and imprisoned in the underworld, necessarily precede the sprouting of the corn, the reunion of mother and daughter. The myth taught primitives to hold sacred and to celebrate their own nature as sexual beings and as creatures who die, and who, like Persephone, in another generation, return from the dead. Even more importantly, the myth acknowledged the incarnation of the divine in the material world.[1]

In *The Sound and the Fury* the myth of eternal recurrence echoes and reechoes like an incantation.[2] Caddy Compson and her daughter together and interchangeably represent Demeter and Persephone, the goddesses of transformation. Conversely, each of Caddy's brothers desires passionately to achieve a mode of existence that is absolute and unchanging, that is outside of generation. They resist the life force and its ceaseless transformative power, and they resist Caddy and her daughter.

No other character seems to have moved Faulkner quite so deeply as Caddy Compson, "the beautiful one," his "heart's darling."[3] To her brothers, she seems to represent the possibility of total gratification; and they seek in vain to know and control her, but she always eludes their grasp. André Bleikasten and John Matthews call her "the absent center" of the novel;[4] but, perhaps more accurately, she is an ever-fading presence. As Benjy's agonized wail reminds us, Caddy seems always to be retreating: *"One minute she was standing in the door."*[5] The door, with its connotation of transition, is one of her symbols; and, like a vegetation goddess, Caddy is constantly undergoing transformations: she is a six-year-old child, an adolescent, a maiden, a mother. Running, swinging in the porch swing, she reproduces the ceaseless motion of the natural world: *"She ran out of the mirror like a cloud"* (100). As critics have frequently observed, she is continually associated with natural images, with trees, with the heavy, ripe smell of honeysuckle, with the muddy water of the branch. And like water and trees, she is another articulation of the inexhaustible, self-regenerative life force.

In particular, Caddy and her daughter's association with trees links them to the transformative goddess. For while Demeter was worshipped as the goddess who made the corn to grow, before Demeter, the ancients believed trees, or the spirits in trees, brought forth the grain. For the primitive mind, the tree is charged with sacred forces because it grows, it loses its leaves, and it periodically regains them. The tree, then, reproduces natural laws of development and transformation. These same laws of regeneration are embodied in the myth of Demeter and her daughter; thus Demeter is intimately connected to trees, even descended from them, a more recent incarnation of an older tree spirit.[6] And like Demeter, Caddy and her daughter are associated with trees. "Caddy smelled like trees" (5), Benjy thinks; among the dark trees Caddy fornicates with Dalton Ames; and Miss Quentin descends the pear tree to meet with her lovers. Even more importantly, as Faulkner repeatedly explained, *The Sound and the Fury* originated with a tree image, the picture of "Caddy climbing the pear tree to look in the window at her grandmother's funeral while Quentin and Jason and Benjy looked up at the muddy seat of her drawers."[7] The tree image from which the novel sprang, an eruption of Faulkner's unconscious, resonates with archetypal significance; it visually renders the myth of the eternal return. In Faulkner's image, Caddy witnesses the rites that commemorate the passing of the old mother; she herself, a female child, embodies the next generation. Her mud-stained drawers are the outward sign of her materiality, marking her as a creature equipped with life-giving powers and biologically pro-grammed to die. Also significant are the relative positions of Caddy and her brothers. High in the tree, Caddy looks directly upon death while her brothers, below her, see only her. In other words, Caddy is possessed of a knowledge of the mysteries of the universe to which her brothers have access only through her. She is their intermediary, their high priestess. They can approach no nearer to the sacred mystery of the universe than to worship her, their eyes straining upward to see and to know Caddy, raised on a tree above them.[8]

In *The Sound and the Fury*, then, Caddy Compson is Faulkner's incarnation of the transformative goddess. Because Persephone, the seed, eventually is transformed into Demeter, the corn, Caddy alternately plays both the role of the ravished daughter and the grieving mother; and her daughter is her double. Like Demeter, Caddy is a mother-figure, surrogate-mother to Benjy, and mother to her own daughter, Quentin, who, like Demeter's child, is taken from her; but Caddy is also Persephone, the lost daughter, the Compson daughter who, like Persephone in the underworld, is a "fallen" woman. For example, Jason recalls a time when Mrs. Compson "happened to see one of them kissing Caddy and all next day she went around the house with a black dress and a veil . . . crying and saying her little daughter was dead" (286). In her veil, Mrs. Compson becomes the veiled corn goddess who mourns the loss of her daughter. The kiss Mrs. Compson witnesses is an articulation of the rape of Persephone; it measures Caddy's budding sexuality, which Mrs. Compson equates with death in accordance with the Demeter myth: Persephone's rape is accompanied by her descent into the world of the dead, a necessary rite of passage in the age-old cycle of renewal.

Mrs. Compson's pairing of sex and death is insistently reiterated throughout Faulkner's novel. Caddy describes her sexual union with Ames as kind of death: "yes I hate him I would die for him I've already died for him I die for him over and over again everytime this goes" (188). And pregnant with new life, Caddy says, "I'm sick" (137), expressing the primordial mystery that the price of renewal is death. Even Caddy's nightly copulations in the dark woods close to the earth counterpoint sex and death. Quentin bitterly objects to his "little sister death's" earthy fornications: *"Why wont you bring him to the house, Caddy? Why must you do like nigger women do in the pasture the ditches the dark woods hot hidden furious in the dark woods*" (113–14). By coupling with her lover in the dirt, Caddy replays the cosmic drama. In the Odyssey, the sea nymph Kalypso recounts how Demeter once took for a lover a mortal and lay with him in a furrow three times ploughed, underscoring her continuity with the earth's substance and reenacting the rape of her daughter who is ravished by Hades beneath the earth's surface. Both acts of copulation are literally attended by descents into the earth to express the cosmic mystery that death is required for regeneration. And the primordial ritual is rehearsed once again as Caddy lies with Dalton Ames in the pasture, and yet again as Caddy's daughter lies in a ditch with the circus man who promises new life away from the Compson place.

Twinned with Persephone by her earth-bound fornications, Caddy enacts the role of Persephone once again when she becomes the bride of Herbert Head, a Hades-figure. In the archetypal drama, Hades plays the role of fecundating phallus, and Herbert's ubiquitous cigar, which threatens to blister Mrs. Compson's mantel, symbolizes the phallus and the threat of sexual violation. Herbert's position as bank president also associates him with Hades, whose Latin name is Pluto, which means "wealth" or "abundance"; appropriately, then, Quentin says to Herbert, "To hell with your money" (136). This incarnation of Hades carries away his reluctant bride, not in a golden, horse-drawn chariot, but in a shiny new car. And like Persephone, the mysterious goddess who is sometimes referred to with awe as "the maiden whose name may not be spoken,"[9] so also Caddy's name is not spoken around the Compson place after she vanishes in the arms of Head.

But Caddy's disappearance marks only a stage in the cyclical drama of recurrence. As a representative of the transformative powers of the cosmos, she metamorphizes endlessly. In her next incarnation she appears as Demeter, the grieving mother goddess. In this version of the primordial story, Jason is Hades and he recreates the central image of the Demeter story—Persephone's abduction in Hades' horse-drawn chariot. When a tearful Caddy, veiled like the disguised goddess of the corn, begs Jason to be allowed to see her child, Jason hires a hack and, whipping the horses and holding Miss Quentin in his arms, thunders past Caddy who runs vainly after them.

Like Hades, lord of the dead, Jason rules the Compson household following the deaths of his brother and father; and, when the narrator provides a physical description of Jason, his "close-thatched brown hair" is "curled in two stubborn hooks one on either side of his head" (348). These "hooks" evoke the image of a demon's horns, calling up, in turn, Dilsey's words to Jason, "I dont put no devilment beyond you" (230), and Miss Quentin's frustrated cry, "I'd rather be in hell than anywhere where you are" (235).

Like Persephone, kept against her will in the realm of the dead, Jason keeps Quentin a virtual prisoner on the Compson place, locking her into her room each night; and, as if the moribund Compson place were the underworld of Persephone's incarceration, the Compsons continually refer to one another as damned souls. In particular, when alluding to Jason, Miss Quentin obsessively runs together the words "god," "damn," and "old"— "You—you old goddamn! . . . You damn old goddamn!" (229)—as if calling Jason an old damned god, a Hades-figure. And, like Hades who ravishes Persephone, Jason threatens his niece with violence rife with sexual intent, "grabbing" and "dragging" her until her kimono comes unfastened, "flapping about her, damn near naked" (228). Also sexually suggestive is Jason's act of removing his pants' belt: "What are you going to do?" Quentin asks. "You wait until I get this belt out and I'll show you" (229), he replies. Obviously he is preparing to whip her, yet another interpretation is implied by his phrasing: with his belt unbuckled, what might he "show" his niece? Moreover, more than once he threatens to "neuter" Caddy's daughter as he already has Benjy: "I says I know what you need, you need what they did to Ben then you'd behave" (315). Jason threatens Quentin with a feminine version of castration; and, according to Freud, in the language of the unconscious,

castration is the symbolic equivalent of death, Persephone's
ceaselessly reiterated fate.

In the Greek myth, Persephone looks to her mother to rescue
her from masculine violation, and in the gloomy underworld of
the Compson household two surrogate mothers, Miss Quentin's
grandmother and Dilsey, intervene when Jason becomes most
abusive. In particular, Dilsey acts the mother's part in Caddy's
absence, telling Quentin, "He aint gwine so much as lay his hand
on you while Ise here" (230). Dilsey's words formulate one essential meaning of the myth: the indissoluble bond between mother
and daughter. And so, like Persephone, separated from her
mother, Quentin protests, "I want my mother" (230). And, like
Demeter, who begs Zeus to return her child, Caddy intones, "Oh
God, oh God" (261).

But the Compson place cannot contain Miss Quentin, as hell
cannot hold Persephone. Periodically the grain erupts from the
earth, the maiden of the spring is released from the underworld, and Quentin breaks free of the Compson place. Significantly, her escape is discovered on Easter Sunday morning,
apparently deliberately invoking a parallel with Christ's resurrection from the dead. According to Neumann, Campbell, and
others, the crucifixion and resurrection of Christ can be compared to primitive fertility rituals celebrating the seasonal change
from winter to spring; and from such rituals the Demeter/Per-
sephone myth is derived.[10] As evidence for a parallel between
Christ's resurrection and primitive fertility rites, mythographers
point to the timing of Easter, which coincides with the time of
ancient festivals celebrating the sprouting of the seed. Interpreted this way, the parallel to Christ's resurrection complements
and reinforces the correspondences to the myth of seasonal recurrence. And Quentin's escape from the Compson domain is un-
mistakably compared to Christ's resurrection. Just as on Easter
morning the disciples and Mary Magdalene find the rock rolled
away from Christ's tomb, the body gone, and Christ's shroud left
behind, so Dilsey, Jason, and Mrs. Compson find Quentin's

window open, Quentin vanished, and a soiled undergarment left behind.

While Quentin's escape from the Compson domain resonates with Christian symbology, it also invokes other associations. For example, her escape—via a tree—pairs her with her mother. As a young girl, Caddy ascends the pear tree and is initiated into the mystery of death—the death of the great mother, the source of life; Caddy's daughter descends the flowering tree and is possessed of new life. When Caddy acquires a knowledge of death, her drawers are muddy, symbolizing her materiality, the inevitability of sex and death. On the other hand, when Quentin climbs down the pear tree seeking new life, she leaves behind her a "soiled undergarment," figuring a periodic release from death's power. Together, the tree and undergarment resonate with mythic significance: Caddy, in her muddy drawers, seeing from her tree perch the death of the great mother, symbolically presents one pole of existence, death, the sowing of the seed, Persephone ravished in the underworld. Conversely, Quentin's escape via a tree from the Compson household, her soiled undergarment left behind, pictorially represents the other pole of existence—rebirth and renewal, the sprouting of the seed, Persephone's resurrection from the world of the dead.

As there is no end to the cycle of death and rebirth, so, even after Miss Quentin's escape from the Compson underworld, the drama of eternal recurrence plays on in the novel. In one particularization of the myth, Benjy takes his turn as Demeter's doomed child. Like Persephone taken from her mother, Benjy is forcibly separated from his surrogate mother, Caddy. And the central image of the Demeter myth—Hades' abduction of Demeter's child in a horse-drawn chariot—is invoked yet again at the end of the novel when Luster drives Benjy to the graveyard in the Compson's ancient surrey. As Luster turns left at the Confederate monument, Benjy howls his outrage, and Jason comes "jumping" (400) up from the Square onto the wagon, seizing the reins. Whipping Queenie to a plunging gallop, Jason strikes Benjy with his fist and breaks his flower, a Narcissus, the same flower which Persephone was picking when Hades erupted from the bowels of the earth and dragged her shrieking away. Like Persephone, violently carried off to Hades' shadowy realm, so Benjy seems bound as Jason shouts at Luster, "Get to hell on home with him" (400). And again like Persephone, raped by the king of the underworld, Benjy is Jason's sexual victim: as Benjy's broken flower stalk emblemizes, at Jason's command, Benjy is castrated, the masculine equivalent of rape, the symbolic equivalent of death, the twinned fate of Demeter's child.

While, at one level, Benjy seems to represent Persephone, Demeter's violated child, at another, he seems to personify the mythic figure of Demophoon, Demeter's adoptive son. As the Greek myth is told, after the abduction of Persephone, Demeter, disguised as a mortal, dwelled for a time in Eleusis and attempted to give immortal youth to Demophoon, the infant son of Metaneira, by nightly placing the baby in the red heart of a fire. One night, Metaneira, seeing her son in the fire, screamed in terror angering the goddess who abruptly abandoned her intention to free the child from old age and death. In the myth, then, Demeter acts as mother-surrogate to Demophoon, just as Caddy is Benjy's mother-substitute. Like the infant Demophoon, who is laid in a fire, so Benjy must be restrained from burning himself, as if Benjy is a Demophoon-come-again, yearning for the fires of everlasting life. Just as the source of eternal life, fire, is associated with the life-giving mother-goddess, Demeter, so Benjy thinks of Caddy and fire together, "Her hair was like fire, and little points of fire were in her eyes" (88). And just as the mother-goddess meant to endow Demophoon with eternal youth, but her attempt is thwarted; so Benjy, whose mental development is arrested in infancy, might seem to be the product of an abortive attempt to bequeath immortality.

Nor does the echoing of the story of Demeter and her child end there. Everywhere in Faulkner's narrative, the myth recurs. Even in the midst of the Christian service, elements of the older pagan cosmogony survive. The central tableau of Reverend Shegog's sermon, for example, pictures Mary, virgin and mother, Persephone and Demeter, sitting in a doorway, Caddy's symbol and symbol also of the transformative goddess. Reverend Shegog evokes Christ's death and resurrection in terms of Mary's separation from her child, terms comparable to Demeter's loss of her child to the god of death: "Ma'y settin in de do' wid Jesus on her lap, de little Jesus. Like dem chillen dar, de little Jesus . . . sees Mary jump up, sees de sojer face. We gwine to kill! We gwine to kill! We gwine to kill you little Jesus!" (369). Similarly, the cross, the instrument of the crucifixion, is repeatedly referred to as a "sacred tree" (370), connecting the Christ story to an older faith, to a time when the regenerative power of trees inspired worship.

The myth which affirms that death is merely a phase in nature's cycle of renewal refuses itself to die in Faulkner's novel. In fact, even after the close of the 1929 novel, the drama of eternal recurrence continues. When in 1945 Faulkner added an appendix to *The Sound and the Fury*, his creative imagination formulates Caddy these many years later as once again a doomed Persephone, the consort of Hades. In this addendum to the novel, Caddy is glimpsed in a photo seated in "an open powerful expensive chromiumtrimmed sports car; beside her a handsome lean man of middle-age in the ribbons and tabs of a German staff-general" (415). The shiny sports car is another in a series of evocations of Hades' golden chariot; the Nazi general, a wartime avatar of the ruler of the dead. Once again, Caddy is death's paramour; once again Caddy, "ageless and beautiful, cold serene and damned" (415), sits beside Hades as they speed toward hell.

Caddy Compson and her daughter strike us with such force because they are modern-day representatives of ancient mythic figures; they are descended from primitive fertility goddesses, and their story has its origins in prehistory, a story that primitive people told to explain the fundamental mystery of existence, creation and dissolution. They are bathed in a "luminous lambent quality of an older light than ours."[11] Radiant, numinous, Caddy and her daughter evoke a pagan cosmogony, the ebb and flow of life, an endless series of deaths and resurrections. In contradistinction to Caddy and her child, all three of Caddy's brothers cling to fixity.[12] Benjy's arrested mental development is itself a rejection of time and change; in him, nature stands still. His section obsessively rehearses successive phases in Caddy's sexual development, and at each progessive stage in this inexorable maturation, he bellows his protest, signalling his opposition to the ceaseless transformation and replacement of life. Jason's resistance to regenerative forces is apparent in his vindictive, vengeful treatment of Caddy and her daughter, avatars of cosmic rhythms, and in his attitude toward the Easter service, a celebration of the universe's ability to renew itself. When Jason objects to eating a cold dinner because the Compson servants are attending the Easter celebration, Mrs. Compson says to her son, "I know it's my fault, . . . I know you blame me," and Jason replies, "For what? . . . "You never resurrected Christ, did you?" (134). If Jason doesn't blame his mother, he does blame the forces at work in the universe which periodically renew life. Finally, Quentin also emphatically refuses cyclical renewal. For him, it is intolerable that a creature endowed with self-awareness should be returned to the earth to be succeeded by a new form. He longs for transcendence of periodic becoming, and he adamantly repudiates the immanence which his sister embodies. Seeking somehow to exempt himself from natural law, he resists the motion of life and clings to virginity, "a negative state . . . contrary to nature" (143), and to death. So that his death by drowning will be final he weights his body with flatirons. He will not allow the waters of life to renew him; for him, there will be no rebirth.

At the very center *The Sound and the Fury*, then, is a conflict between transcendent and immanent divinity, between individual and collective meaning, between patriarchal religions and older fertility rites. To make concrete and to particularize this dichotomy, Faulkner draws on the myth of Demeter and Persephone. Faulkner's use of the Greek myth, however, is not limited to *The Sound and the Fury.* In novel after novel, Faulkner invokes the old faith which deifies the natural order. In *As I Lay Dying,* even the name, Addie, one who adds, suggests Addie Bundren's role as Demeter, the reproductive mother. But Addie is also Persephone reenacting Persephone's subterranean rape, lying close to the earth with her lover, the Reverend Whitfield, "hearing the dark land talking with voiceless speech" (167)[13] as they make love. Like Persephone, Addie ceaselessly dies and is reborn. When Addie's corpse is immersed in the raging river, she undergoes a ritual dissolution, a return to original chaos; her emergence after this disintegration signals a new creation. And Addie suffers death again in the burning barn. Like water, fire disintegrates, abolishes forms, but from this conflagration Addie emerges reborn. And Addie dies yet again, when, like Persephone imprisoned in the underworld, she is buried in the earth, but no sooner is the last shovelful of earth heaped upon her than she reappears: "Meet Mrs. Bundren" (250), Anse says as the novel cyclically closes with a new beginning and a new Mrs. Bundren.

Just as Addie is a representative of the transformative goddess, so also is her daughter. When Dewey Dell picks on down the row to "the secret shade" (26), where she is impregnated by Lafe, she too ritually repeats Persephone's rape in Hades' shadowy realm beneath the earth. And Dewey Dell's pathetic attempts to halt the ceaseless cycle of regeneration, to abort new life, result ironically in yet another recreation of Persephone's descent and rape in the underworld: in the underworld of the drug store basement Dewey Dell is Persephone ravished again. Intuiting her participation in an inexorable natural order or, in mythic terms, her role as Persephone doomed to an endless series of deaths and resurrections, Dewey Dell says, "I feel like a wet seed wild in the hot blind earth" (61).

The myth of eternal recurrence is invoked yet again in *Sanctuary,* as Thomas McHaney has demonstrated. In this manifestation of the myth, Temple is Persephone raped by Popeye and carried off in his "canary-colored" (263) car to the underworld of a Memphis brothel. The veiled Ruby Lamar, who broods above her sickly child, is Demeter, the mother goddess, whose child is fated to die. Ruby's child also resembles Demophoon, the infant placed in a fire by Demeter. In an ironic inversion of the myth, Ruby keeps her baby in a box near the fire, not to confer eternal life, but to protect the child from rats.

Yet another Faulkner novel, *Light in August*, also can be read as the drama of two women who embody seasonal recurrence. Lena Grove, the reproductive mother, a Demeter-figure, represents one side of nature's inescapable equation; and Joanna Burden, who is plunged into an abyss where she is ravished and dies, is Persephone, the dark side of natural law. Finally, even as late as 1940, Faulkner still draws on the myth of the eternal return. In *The Hamlet* Eula Varner combines in herself the figures of Demeter and Persephone. The fecund mother, she reproduces Demeter's role, but, as the maiden whom Labove attempts to rape, she also incarnates Persephone. In this novel too Faulkner recreates once again Persephone's abduction in Hades's chariot as Eula rides away in the Varner surrey with her bridegroom, Flem Snopes, a hellish figure up out of the underworld of Frenchman's Bend.

In a number of novels in addition to *The Sound and the Fury* Faulkner informs his narrative with the Demeter/Persephone myth, a more recent incarnation of an older pagan fertility rite which deifies nature's cycle of death and rebirth. Set against this pagan cosmogony, Faulkner invokes a modern religious world view, a god who transcends natural law and who offers human beings the possibility of an escape from cyclical renewal. Most often, Faulkner expresses this conflict in male/female terms. Like the ancients, who perceived an affinity between the earth and women and who worshipped not gods, but goddesses, as representatives of nature's cycle of regeneration, so Faulkner's women embody the power of cyclical renewal, and Faulkner's men seek the status of an almighty father-god, with the power to control nature and women. This tension between Faulkner's men and women, between transcendence and immanence may help to explain the often observed misogyny in Faulkner's fiction. For example, Quentin's indictment, "the dungeon was mother herself" (215), may allude to his mother's role as a channel of the life force. In other words, the mother is perceived as dungeon because she embodies the trap of cyclical renewal. Women are hated as representatives of nature's power to transform and replace.

As for Faulkner's own attitude toward these conflicting religious impulses in his novels—one postulating a god in nature, the other, a god above nature—from what we know about Faulkner's life and from his public statements, it would seem safe to conclude that Faulkner, like Quentin Compson, yearned for transcendence of seasonal renewal. More specifically, the myth of the eternal return teaches that death is the necessary precondition for the appearance of a new form and therefore human beings should aspire to a collective, rather than individual immortality. But the express goal of Faulkner's whole life's work, his career as a novelist, was to "say No to death,"[14] to achieve personal immortality, to scribble " 'Kilroy was here' on the wall of the final and irrevocable oblivion which he must someday pass."[15] Moreover, the myth of eternal recurrence holds that there is no transcendent god who controls nature, that there is no god but nature; but Faulkner, through fiction-writing, achieved his own transcendence of natural law, as author, the transcendent god of his fictional world. In an interview with Jean Stein, he explained the godlike omnipotence of the writer, "so I created a cosmos of my own. I can move these people around like god, not only in space but in time too."[16] Through fiction-writing, Faulkner achieved what Quentin Compson longed for, transcendence of the natural order. And the products of his creation, his novels, as artifacts, exist outside of periodic becoming.

On the other hand, the repeated appearance of the Demeter myth in so many Faulkner novels suggests that, while he might resist, he could never dismiss the power of periodic becoming or its mythic expression. The goddesses of transformation, Demeter and her daughter, archetypes buried in Faulkner's unconscious along with the notion of ceaseless cosmic transformation, erupted in novel after novel, in a return of the repressed. In the end, then, Faulkner could perhaps be characterized as a reluctant exponent of the myth of the eternal return.

NOTES

1. For my discussion of Demeter and Persephone as personifications of the corn, I am indebted to James G. Frazer, *The Golden Bough*, 1 vol. (1890; New York: Avenel, 1981), 330–62. My interpretation of archaic ontology owes much to Mircea Eliade's *Patterns in Comparative Religion*, trans. Rosemary Sheed (1958; New York: New American Library, 1974) and *The Myth of the Eternal Return or, Cosmos and History*, trans. Willard R. Trask (1949; Princeton: Princeton University Press, 1954). Demeter is of course one avatar of the Great Goddess, the subject of Erich Neumann's authoritative study, *The Great Mother: An Analysis of the Archetype*, trans. Ralph Manheim (Princeton: Princeton University Press, 1972).

2. Critics who have suggested the importance of a primitive cosmogony in Faulkner's novels include Barbara M. Cross, "*The Sound and the Fury:* The Pattern of Sacrifice," *Arizona Quarterly* 16 (Spring 1960): 5–16; Virginia V. Hlavsa, "The Levity of *Light in August*," *Faulkner and Humor*, ed. Doreen Fowler and Ann J. Abadie (Jackson: University Press of Mississippi, 1986), 47–56; and Glenn Meeter, "Male and Female in *Light in August* and *The Hamlet:* Faulkner's 'Mythical Method,'" *Studies in the Novel* (Winter 1988): 404–15. In *Faulkner's Women: The Myth and the Muse* (Montreal: McGill-Queen's University Press, 1977), 61–95, David Williams discusses avatars of the Great Goddess in Faulkner's fiction. My essay builds on Williams's findings by examining Faulkner's use of a specific mythic pattern: the Demeter/Persephone story. Williams's study, in turn, builds on an early article by Karl E. Zink, "Faulkner's Garden: Women and the Immemorial Earth," *Modern Fiction Studies* 2 (1956): 139–49, which proposes that women are identified with "the old earth" in Faulkner's novels. A number of critics have observed that the myth of Demeter and Persephone informs Faulkner's fiction. In *Faulkner: Myth and Motion* (Princeton: Princeton University Press, 1968), 59, Richard P. Adams argues that Faulkner's novels employ Eliot's mythic method and that the Demeter/Persephone paradigm structures and organizes *Sanctuary.* References to the Demeter story in *Sanctuary* are also analyzed by Thomas L. McHaney in his essay, "*Sanctuary* and Frazer's Slain Kings," *Mississippi Quarterly* 24 (971): 223–45; rpt. in *Twentieth Century Interpretations of "Sanctuary,"* ed. J. Douglas Canfield (Englewood Cliffs: Prentice-Hall, 1982), 79–92. In "The Pairing of *The Sound and the Fury* and *As I Lay Dying*," *Princeton University Library Chronicle* 18 (Spring 1957): 119–20, Carvel Collins observes Faulkner's use of the mother-daughter myth in *As I Lay Dying.* And in *Faulkner's Olympian Laugh* (Detroit: Wayne State University Press, 1968), 64, 101, Walter Brylowski notes allusions to the Demeter myth in both *The Sound and the Fury* and *The Hamlet* and contends that Horace Benbow in *Sanctuary* represents Demeter, the grieving mother-goddess. In a recent essay, "Mothers and Daughters in Endless Procession: Faulkner's Use of the Demeter/Persephone Myth," *Faulkner and Women,* ed. Doreen Fowler and Ann J. Abadie (Jackson: University Press of Mississippi, 1986), 100–11, Mimi Gladstein argues that "it is in his manipulation of the Demeter/Persephone myth that some of [Faulkner's] strongest optimistic messages are transmitted."

3. *Faulkner in the University*, ed. Frederick L. Gwynn and Joseph L. Blotner (Charlottesville: University of Virginia Press, 1959), 6.

4. André Bleikasten, *The Most Splendid Failure: Faulkner's "The Sound and the Fury"* (Bloomington: Indiana University Press, 1976), 51–66; John T. Matthews, *The Play of Faulkner's Language* (Ithaca: Cornell University Press, 1982), 72.

5. William Faulkner, *The Sound and the Fury* (1929; New York: Vintage, 1956), 109. Subsequent pages references to this work will be shown in parentheses in the text.

6. The tree, as Caddy's symbol and symbol also of the transformative goddess, is discussed by Williams, 75–78.

7. William Faulkner, "An Introduction for *The Sound and the Fury*," ed. James B. Meriwether, *Southern Review* 8 (Autumn 1972): 708–10.

8. In discussing this tree image, Bleikasten finds the relative positions of Caddy and her brothers a "reminder, perhaps, of the mythic mediating function of woman through whom, for man, passes all knowledge about the origins, all knowledge about the twin enigmas of life and death" (34).

9. Edith Hamilton, *Mythology* (New York: New American Library, 1940), 54.

10. See, for example, Neumann, 252, 259; and Joseph Campbell, *The Hero with a Thousand Faces* (1949; Princeton: Princeton University Press, 1968), 249–51, 319, 374–78.

11. *Faulkner in the University*, 199. Faulkner is referring, of course, to the title, *Light in August*, which, he implies, was inspired by Lena Grove's "pagan quality."

12. Williams explains this opposition in terms of the "antivital fanaticism" of "the male spiritual principle" which is "directed against life itself." "Whatever creates, sustains, and increases life—and the feminine is its archetype—is regarded negatively because male consciousness desires permanence not change; it wants eternity and not transformation, law and not creative spontaneity" (82).

13. I cite from the Vintage editions of *As I Lay Dying, Sanctuary, Light in August*, and *The Hamlet*.

14. Quoted in Joseph Blotner, *Faulkner: A Biography* (New York: Random House, 1974), 1461.

15. James B. Meriwether and Michael Millgate, eds., *Lion in the Garden: Interviews with William Faulkner, 1926–1962* (New York: Random House, 1968), 253.

16. Ibid., 255.

"A Passion Week of the Heart": Religion and Faulkner's Art

Evans Harrington

My purpose in this paper is to examine a statement concerning genius which occurs in one of Faulkner's novels, to throw as much light on that statement as possible, and to argue that religion, which is strongly suggested in the language of the statement, played a stronger and somewhat different role in Faulkner's artistic practice than has usually been understood. As is well known, the phrase "A Passion Week of the heart" occurs in a drunken monologue delivered by Dawson Fairchild, a character based on Sherwood Anderson, toward the end of Faulkner's second novel, *Mosquitoes,* and it can be argued that Faulkner was parodying Anderson's naiveté there as he usually did in that novel and was to do later in *Sherwood Anderson and Other Famous Creoles.* But I think—and many Faulkner scholars agree with me—that Faulkner was not mocking Anderson or Fairchild's speech—at least not only mocking them.

The statement occurs on a night when Mark Gordon, a sculptor, Dawson Fairchild, a writer rather like Anderson, and a "semitic man" are drinking and wandering through the streets of the French Quarter in New Orleans. They pass a dead beggar, from whose hand rats are trying to steal a crust of bread. Priests in threesomes mysteriously pass through. Prostitutes accost the drinking strollers, and Gordon eventually goes into a brothel with one. Faulkner also weaves through this real scene a fantastic bacchanal, though the three real characters ostensibly are unaware of it. Fairchild is drunker than the other two and begins to

babble about the life in the dark streets and houses around them.
I quote in part:

> "That's it. That's it! . . . The dark is close and intimate about you,
> holding all things, anything—you need only put out your hand to
> touch life to feel the beating heart of life. Beauty: a thing unseen,
> suggested: natural and fecund and foul". . . .
>
> A voice, a touch, a sound: life going on about you unseen . . .
> beyond these walls, these bricks . . . in this dark room or that dark
> room. You want to go into all the streets of all the cities men live in. To
> look into all the darkened rooms in the world. Not with curiosity, not
> with dread nor doubt nor disapproval. But humbly, gently, as you
> would steal in to look at a sleeping child, not to disturb it. . . .
>
> "That's what it is. Genius." He spoke slowly, distinctly, staring into
> the sky. "People confuse it so, you see. They have got it now to where
> it signifies only an active state of the mind in which a picture is painted
> or a poem is written. When it is not that at all. It is that Passion Week
> of the heart, that instant of timeless beatitude which some never
> know, which some, I suppose, gain at will, which others gain through
> an outside agency like alcohol, like tonight—that passive state of the
> heart with which the mind, the brain, has nothing to do at all, in
> which the hackneyed accidents which make up this world—love and
> life and death and sex and sorrow—brought together by chance in
> perfect proportions, take on a kind of splendid and timeless beauty.[1]

Despite its appearance in what is generally considered a bad
novel, spoken by a drunk who vomits immediately after deliver-
ing it, this passage has long and widely been counted as a serious
and significant statement of the young Faulkner's aesthetic credo.
In 1962 Richard P. Adams observed that "the story of the Passion
Week is so tightly woven into so many of Faulkner's works that we
can almost take as a literal statement of his policy and practice
[Fairchild's pronouncement]."[2] In 1966 Michael Millgate said of
the passage, "Here . . . we find the statement of artistic principle
and belief which seems most fully to embody Faulkner's own
position. Almost as if [*Mosquitoes*], with its exploration and exposition of many different viewpoints, had been the means by
which he had argued out his own uncertainties and arrived

eventually at a clearer conception of his role as artist."[3] In 1976 André Bleikasten compared Fairchild's statement to the artistic theory of Stephen Daedalus in James Joyce's *A Portrait of the Artist as a Young Man*, seeming to take for granted that Fairchild enunciates Faulkner's own view of genius and art.[4] In 1978 Cleanth Brooks described the passage as "the celebrated definition of genius as the 'Passion Week of the heart,' a phrase that was to make its fortune and almost certainly represents Faulkner's own definition of genius."[5]

The passage therefore seems to deserve consideration, and three of the critics I have cited have made interesting additional comments about it. Brooks, asserting that Faulkner was still "an unregenerate romantic" when he wrote *Mosquitoes*, yet notes that Faulkner "insists upon undercutting all romantic expressions and exaltations," including the Fairchild speech in question. Brooks's attempt in that discussion to prove Faulkner's intention of undercutting the passage unfortunately not only contradicts itself but fails to prove his point. But his point itself seems valid. Faulkner does undercut the speech both by having it uttered by a drunk and by assigning it to Fairchild, whom he has portrayed often in the book as somewhat limited. And the rest of Brooks's discussion is very pertinent. "Genius," he states, "is here being described . . . not as an act of making but as an act of vision." He observes, too, that "seeing into the heart of things" is "what Wordsworth called 'spots of time.'" And he comments about Fairchild's vomiting immediately after the vision that "the retching of the body does not necessarily obliterate the sense of 'timeless beatitude,'" but "Faulkner is making the point that our transcendent visions are dependent upon a thoroughly earthy body."[6]

André Bleikasten sees *Mosquitoes* as Faulkner's portrait of the artist, and inferior in literary merit to Joyce's *A Portrait of the Artist as a Young Man*, but he sees "close analogies" between Joyce's and Faulkner's definitions of aesthetic experience and creation: "Joyce's 'enchantment of the heart' is echoed by Faulkner's 'Passion Week of the heart,'" and Joyce's 'silent stasis' is . . .

parelleled in Faulkner's 'frozen time.'" But Bleikasten finds great
differences between the two young writers. Though "both are
indebted in their theorizings to the tradition of romantic idealism,
and both borrow part of their aesthetic vocabulary from Christianity," he writes, "Faulkner's reflections owe nothing to scholastic
philosophy and Thomist theology, and they are far more sketchy
than the highly ambitious speculations attributed to Stephen
[Daedalus]." He comments further:

> In *Mosquitoes* there is no trace whatever of [Stephen's] cold intellec-
> tual arrogance and narcissistic elation; what is stressed is not so much
> the "ectasy" of artistic creation as its "agony": to Faulkner art is a
> "passion" in the two senses of the word. Sorrow and suffering are seen
> to be at the dark core of art as well as of life: "Only an idiot has no
> grief," Gordon says at the close of the novel, "only a fool would forget
> it. What else is there in this world sharp enough to stick to your guts?"
> Stephen's theory of art—not to be mistaken for that of Joyce himself
> when he wrote the PORTRAIT—is still pretty close to pure aesthet-
> icism (as can be seen from its contemptuous dismissal of kinesis).
> Faulkner, on the other hand, is already moving from the shallow
> idealism of his literary beginnings to the tragicomic realism of his
> major works.[7]

Yet Richard P. Adams's comments focus most clearly on the
point at hand. In addition to his previously cited statement about
the story of the Passion Week being "tightly woven into so many of
Faulkner's works," he quotes Fairchild's statement about "the
hackneyed accidents which make up this world [being] brought
together by chance in perfect proportions," and adds:

> Except that when an author consciously, deliberately uses the struc-
> ture and feeling of the Christian legend as a forming principle at the
> heart of his creative activity, as Faulkner repeatedly does, it can hardly
> be "by chance" if he succeeds in achieving something of that "splendid
> and timeless beauty" that Fairchild is talking about. The legend of the
> Fall of Man is almost as ubiquitous, and other Bible matters, such as
> the story of David and Absalom, are clearly present. Faulkner's use of

the Bible is worth a long book by itself, and I have no doubt that some day such a book will appear.[8]

Certainly Adams is right in insisting on the centrality of Christian and other Biblical matter in Faulkner's work. In the present volume there are discussions of, to select just a few, *The Sound and the Fury*, in which the Passion Week not only provides the structural organization but—in Reverend Shegog's Easter sermon—what is often regarded as the structural and thematic resolution; of *Light in August*, again with its evocation in Joe Christmas of Christ's Passion, not to speak of the many other Christian and Biblical references; of *Absalom, Absalom!*, with not only its Biblical title but what Glenn Meeter finds to be a parallel of the creation of the Bible and William Lindsey sees as an edifying inversion of the Judeo-Christian Creation Myth. This conference has provided readings from *A Fable*, concerned completely with the Passion Week—so intensely that the days of that week and the actions described in them were written by Faulkner on his study wall; and from Reverend Shegog, Reverend Goodyhay, and Brother Fortinbride, just three of the dozen vivid minister figures whom Charles Wilson tells us Faulkner created.[9]

At the same time, all students of Faulkner know that he denied again and again being primarily interested in the Christian symbolism in even *The Sound and the Fury, Light in August*, and *A Fable*. Repeatedly he maintained that people, his characters, come first, symbolism second. He stated that the story of Christ was a part of his small-town Mississippi background, that it was just there and his use of it had nothing to do with whether he believed it or not.[10] Add to that his frequent statement that an individual's only immortality is whatever memorable thing he achieves in this life before passing into oblivion[11] and you have to conclude that he did not—most of the time—believe in a heaven, and therefore in Christianity. (I say "most of the time" because, like Nancy Mannigoe in *Requiem for a Nun*, he seems sometimes, even in his late years, to have "grabbl[ed] back at hoping" in a heaven).[12]

So we are left with a baffling question. Why did this author, who consistently denied intentional Christian symbolism in his work, and most of the time denied belief in Christianity, write so often—one might even say obsessively—about Christ, Christians, and Christianity? It is not satisfying to stop with a speculation that he was still playing his infamous, youthful tricks of role-playing and self-misrepresentation, though that possibility cannot be ruled out. Nor is it enough just to make the more cogent guess that his obsession with Christianity came from his doubts about it, that he was pursued by a Southern Baptist or Methodist Hound of Heaven. (His mother's family religion was Baptist; he was baptized a Methodist.)[13]

At this first consideration of the question, however, we should remember Faulkner's occasional variation on his repeated insistence that he was merely using Christian symbolism as a tool, as the best way to tell his story, as when, in Manila, he stated that

I believe that what drives anyone to write is the discovery of some truth that had been in existence all the time, but he discovered it. It seems so moving to him, so necessary that it be told to everyone else in such a way that it would move them to the same extent that it moved him. He is trying to tell that truth in the best way he can. He may know that he will probably fail, that he cannot tell that truth in a way that will seem as true, as moving, as beautiful, as passionate, as terrible to anyone else as it seemed to him, but he will try. He will try through methods, through style, because simply he is not trying to be difficult, to be obscure, he is not trying to be stylish, he is not trying for method, he is simply trying to tell a truth, that which troubled him so much he had to tell it in some way that it will seem troubling or true enough or beautiful or tragic enough to whoever reads it.[14]

"The discovery of some truth . . . so necessary that it be told to everyone else [so] that it would move them to the same extent that it moved him." Again and again Faulkner has spoken of having to write, of being driven by a demon. He said often, as he implied in the quotation above, that if an author has something important to say he cannot be bothered with style.[15] Could it be that what drove him was this Passion Week of the heart, this vision of timeless beatitude which some never know, which some, Fairchild/Faulkner supposes, gain at will, which others gain through an outside agency like alcohol, this splendid and timeless beauty?

More about all this, including alcohol, a bit later. First, it seems advisable to remind ourselves of the intellectual and cultural atmosphere of Faulkner's formative years, say 1910–1925. Scientific Determinism and its literary offspring, Naturalism, had been dominant for decades in France and England and would reach their peaks in America during this period with the Scopes trial and the novels of Dreiser. O'Neill would compound Naturalism and Freudianism with his personal Romanticism. Pound would push Imagism, Vorticism, and T. S. Eliot. Eliot would give a name to the era with *The Waste Land,* and in the same work call attention to the study of primitive religions by Jessie Weston in *From Ritual to Romance* and by Sir James Frazer in *The Golden Bough.* The same year Joyce would bring out *Ulysses* and Eliot would declare in a review of it that Joyce's method of tying his present-day material to ancient myth (the same method Eliot had used in *The Waste Land*) was the only method for ordering literary art in the present chaotic age.

But in the middle of this period came Henri Bergson, a French philosopher who attacked scientific materialism with an argument that had enormous appeal for many intellectuals of the day, including Faulkner. Bergson wrote an unusually lucid prose, using vivid images and metaphors, and his message that mankind was the means of continuing God's initial creation by responding to the vital impulse and creating new works of their own appealed to a wide variety of intellectuals, among them (besides Faulkner) writers Marcel Proust and Bernard Shaw; political philosopher George Corel; painter Claude Monet; and musician Claude Debussy. Perhaps even more noteworthy in the present discussion, many French Catholics were so impressed with the spiritual values in his work that they threatened to substitute his teachings for the traditional philosophical preparation for theology.[16]

Faulkner acknowledged freely Bergson's influence on him,[17] and since Bergson radically questioned the scientific conception of time—most readily designated as clock time—and since Faulkner radically flaunted clock time in his novels, scholars have focused on Bergson's influence on Faulkner's conception of time. Thomas McHaney has pointed out Faulkner's use of Bergsonian metaphors of time in the Elmer papers, which preceded *Mosquitoes*,[18] and Frederick Karl, in his recent critical biography of Faulkner, has demonstrated Faulkner's elaborate and profound use of an understanding of Bergson's conception of time. Indeed, Karl exclaims at one point, "It was as though the Southern writer, despite his brief education, had reached back and touched the mind of the French philosopher," but he immediately seems to belittle Bergson's direct impact on Faulkner by adding that Faulkner had merely picked up "through his early homage to French symbolists and to Mallarmé in particular . . . what was Bergsonian in their practices."[19]

Certainly, Karl has a point about the symbolists. They—particularly Mallarmé—did influence Faulkner greatly. But Bergson's questioning of the scientific conception of time was not his only challenge to intellectual conceptions of his day. In 1907 he published *L'Evolution Creatrice*, brought out in English in 1911 as *Creative Evolution*, and there is ample evidence that Faulkner was familiar with it.[20] This was Bergson's most famous exposition of his "revolt against reason." In it, though he argued that life was an evolutionary process, he not only reiterated his arguments in previous books that science, and also philosophy dominated by science, has an artificial conception of time, and thus of all living reality, but that the origin of life was an *elan vital*, a vital impulse initiated by God. Evolution, therefore, was not mechanistic but creative, and the vital creative impulse was at work everywhere in the world. Moreover, one should not rely on science to understand life, since science was dominated by the intellect, which could only analyze life from the outside. Rather, intuition—a higher form of instinct—was the true channel to the heart of life. When life entered matter it tried using both instinct and intelligence to understand matter and therefore itself. But intelligence far outstripped instinct in dealing with matter, and instinct was left largely to insects while intelligence found its highest development in man and his science. But life needs both faculties to understand itself completely, and its consciousness retains a knowledge of both. In a passage strongly evocative of Faulkner, Bergson writes:

> We trail behind us, unawares, the whole of our past; but our memory pours into the present only the odd recollection or two that in some way complete our present situation. Thus the instinctive knowledge which one species possesses of another on a certain particular point has its root in the very unity of life, which is, to use the expression of an ancient philosopher, a "whole sympathetic to itself."

And a few pages later he goes on:

> Instinct is sympathy. . . . [Intelligence] goes all round life, taking from outside the greatest possible number of views of it, drawing it into itself instead of entering it. But it is to the very inwardness of life that *intuition* [his emphasis] leads us—by intuition I mean instinct that has become disinterested, self-conscious, capable of reflecting upon its object and of enlarging it indefinitely.
>   That an effort of this kind is not impossible, is proved by the existence in man of an aesthetic faculty along with normal perception. Our eye perceives the features of the living being, merely as assembled, not as mutually organized. The intention of life, the simple movement that runs through the lines, that binds them together and gives them significance, escapes it. This intention is just what the artist tries to regain, in placing himself back within the object by a kind of sympathy, in breaking down, by an effort of intuition, the barrier that space puts up between him and his model.[21]

If Faulkner could have reached back and touched the French philosopher's mind concerning his concepts of time, he could equally have absorbed his concepts of intuition and creativity. One thinks, of course, of any number of characters Faulkner seems effortlessly to intuit, particularly of Darl Bundren, whose own intuition troubles so many characters in *As I Lay Dying*— and not a few readers. Or of Faulkner's empathy with the ice in an ice rink: "The vacant ice looked tired, though it shouldn't have. They told him it had been put down only ten minutes ago following a basket-ball game. . . . But it looked not expectant but resigned."[22] Or of his letter to the *New York Times* about the crash of an airplane which had failed three times to hold its instrument glide path:

> I imagine that even after the first failure to hold the glide-path, certainly after the second one, [the pilot's] instinct—the seat of his pants, call it what you will [intuition?]—after that much experience . . . told him something was wrong. . . . But he dare not trust that knowledge. . . . He dared not so flout and affront, even with his own life at stake, our cultural postulate of the infallibility of machines, instruments, gadgets—a Power more ruthless even than the old Hebrew concept of its God, since ours is not even jealous and vengeful, caring nothing about individuals.[23]

I should add, perhaps, that Bergson conceded that science was more efficient and effective in running the practical world; he reserved intuition for the knowledge of the real, inner truth. The last passage quoted leaves some doubt whether Faulkner followed him in that concession.

But Bergson's influence could have gone even further than the challenge to scientific time and the encouragement of intuition. The vital impulse by which God initiated life, according to him, was the result of love, and moreover was love itself. Furthermore, vertebrate life, with mankind its chief leader, was imbued with this vital love, and special human beings—specifically mystics— were most attuned to the impulse. They were the creators, the artists, through whom the vital impulse—what Bernard Shaw called the Life Force[24]—realized itself, gained self-knowledge, the ultimate expression of love. And in a later book, *Two Sources of Morality and Religion,* Bergson would go on to assert that "the complete mysticism is that of the great Christian mystics."[25]

Now I am only two disclaimers short of being ready to present my concept of the role of religion in Faulkner's art, accompanied by some suggestions about how he came to such an attitude. Disclaimer one: fully aware of the difficulties of establishing influences on an author, I do not insist on most of the possible influences I have planted above and will suggest in my argument. My suggestions themselves should make that clear. Disclaimer two: as important as I think Faulkner's religious vision was in his writings, I am fully aware that the vision alone did not make, could not have made, him the great writer he was—something I think he himself tended to forget, or anyway minimize, in his later years, when he emphasized having something to say and cavalierly dismissed style and method. Joseph Blotner,[26] George Garrett,[27] Judith Sensibar,[28] Lothar Hönnighausen,[29] and others have made us aware of the many years—six to eight at least—of diligent poetic apprenticeship he sentenced himself to, wrestling with rhythm, tone, metaphors, figures of speech in revision after revision. And this was before the first two novels. Anyone who has ever had any success with writing knows that one learns the basic rules and methods by just such hard literary labor and then they become instinctive and one can think—unless he or she is a teacher or editor and is forced to observe almost daily how novices do not apply them—that he or she has abondoned them, even forgotten them, which one never does.

My belief is that throughout Faulkner's career his vision was basically what he expressed in Fairchild's drunken epiphany, an epiphany presented in the drunken, limited Fairchild probably because it most often came to Faulkner himself at some stage of drunkenness and because, in his fundamental humility, he felt he was limited (I think he was fundamentally humble, though he certainly was as proud as, if not prouder than, most people). For the relationship between Faulkner's drinking and his literary achievement see Frederick Karl's *William Faulkner: An American Writer.* Karl is the first major critic I have read who insists that Faulkner did not drink just between books but that he drank while he wrote and that he would not have been the writer he was without his drinking.[30] In this connection also it is worth noting that in 1953, after extensive tests, including an electroencephalogram, the chairman of the department of psychiatry and neurology at New York University Medical School concluded that Faulkner

> had an intense emotional responsiveness which was different from that of ordinary people. He had such receptiveness for others that their problems hurt him. On another level, he suffered with problems of the South which were somehow related to his own tensions. He was so sensitive . . . that life must have been very painful for him. Obviously, his alcoholism was a narcotizing device to make it almost bearable for him, but there was not the aggressiveness in drinking found in so many others.[31]

See also Tom Dardis's new book *The Thirsty Muse,* which deals with the alcoholism of Faulkner, Hemingway, Fitzgerald, and O'Neill.[32]

Returning to Faulkner's vision, one might ask if, since his writing changed (many good critics limit his major achievements to the period 1929–1936), did his vision not change also? It modified, mellowed gradually. In those first, great years the spirit of beatitude, love, had a zest, almost a fierceness, so that even the "villains" were embraced in it and imbued with a humanness which is disturbing—perhaps that quality in *Light in August* which Richard King remarks on.[33] Jason Compson in his meanness is so thoroughly realized, so human, that we are embarrassed by him, or for him. Simon McEachern is not unkind, just without human self-doubt and pity, therefore ruthless. Percy Grimm is inspired, almost exalted—his face angelic in his pursuit and destruction of Joe Christmas. And the Player or Providence that moves him unerringly on his brutal mission is the same God who made Joe or Byron Bunch or Lena Grove—or Hitler. Faulkner said of Grimm he created a Nazi before Hitler did,[34] but perhaps he had a model for a Nazi in ex-United States Senator from Mississippi W. V. Sullivan, who in Oxford when Faulkner was eleven years old exhorted a mob to take Nelse Patton, a black man, out of jail and castrate him and drag him around and around the square and hang him on a tree limb across the street from and just to the east of the Confederate statue in front of the Court House.[35] Faulkner must have wondered why God loved W. V. Sullivan.

Bergson's concept of a God of vital love might have given some of this zest to Faulkner's vision and also helped to free it of the God-versus-Satan limitations of the protestantism he heard Hightower deplore (or maybe Hightower was speaking for him;[36] maybe that was not one of the times when, as he described it, the characters took over and he just ran along behind them putting down what they said.[37]) And the studies of Jessie Weston and Sir James Frazer almost certainly helped broaden his concept of the Prime Mover of the universe, particularly with the promptings of Eliot and Joyce in *The Waste Land* and *Ulysses,* just as these rivals' use of myth—and Eliot's pronouncement on the structural value of myth—may have helped him to see how "that Christ story," as he once described it, "is one of the best stories man has invented, assuming he did invent it."[38] And that last phrase, "assuming [man] did invent it," reminds me at least that the vision we are discussing originated in and remained anchored in a Mississippi consciousness. I can easily conceive that it might have been easier for someone born and bred outside the Bible Belt to forget that that story might *not* have been invented and avoid the sensation that Jesus *might* be right up there in a very close heaven feeling hurt at such a thought. But then there was Stephen Daedalus's *agenbite of inwit,* agony of conscience, over not praying at his mother's death bed.[39]

"Oh," one might argue, "but that's Catholic Ireland. That's as bad as the Bible Belt." All right, shall we take a real cosmopolite, say T. S. Eliot, the most celebrated literary convert to Christianity of this century, or his mentor Henry Adams who agonized over the replacement of the Virgin with the dynamo? And could not Faulkner have looked at the pull of that story in contemporaries and near-contemporaries like these and—aside from his own Bible Belt tuggings, or rather in addition to them—recognize the story's power, and also recognize in it, as the anthropologists were heralding, the culmination of what he called near the end of his first novel "all the longing of mankind for a Oneness with Something, somewhere"?[40]

So the zest in the benevolence during those great years may have owed something to Bergson's *élan*, heightened by Eliot's, Joyce's, and the anthropologists' influence, or it may not have needed these, may have come from Mississippi evangelism, which can be very zestful, too. Or, quite probably, the vision might have stayed the same throughout, but the newness, the ecstasy he spoke of feeling in writing the Benjy section of *The Sound and the Fury* and the vigor of his first maturity—"the cold satisfaction in work well and arduously done"[41]—may account for the zest, just as its diminution, perhaps hastened by his drinking, may account for the mellowing and more overt moralizing by the time of *Go Down, Moses*. That makes most sense to me.

But did this vision of Christian beatitude mean that Faulkner believed in Christianity? Not necessarily. Cleanth Brooks spoke, in a passage previously quoted, of the vision's kinship with Wordsworth's "spots of time," and T. E. Hulme (a disciple of Bergson, by the way, and a Catholic) was not alone in seeing Wordsworthian Romanticism as "spilt religion,"[42] a distasteful transgression and obfuscation by art in the realm of religion. In the present volume, moreover, Giles Gunn, Richard King, and Alfred Kazin,[43] in different ways, characterize Faulkner's religion as heterodoxy. And I have no quarrel with their positions. I do not know of an orthodox Christian church which, if it held strictly to its creed and held Faulkner strictly to his public statements and the implications—and explications, in some cases—of his work, could accept him as a bona fide member.

Yet I maintain that Faulkner's work was motivated—driven, as he ofen said—in large part at least, by the beatific vision he expressed in Fairchild's speech. What part was the dream of fame, Milton's "last infirmity of noble mind," I will not try to determine, though a recurrent grandeur of concept in his work—that buck-skin pony in "Carcassonne," for instance, with "eyes like blue electricity and a mane like tangled fire, galloping up the hill and right off into the high heaven of the world"[44]—makes me take note of fame, as do a number of Faulkner's comments like the very early one, reported by Phil Stone, that whereas Amy Lowell and her "gang" had one eye on the ball and the other on the grand-stand as poets, Faulkner had one eye on the ball and the other on Babe Ruth.[45] I have freely conceded that this vision did not account alone for Faulkner's greatness as a writer, and I have spoken of how it mellowed and modified but stayed basically the same as the years wore on. As I approach my conclusion, I want to cite several facts from Faulkner's career and an important obser-vation from another critic, all of which seem to me to bear out my belief.

In the prologue, we might call it, to his vision, Fairchild speaks of beauty as "natural, fecund and foul." That last quality, though often blown out of proportion by his detractors, is celebrated realistically by Faulkner in work early and late, it seems to me—as apparenly to the late Hannah Arendt, according to Alfred Kazin in a comment at the 1989 Faulkner and Religion conference.[46] Fairchild also speaks of wanting to look into all the "darkened rooms." That, too, is a consistent element in Faulkner's works, as critics have often noted; some have even termed some of his works voyeuristic.[47] Fairchild's vision has nothing to do with "the mind, the brain." It is "a passive state of the heart." Aside from how much this might partake of Bergson's condemnation of analytic science and affirmation of intuition, Faulkner always spoke of trusting the heart, not the head; he gave Caddy's effective, if resented, lover a last name which in French means soul—Dalton Ames—and her merely despicable husband the last name Head; and he had Isaac McCaslin explain erroneous statements in the Bible as the result of writings by simple people who had hearts and could reach the hearts of other simple people because "he didn't have His Book written to be read by what must elect and choose, but by the heart, not by the wise of the earth because maybe they dont need it or maybe the wise no longer have any heart."[48]

As early as 1963, though he did not mention the vision of genius in *Mosquitoes,* Lawrence Bowling seems to have conceived the motivation of Faulkner's work very much as I have been trying to describe it. In an article entitled "William Faulkner: The Importance of Love," he noted the argument, frequent even then, that the celebration of the old verities of the human heart—"love and honor and pity and pride and compassion and sacrifice"—in Faulkner's Nobel Prize Acceptance Speech "bears no resemblance to the author's literary practice." Bowling points out, however, that love is the first of the universal truths mentioned in Faulkner's list and that "it is repeated and amplified in three of the other five terms, 'pity' and 'compassion' and 'sacrifice,' which are merely different aspects of love." He then writes:

> If we examine Faulkner's writings in the light of these universal truths . . . we find that love really is the central subject of all his greatest work. We may go even further and say that all of Faulkner's significant writings constitute merely a series of variations on a single idea: *the importance of love.*
>
> This fact has generally been overlooked, for two reasons. First, because of the romantic tradition in literature, most readers tend to identify love with romantic courtships and illicit sexual activity, whereas Faulkner conceives of love in terms of pity and compassion and sacrifice and faith and patience and endurance. To him, the greatest love is based not upon sensation but upon the spiritual affinity between man and nature, between man and his fellow man, and among the members of a family. Another reason why readers overlook the significance of love in Faulkner's writing is that its

importance is often emphasized indirectly through its absence or perversion. The need for love is the central issue in the most un-lovely of Faulkner's books—such as *The Sound and the Fury, Absalom, Absalom!* and *Sanctuary*—in which we behold the depravity and desperation and horror of human actions divorced from pity and compassion and sacrifice.[49]

Finally, the vision, as André Bleikasten noted, is not only of love but of sorrow and suffering—and one might add of pity, which Bowling has noted as another aspect of love and which Faulkner not only mentioned over and over in his later works and public utterances but evoked strongly in his work from his first novel, *Soldiers' Pay,* onward. In his Nobel Prize Acceptance Speech he admonished young writers to make their works grieve on universal bones, and two years later he praised Hemingway's *The Old Man and the Sea* in terms which I think far better describe his own works, from first to last. Hemingway "found God, a creator," he said.

> [H]e wrote about pity: about something somewhere that made them all: the old man who had to catch the fish and lose it, the fish that had to be caught and then lost, the sharks which had to rob the old man of his fish; made them all and loved them all and pitied them all. . . . Praise God that whatever made and loves and pities Hemingway and me kept him from touching it any further.[50]

Substitute for the characters and creatures in the Hemingway story those in Faulkner's "The Bear": The old bear that had to be caught; the big dog which had to catch the bear; the old, poly-blooded man who did not want the bear caught but had to train the dog to catch him. . . . Or substitute the characters in *Light in August.* The old sin-shouter who had to put his grandson in an orphanage, the ruthless man who had to adopt and brutalize him; the tormented grandson who had to kill the woman, who, twisted herself, had to make him kill her, and the young puritan who had to kill and emasculate the grandson. . . . Or Caddy Compson who had to find life and disgrace, and Quentin who had to escape his torment, and Jason who had to live only for selfish gain, alienated from everything and everyone around him.

Faulkner made all these characters and loved them all and pitied them all, and I think he was moved by "that Christ story," moved by it first of all because it is the finest ideal of Western man, even if he or she stops believing it, even if they are romantics dabbling in "spilt religion" or despairing moderns seeing it as man's invention out of his and her desperate need for a "Oneness with Something somewhere." He was moved by it even more poignantly, probably, because of his perception—this man with "an intense emotional responsiveness which was different from that of ordinary people"—that most men and women have never felt it, that "we've never tried it yet, but we must use it—it's a nice glib tongue but we have never really tried Christianity."[51] And with this perception almost certainly came the painful knowledge that even if man had not invented Christianity, even if it were true and available to all mankind, it would be of no help to most people, to the Sartorises and Compsons and Bundrens and Sutpens and McEacherns, to Joe Christmas and Percy Grimm and Flem Snopes—and, yes, probably even to Gavin Stevens. If, to Wallace Stevens, "Death is the mother of beauty,"[52] to Faulkner, its seems, blind death is the mother of anguishing beauty—and, it could be argued, of a new, post-Christian concept of tragedy.

NOTES

1. William Faulkner, *Mosquitoes* (New York: Liveright, 1927), 335–39.

2. Richard P. Adams, in *William Faulkner: Four Decades of Criticism*, ed. Linda Welshimer Wagner (Lansing: Michigan State University Press, 1973), 14.

3. Michael Millgate, *The Achievement of William Faulkner* (New York: Random House, 1966), 74.

4. André Bleikasten, *The Most Splendid Failure* (Bloomington: Indiana University Press, 1966), 28–29.

5. Cleanth Brooks, *Toward Yoknapatawpha and Beyond* (New Haven: Yale University Press, 1978), 144.

6. Ibid., 150.

7. Bleikasten, 29.

8. Adams, 14.

9. See elsewhere in this volume Glenn Meeter, "Quentin as Redactor: Biblical Analogy in Faulkner's *Absalom, Absalom!*"; William D. Lindsey, "Order as Disorder: *Absalom,*

Absalom!'s Inversion of the Judeo-Christian Myth"; and Charles Reagan Wilson, "Faulkner and the Southern Religious Culture."

10. See, for instance, *Faulkner in the University*, ed. Frederick L. Gwynn and Joseph L. Blotner (New York: Vintage Books, 1965), 17, 68, 85–86, 117; and *Lion in the Garden*, ed. James B. Meriwether and Michael Millgate (Lincoln: University of Nebraska Press, 1980), 178–79, 246.

11. Gwynn and Blotner, 61, 65; and Meriwether and Millgate, 193, 106, 227, 253.

12. *Requiem for a Nun* itself may be such a groping; see also Gwynn and Blotner, 100.

13. Joseph Blotner, *Faulkner: A Biography*, 1-vol. ed. (New York: Random House, 1984), 3, 7.

14. Meriwether and Millgate, 204.

15. Ibid., 10–11, 20, 71–72, 220, 239.

16. Irwin Edman, Foreword, *Creative Evolution* by Henri Bergson, trans. Arthur Mitchell (New York: The Modern Library, 1944), passim; Pete A. Y. Gunter, Introduction to the UPA Edition, *Creative Evolution* by Henri Bergson, trans. Arthur Mitchell (Lanham, Md.: University Press of America, 1983), xvii–xviii; Albert Thibaudet and Otto Allen Bird, "Bergson," *Encyclopaedia Britannica*, 15th Edition.

17. Blotner, 511; and Meriwether and Millgate, 70.

18. Thomas L. McHaney, "The Elmer Papers: Faulkner's Comic Portraits of the Artist," in *A Faulkner Miscellany*, ed. James B. Meriwether (Jackson: University Press of Mississippi, 1974), 54–58.

19. Frederick P. Karl, *William Faulkner: American Writer* (New York: Weidenfeld and Nicholson, 1989), 739.

20. Ibid., 1023.

21. Henri Bergson, *Creative Evolution*, trans. Arthur Mitchell, 167, 176–77.

22. William Faulkner, "An Innocent at Rinkside," in *Essays, Speeches, and Public Letters*, ed. James B. Meriwether (London: Chatto and Windus, 1967), 48.

23. William Faulkner, "To the Editor of the *New York Times*," December 26, 1954, in *Essays, Speeches, and Public Letters*, 213.

24. See, for instance, George Bernard Shaw, *Man and Superman*.

25. Henri Bergson, *Two Sources of Morality and Religion*, trans. R. Ashley Ausra and Cloudesley Brereton with the assistance of W. Horsfall Carter (Notre Dame: University of Notre Dame Press, 1977), 227.

26. Blotner, 43–135.

27. George P. Garrett, Jr., "An Examination of the Poetry of William Faulkner," in *Princeton University Library Chronicle*, 18 (Spring 1957), 124–35.

28. Judith L. Sensibar, *The Origins of Faulkner's Art* (Austin: University of Texas Press, 1984), passim; William Faulkner, *Vision in Spring*, ed. Judith L. Sensibar (Austin: University of Texas Press, 1984), x–xxviii, xxxiii–xivi.

29. Lothar Hönnighausen, *William Faulkner: The Art of Stylization in His Early Graphic and Literary Work* (Cambridge: Cambridge University Press, 1987), passim.

30. Karl, 131–32.

31. Joseph Blotner, *William Faulkner: A Biography*, Two-Volume Edition (New York: Random House, 1974), 1454.

32. Tom Dardis, *The Thirsty Muse: Alcohol and the American Writer* (New York: Ticknor and Fields, 1989), 1–95.

33. See elsewhere in this volume Richard H. King, "Gnosticism and Incarnation: World-Rejection in Faulkner's Early Ficiton."

34. Malcolm Cowley, *The Faulkner-Cowley File: Letters and Memories, 1944–1962* (New York: The Viking Press, 1966), 32.

35. John B. Cullen in Collaboration with Floyd C. Watkins, *Old Times in the Faulkner Country* (Baton Rouge: Louisiana State University Press, 1976), 91–98.

36. William Faulkner, *Light in August* (New York: Random House, 1967), 347–48.

37. Gwynn and Blotner, 120.

38. Ibid., 117.

39. James Joyce, *Ulysses* (New York: Random House, 1934), 240, 564–67.

40. William Faulkner, *Soldiers' Pay* (New York: Boni and Liveright, 1926), 319.

41. William Faulkner, "An Introduction to *The Sound and the Fury*" in Meriwether (ed.), *A Faulkner Miscellany*, 160–61. The whole pasage, written in 1933, presumbably at the height of Faulkner's powers, is of much interest here: "[W]hen I wrote Benjy's section, I was not writing it to be printed. . . . And I have learned but one thing since about writing. That is, that the emotion definite and physical and yet nebulous to describe which the writing of Benjy's section of *The Sound and the Fury* gave me–that ecstasy, that eager and joyous faith and anticipation of surprise which the yet unmarred sheets beneath my hand held inviolate and unfailing _____ will not return. The unreluctance to begin, the cold satisfaction in work well and arduously done, is there and will continue to be there as long as I can do it well. But that other will not return. I shall never know it again."

42. T. E. Hulme, *Speculations: Essays on Humanism and the Philosophy of Art*, ed. Herbert Read (Harcourt, Brace and Company, 1936), xi, 118.

43. See elsewhere in this volume Alfred Kazin, "Determinism, Compassion, and the God of Defeat."

44. William Faulkner, "Carcassonne," in *Collected Stories of William Faulkner* (New York: Random House, 1950), 895.

45. Phil Stone, Preface to *The Marble Faun*, in William Faulkner, *The Marble Faun and A Green Bough*, First Random House Edition (New York: Random House, 1965), 8.

46. In answer to a question after his address at the Faulkner and Religion conference at the University of Mississippi on August 2, 1989, Professor Kazin mentioned Ms. Arendt's defence of Faulkner's portrayal of dark elements in human nature.

47. See, for instance, Robert Dale Parker, *Faulkner and the Novelistic Imagination* (Urbana: University of Illinois Press, 1985), 71–79.

48. William Faulkner, *Go Down, Moses* (New York: Random House, 1942), 260.

49. Lawrence Bowling, "William Faulkner: The Importance of Love," in Wagner, 109–110.

50. William Faulkner, "Review of *The Old Man and the Sea*," in *Essays, Speeches, and Public Letters*, 193.

51. Gwynn and Blotner, 100.

52. Wallace Stevens, "Sunday Morning," in *The Collected Poems of Wallace Stevens* (New York: Alfred A Knopf, 1967), 68.

The Dream Deferred: William Faulkner's Metaphysics of Absence

ALEXANDER J. MARSHALL, III

Over the years, critics such as André Bleikasten, John T. Matthews, and Gail L. Mortimer have cited loss as a central thematic and rhetorical concern of William Faulkner.[1] Indeed, Faulkner's major novels often develop around the loss or absence of a major character or event: Caddy Compson (not) in *The Sound and the Fury;* Addie Bundren (not) in *As I Lay Dying;* the rape of Temple Drake (not) in *Sanctuary;* Thomas Sutpen and "the shot heard only by its echo" (not) in *Absalom, Absalom!* As these critics have been quick to note, this decentering has a direct corollary in language in general and in Faulkner's rhetorical and narrative strategies in particular. Loss is inherent in the semiotics of language, in the differing and deferring nature of the sign, in the essential absence of the signified in written discourse.[2] This is not simply poststructural hindsight; these are concerns about which Faulkner himself was rather explicit.

Asked once in a Japanese interview (1955) to describe his ideal woman, William Faulkner replied:

> Well, I couldn't describe her by color of hair, color of eyes, because once she is described, then somehow she vanishes. That the ideal woman which is in every man's mind is evoked by a word or phrase or the shape of her wrist, her hand. Just like the most beautiful description of anyone . . . is by understatement. . . . And every man has a different idea of what's beautiful. And it's best to take the gesture, the shadow of the branch, and let the mind create the tree.[3]

Faulkner's fiction may be understood as a discourse mediating the terms in this quotation, particularly an elaboration of the semiotic ambivalence: Faulkner's "ideal woman" testifies to a belief in some transcendental signified, some metaphysical "Truth"; however, the fact that this "Truth" can only be approached indirectly, by evocation, implies a clear distrust of the signifier's ability to signify adequately. The solution lies in "the gesture, the shadow of the branch," that is, in indirection, evocation, suggestion—all modes of what is generally known as defamiliarization. In short, the familiar is made defamiliar in order that it may be revitalized and seen anew; but inversely, the totally unfamiliar, that which cannot be approached directly—a transcendental signified, for example—must perforce be intimated, suggested, obliquely evoked. [4] In an almost Heisenbergian sense, to depict the tree lessens the tree, while the evocative force of the shadow energizes the text, allowing for the plenitude of imagination. This is finite, fallen man's only way of approaching the infinite; it is the approach Faulkner characteristically takes in pursuit of his dream of perfection.

Indirection is central to Western metaphysics: we think of Zeus who had to disguise his radiant splendor when wooing mortal women. For Leda he assumed the form of a swan; for Semele he appeared variously as a lion, a leopard, a snake, a white bull, knowing full well that no mortal could look upon him in his "awful glory of burning light"[5] and survive—as Semele unfortunately discovered. And the Judaeo-Christian tradition has its own examples, most prominently, Adam, who "dared to eat a peach," as Eliot might say, who dared to directly obtain absolute knowledge, and the rest is, quite literally, the history of fallen man. These lessons in indirection teach us that absolute truth lies beyond the capacities of mortal man. Truth can only be "approached" in this life, and approached only "gradually" and "circuitously," as Emily Dickinson pointed out. Modernists and postmodernists teach much the same thing: truth, if it exists at all, is elusive, ephemeral, fleeting. This should sound familiar to readers of William Faulkner; the elusiveness of truth is one of his major themes and dominant concerns: he too recognized that "no one individual can look at truth. It blinds you."[6]

Faulkner once said that "a proof of God is in the firmament, the stars. . . . a proof of man's immortality, that his conception that there could be a God, that the idea of a God is valuable, is in the fact that he writes the books and composes the music and paints the pictures. They are the firmament of mankind."[7] In effect, Faulkner here is treating literature semiotically, as a signifier of God. Incapable of viewing God directly, man must look upon Him "slant," inferring His presence from Yeats's swan, Bellow's lion, Hemingway's leopard—all transformations of the "white bull," that blank page which is the writer's Chaos.

In his 1933 introduction for a proposed edition of *The Sound and the Fury*, Faulkner tried to explain "the other quality" he had experienced in writing that novel: "that emotion definite and physical and yet nebulous to describe: that ecstasy, that eager and joyous faith and anticipation of surprise which the yet unmarred sheet beneath my hand held inviolate and unfailing, waiting for release."[8] It is Faulkner's "white bull," his blank and thus "unmarred" page that holds his "eager and joyous faith." In the silence that is the unmarred page lies the potential for ecstasy, for surprise, for perfection. The silence that precedes creation also precludes violation and failure—the inevitable results of finite human endeavor. The writer's approach to the silence of the blank page is tantamount to a fall into consciousness—or, as Karl Zender puts it, "silence was for [Faulkner] an ideal condition, a paradisaical state out of which one falls into the imperfection of language."[9] Desiring some prelapsarian (or prenatal) fulfillment, the writer inscribes his being on the silent page, hopefully "scribbling 'Kilroy was here' on the wall of the final and irrevocable oblivion."[10] In this finite world of contingency, desire goes on and on with, at best, only partial and temporary fulfillment. The end of desire is the end of consciousness, the end of language. The fulfillment of desire, the attainment of perfection, is the transcendence back into silence. Everything in between is doomed, in

Faulkner's terms, to failure: "I think that the writer must want primarily perfection. . . . He can't do it in this life because he can't be as brave as he wishes he might, he can't always be as honest as he wishes he might, but here's the chance to hope that when he has pencil and paper he can make something as perfect as he dreamed it to be."[11]

But the dream of perfection is frustrated by the limitations of language, what Faulkner called "the damndest clumsiest frailest awkwardest tool he could have been given."[12] His explicit goal was to "try to express clumsily in words what the pure music would have done better."[13] The pure music would evoke or suggest, and as Faulkner learned from the Symbolists, "to name is to destroy, to suggest is to create."[14] Indirection may perhaps suggest the ineffable and in so doing transcend the limits of verbal discourse that confine the writer to, at best, "splendid failures." For indirection functions by taking advantage of the very contingencies that problematize and undermine language: indirection attempts to manipulate the play of *differance;* it counts on paradigmatic and syntagmatic (associative and combinative) play to evoke that which is not in order for the reader to supply that which is unstated, silent, and hence absent. As Jacques Derrida points out,

> play is the disruption of presence. The presence of an element is always a signifying and substitutive reference inscribed in a system of differences and the movement of a chain. Play is always play of absence and presence.[15]

> The sign represents the present in its absence. It takes the place of the present. When we cannot grasp or show the thing, state the present, the being-present, when the present cannot be presented, we signify, we go through the detour of the sign. . . . The sign, in this sense, is deferred presence. . . . the circulation of signs defers the moment in which we can encounter the thing itself, make it ours, consume or expend it, touch it, see it, intuit its presence.[16]

We might consider, for example, the way Faulkner suggests changes in Caddy Compson by using Benjy as a barometer of her maturation: the way he cries when his sister no longer smells like trees. In fact, Caddy's entire character is evoked by this kind of indirection, by Faulkner showing the effects she has on others and associating her with water, fire, wind, moonlight, leaves, and trees. Or we could consider how Faulkner uses displaced or indirect discourse to suggest Quentin's suicide, what John T. Matthews calls "the great unspoken fact of his monologue."[17]

In *Faulkner's Rhetoric of Loss* Gail L. Mortimer explains this process in terms of the figure-ground reversal, those optically illusive pictures "in which two faces in profile facing one another become, in an alternate view, a vase, the same boundary defin[ing] both entities."[18] By delineating the field, one implicitly defines the object, and, as Mortimer points out, Faulkner "often turns to the *less important* thing (the field or ground) of the two possible focuses because the obliquity of such a description allows the important thing (the object, whichever thing he wants to preserve) to retain its vitality. The object is thus experientially potent for the reader because it is never limited by the inherent finitude of direct description. It is evoked instead."[19]

The result of this technique is a dual and shifting focus: background becomes foreground and vice versa. There is a complementary relationship of content and form, each reinforcing the other, which parallels the near-perfect complement of text and reader. Faulkner presents the shadows, the effects, the boundary of the field; the reader must create or ideate character and act.

This narrative strategy attempts to counteract what Dawson Fairchild in *Mosquitoes* calls the "sterility" of words:

"You begin to substitute words for things and deeds . . . and pretty soon the thing or the deed becomes just a kind of shadow of a certain sound you make by shaping your mouth a certain way. But you have a confusion, too. I don't claim that words have life in themselves. But words brought into a happy conjunction produce something that lives, just as soil and climate and an acorn in proper conjunction will produce a tree. Words are like acorns, you know. Every one of 'em won't make a tree, but if you just have enough of 'em, you're bound to get a tree sooner or later." [20]

In fact, Faulkner did achieve such happy conjunctions more often than not. Largely through indirection, his words did indeed produce a tree, his Tree of the Knowledge of Good and Evil, from whose branches sprouted the "ripe peach" Eula Varner, the arboreal Caddy Compson, and that archetypal bad apple, Flem Snopes, not to mention Lucas Burch, Lena Grove, and the varieties of Beauchamps. Faulkner's garden is "spring-rife" with honeysuckle, wisteria, verbena, and a tanglewood of fallen (and some perhaps unfallen) characters struggling to affirm the "eternal verities of the human heart" in the very midst of the wasteland. Such is Faulkner's "little postage stamp of native soil," the "cosmos" in which he could "move people around like God," [21] the cosmos he created, á la Thomas Sutpen, "like the oldentime *Be Light*," [22] complete with firmament and waters and topography and genealogies: "Jefferson, Yoknapatawpha Co., Mississippi. Area 2400 sq. miles. Population, Whites, 6298, Negroes, 9313. William Faulkner, Sole Owner & Proprietor." [23]

Perhaps the most appropriate example of Faulkner's "metaphysics of absence" [24] can be found in his handling of Easter, the cornerstone of Christendom, and in the sermon of the black minister he apparently named, in an interesting bit of prefiguration, after "the Shegog place," the dilapidated antebellum home Faulkner would move into almost two years after writing *The Sound and the Fury* and, ever the Adamic namer, rechristen Rowan Oak. [25]

The work whose title alludes to "sound and fury signifying nothing" exemplifies Faulkner's ambivalence toward language. While the novel may, in a pessimistic reading, signify *nothing*, i.e., a bleak, nihilistic world in entropic decay, that is not the same as failing to signify. It signifies, among other things, the difficulties of signification itself, the frustrations of "trying to say," of verbal impotence; and in so doing, *The Sound and the Fury* ultimately is a testament of hope and faith, an optimistic affirmation of language in keeping with Jacques Lacan's speech-act theory: "even if it communicates nothing, the discourse represents the existence of communication; even if it denies the evidence, it affirms that speech [read "language"] constitutes truth; even if it is intended to deceive, the discourse speculates on faith in testimony."[26]

The fourth section of the novel presents Easter Sunday, 1928, in a manner designed to subvert and even deconstruct our habitual responses to this holiday. "The day dawned bleak and chill" immediately shakes up our conventional notions of grammar and syntax, and, consequently, our habitual way of ordering reality. We *want* to read "bleak and chill" as adverbs rather than noun complements; the result is a tension between reading strategies, between the prose we believe we see and the poetry we are forced to recognize. The syntactic irony reinforces (and is reinforced by) the semantic irony of the nearly oxymoronic "bleak dawning." And remembering the religious significance of this day only enriches the feeling of dislocation.

As the passage continues, the irony is developed through a series of wasteland images that invert our usual conceptions of April and Easter in ways reminiscent of Eliot's condemnation:

> The day dawned bleak and chill, a moving wall of grey light out of the northeast which, instead of dissolving into moisture, seemed to disintegrate into minute and venomous particles, like dust that, when Dilsey opened the door of the cabin and emerged, needled laterally into her flesh, precipitating not so much a moisture as a substance partaking of the quality of thin, not quite congealed oil. (158)

Rather than awakening in botanical and spiritual rebirth, this April seems cruel indeed; nature is topsy-turvy, "grey," "dissolving," "disintegrating" into "venomous particles, like dust." The symbolic implications are clear: the decay, destruction, and inversion of the natural order parallels that of the social order; yet as the world of the Compsons declines, Dilsey "emerges"—the verb is repeatedly associated with her (159, 171, 178)—"emerges" as narrative center, heroine, earth mother, and repository of what remains of moral and spiritual values in this wasteland.

But even Dilsey herself is portrayed in complex, almost paradoxical terms. She is queenlike yet rustic in her turban and "maroon velvet cape with a border of mangy and anonymous fur above a dress of purple silk, . . . her myriad and sunken face lifted to the weather, and one gaunt hand flac-soled as the belly of a fish" (158). Faulkner's adjectival pairs—"mangy and anonymous," "myriad and sunken"—function almost like merisms, seeming to be inclusive in scope by encompassing abstract vagueness and concrete precision. At once inappropriate and strangely apt, they read with the finality of epithet. "Flac-soled" is another case in point: the odd, apparently meaningless compound conjures a clear image of loose palm-skin, the flaccid sole not of a foot but an aging hand, pale and convex as a fish belly. The strange metalepsis seems incomprehensible denotatively, yet poetically congruent.

This tension between poetry and prose characterizes the continuing description of Dilsey:

> The gown fell gauntly from her shoulders, across her fallen breasts, then tightened upon her paunch and fell again, ballooning a little above the nether garments which she would remove layer by layer as the spring accomplished and the warm days, in color regal and moribund. (158)

Again we confront a dislocating grammar and syntax: what is the object of the transitive "accomplished"? (Or is it a participle?) How do we process the anacoluthic "and the warm days"? And are the "days" "regal and moribund"? Or the gown? These gaps require interpretive choices; we must "rewrite" the sentence in ways commensurate with our personal reading strategies. For many of us, the sentence may make its sense rhythmically more so than grammatically; Faulkner seems indeed to be approaching the suggestivity of music.

In fact, Dilsey's section is energized by Faulkner's Symbolist techniques. Narratively, he attempts something like Dilsey's song "without particular tune or words" (161)—or perhaps, more appropriately, like Luster's trying to coax a tune out of a saw (171). Nowhere is the evocative musicality of language invoked with more force than in the sermon of Reverend Shegog. This "insignificant looking" visitor begins speaking with the voice of "a white man. His voice was level and cold. It sounded too big to have come from him and they listened at first through curiosity, as they would have to a monkey talking" (175). Shegog is, in fact, practicing his own brand of defamiliarization on his "readers" as Faulkner triangulates the effect to his. Faulkner's reader, consequently, is suspended in a paradoxical narrative space: watching both Shegog and the congregation watching Shegog; experiencing both the sensations of the congregation and those of an objective bystander; being both character and reader. We have moved, in effect, from the interior perspectives of the first three sections to a point of view vacillating between interior and exterior as we must read on at least two textual levels.

As Shegog continues his sermon, the audience forgets "his insignificant appearance in the virtuosity with which he ran and posed and swooped upon the cold inflectionless wire of his voice"; they are spellbound until, like "an empty vessel," he pauses and gives them moment to sigh as if waking from "a collective dream" (175). "Then a voice said, 'Brethren.' . . . It was as different as day and dark from his former tone, with a sad, timbrous quality like an alto horn, sinking into their hearts and speaking there again when it had ceased in fading and cumulate echoes" (175). Shegog is modulating his voice, transposing his message from the rational, denotative, conventional "white man's" language to the transrational, suggestive, evocative language of music. It is a magical transformation, a move toward wordless communication. " 'I got the recollection and the blood of the Lamb!'" he says; but the words do not signify denotatively as much as connotatively or even mystically. In effect, Shegog becomes a medium for the music that transcends rational discourse:

He was like a worn small rock whelmed by the successive waves of his voice. With his body he seemed to feed the voice that, succubus like, had fleshed its teeth in him. And the congregation seemed to watch with its own eyes while the voice consumed him, until he was nothing and they were nothing and there was not even a voice but instead their hearts were speaking to one another in chanting measures beyond the need for words. (175–76)

Then the music modulates once more, "his intonation, his pronunciation," becoming "negroid," the congregation "swaying in their seats as the voice took them into itself." Shegog launches into a litany of religious code words, syntactically and semantically incoherent, yet speaking eloquently to a knowledgeable community.[27] His words evoke a realm of Biblical references—Genesis, the Gospels, Revelations—that each member of the congregation could be expected to understand. They can fill in the gaps and re-create the entire range of Christian and slave experiences:

> "When de long, cold—Oh, I tells you, breddren, when de long, cold. . . . I sees de light en I sees de word, po sinner! Dey passed away in Egypt, de swingin chariots; de generations passed away. Wus a rich man: whar he now, O breddren? Wus a po man: whar he now, O sistuhn? Oh I tells you, ef you aint got de milk en de dew of de old salvation when de long, cold years rolls away!"
> "Yes, Jesus!"
> "I tells you, breddren, en I tell you, sistuhn, dey'll come a time. Po sinner sayin Let me lay down wid de Lawd, lemme lay down my load. Den whut Jesus gwine say, O breddren? O sistuhn? Is you got de ricklickshun en de Blood of de Lamb? Case I aint gwine load down heaven!" (176)

The sermon evokes the ultimate nonverbal response, a "concerted" "Mmmmmmmmmmmmm!" from the congregation, "and still another, without words, like bubbles rising in water" (176–77). Even one member's attempt at analysis finds language insufficient—"'He sho a preacher, mon! He didn't look like much at first, but hush!'" (177)—the concluding imperative a colloquial inexpressibility topos. The entire movement of the sermon has been towards this silence, the effective death of the Word. It is Faulkner's religious paradox: only through its apparent death can the finite signifier hope to transcend its limitations; the death of Word is the precondition of its resurrection. Like the soul that comes from God and only through death can return to everlasting life, the word comes from the silence of the writer's creative imagination and can only find meaning in the silence of the reader's re-creation.

To this end, Reverend Shegog's sermon recapitulates in reverse the narrative strategies of the novel itself, from the cold, rational "white man's language" of Jason to the irrational language of Quentin to the meaningless yet meaning-full moan of Benjy. The sermon is an eloquent example of transcendent, nonverbal communication in a world of verbal impotence. As these assertions imply, Shegog's discourse is a distillation of Faulkner's characteristic narrative technique, i.e., indirect discourse that *presents* its message through evocative play. The sermon relies heavily upon the suggestive power of metaphor and metonymy, the two "poles" of language Jakobson equates with the paradigmatic and syntagmatic axes of similarity and contiguity:[28] "The blood of the lamb!" (175); "de blastin, blindin sight!" (177); "Calvary, wid de sacred trees"; "de thief en de murderer en de least of dese"; "de resurrection en de light"; "de doom crack en de golden horns shoutin down de glory" (177). One of Shegog's tropes—"I sees de light en I sees de word" (176)—alludes to the opening of The Gospel According to John:

> In the beginning was the Word, and the Word was with God, and the Word was God. He was in the beginning with God; all things were made through him, and without him was not anything made that was made. In him was life, and the life was the light of men. The light shines in the darkness, and the darkness has not overcome it. (1:1–5)

This equation of the Word with God, a substitution emphasized by the personifying pronouns, reminds us that either may be said to be "the Alpha and the Omega, the first and the last, the beginning and the end" (Revelations, 22:13). One might argue that whatever we know of virtually anything begins and ends with language, just as one might argue the same for God. Moreover, both the Word and God are "deferred presences": With neither can we "encounter the thing itself, make it ours, consume it or expend it, touch it, see it, intuit its presence."[29] Both are marked by "the very principle of difference which," according to Derrida, "holds that an element functions and signifies, takes on or conveys meaning, only by referring to another past or future element in an economy of traces."[30] Shegog's agenda (and Faulkner's) calls for the metaphorical evocation of the absent "element," what Derrida would call the "transcendental signified," that which "in its essence, would refer to no signifier, would exceed the chain of signs, and would no longer itself function as a signifier."[31] Such transcendence would mark the place where semiosis, *differance,* play, displacement, disjunction, irony, absence, and so forth, all come to an end in the thing itself, absolute presence. It would mark the transition from this finite world of contingency to the ideal world of unironized absolute meaning. Appropriately, the Easter Sunday section of the novel concludes a cubistic vision of verbal inadequacy and loss, with Dilsey and Shegog suggesting the possibilities of transcendent signification, while the Compson (conventional) world declines into Benjy's arbitrary, unmotivated semiotic order ("cornice and facade flow[ing] smoothly . . . from left to right, post and tree, window and doorway and signboard each in its ordered place" [191]).

But this section is simply the most explicitly religious example of the metaphysics of absence. The same mediating discourse can be found throughout Faulkner's works; that is what energizes the Faulknerian voice; it is apparent every time he "revs up" to indicate that something significant is occurring. We may look, for instance, at what appears to be a purely secular and even profane example—Ike Snopes's union with his beloved (and perhaps sacred?) cow—and find the same evocative intensity.

In *The Hamlet,* Faulkner describes Ike waiting for his love:

He would lie amid the waking instant of earth's teeming life, the motionless fronds of water-heavy grasses stooping into the mist before his face in black, fixed curves, along each parabola of which the marching drops held in minute magnification the dawn's rosy miniatures, smelling and even tasting the rich, slow, warm barn-reek milk-reek, the flowing immemorial female, hearing the slow planting and the plopping suck of each deliberate cloven mud-spreading hoof, invisible still in the mist loud with its hymeneal choristers.[32]

Through lyrical, synaesthetic language Faulkner evokes a pastoral scene of religious rapture. In this epithalamium, the consummation is depicted elliptically, metaphorically:

It was as if the rain were actually seeking the two of them, . . . finding them finally in a bright intransegent [sic] fury. The pine-snoring wind dropped, then gathered; in an anticlimax of complete vacuum the shaggy pelt of earth became overblown like that of a receptive mare for the rampant crash, the furious brief fecundation which, still, rampant, seeded itself in flash and glare of noise and fury and then was gone, vanished; then the actual rain. . . . (184)

Following the "storm," Ike "breaks with drinking the reversed drinking of his drowned and faded image" in the spring, the "well of days" that "holds in tranquil paradox of suspended precipitation dawn, noon, and sunset; yesterday, today, and tomorrow" (186). Because of the similarities between Ike and his cow, we may interpret this scene in terms of narcissism and the immortality of reciprocating mirror images. In any event, Ike has found a kind of immortality through love, the symbolic death which leads, under most circumstances, to the creation of new life and the synecdochic perpetuation of the self. Faulkner has found his immortality through a similar "rampant crash" and "furious brief fecundation," through displaced discourse and the kinds of indirection and defamiliarization that attempt to revalue the fallen sign and transform arbitrary signifiers into meaningful scratches on the wall of oblivion.

What I have been calling Faulkner's "metaphysics of absence" is clearly a discourse of faith and doubt. Through indirection in its many forms—especially elliptical, displaced, and lyrical discourse—Faulkner's language attempts to reconcile those two poles. Obviously this involves a kind of sleight of hand: like the proverbial sailors in their leaky boat, language must repair itself without abandoning ship. However, indirection, by compelling active reader participation, provides one way of overcoming this apparent paradox—or of "overpassing," as Faulkner would say in *Absalom, Absalom!*, a work that functions as a kind of paradigm of the interaction between text(s) and reader. And in terms of reader-response, we should not overlook the obvious experiential value: the difficulties and enigmas of the phenomenological world are replicated in those of Faulkner's language, in the way it disorients the reader, places us in that twilight state so prevalent among Faulkner's characters, forces new and unexpected modes of reading upon us, asks us to fill in the gaps and come to terms with indeterminacies. First our expectations are shattered, our very conceptions of how we are supposed to read deconstructed. Consequently, we are forced to question our relation to literature, the relation of literature to life, and even our conception of ourselves. (Notwithstanding the "fallacy of expressive form," it seems fair to say that the reader at the end of *Absalom, Absalom!*, for example, *does* experience the kind of psychological oxymoron evident in Quentin's *"I don't hate it!,"* as I hope I've shown we participate in the Easter sermon.)

In effect, the dream of perfection is always the dream *deferred:* deferred ultimately, perhaps, to some "Other" realm of pure meaning; deferred immediately, at least, to the reader who must decode both the said and the unsaid and thereby translate the inscribed text back into a meaningful silence. That is what Faulkner understood when he said "it takes two to make the book,"[33] and when he said, when asked if anyone in *Absalom, Absalom!* had the right view, that "the truth . . . comes out, that when the reader has read all these thirteen ways of looking at the blackbird, the reader has his own fourteenth image of that blackbird which I would like to think is the truth."[34] Nevertheless, the writer and reader's medium, the Word, is fraught with doubt, its inherent absence a constant temptation to apostasy. Faulkner *qua* writer lives literally and figuratively on a papered over abyss, as frozen on the problematic side of epistemology and meaning as Keats's figures on Faulkner's beloved urn. Yet, as a writer, he is compelled to believe, compelled to put one word after the other in the hope that they will "produce something that lives," that through some "happy conjunction" of words he may indeed realize the dream of perfection and those "eternal verities" he was so fond of invoking, "the old verities and truths of the heart, the old universal truths lacking which any story is ephemeral and doomed."[35] Finally (or Ultimately), Faulkner must believe in the face of doubt. He must confront language on its own terms, face the abyss of absence and loss, and attempt to transcend in the only way a writer can, one word at a time, each an implicit leap of faith.

NOTES

1. André Bleikasten, *The Most Splendid Failure: Faulkner's "The Sound and the Fury"* (Bloomington: Indiana University Press, 1976). John T. Matthews, *The Play of Faulkner's Language* (Ithaca: Cornell University Press, 1982). Gail L. Mortimer, *Faulkner's Rhetoric of Loss: A Study in Perception and Meaning* (Austin: University of Texas Press, 1983).

2. Jacques Derrida, *Of Grammatology*, trans. Gayatri C. Spivak (Baltimore: Johns Hopkins University Press, 1976), and *Writing and Difference*, trans. Alan Bass (Chicago: University of Chicago Press, 1978). See also Robert Scholes, *Semiotics and Interpretation* (New Haven: Yale University Press, 1982), and Allen Thiher, *Words in Reflection: Modern Language Theory and Postmodern Fiction* (Chicago: University of Chicago Press, 1984).

3. *Lion in the Garden: Interviews with William Faulkner, 1929–1962*, ed. James B. Meriwether and Michael Millgate (Lincoln: University of Nebraska Press, 1980), 127–28.

4. Victor Shklovsky, "Art as Technique," in *Russian Formalist Criticism: Four Essays*, trans. Lee T. Lemon and Marion J. Reis (Lincoln: University of Nebraska Press, 1965), 3–24. See also R. H. Stacy, *Defamiliarization in Language and Literature* (Syracuse: Syracuse University Press, 1977).

5. Edith Hamilton, *Mythology* (New York: New American Library, 1969), 55.

6. *Faulkner in the University: Class Conferences at the University of Virginia, 1957–58*, ed. Frederick L. Gwynn and Joseph L. Blotner (New York: Vintage, 1965), 273.

7. *Lion in the Garden*, 103.

8. William Faulkner, *The Sound and the Fury*, a Norton Critical Edition, ed. David Minter (New York: W. W. Norton and Co., 1987), 219.

9. Karl F. Zender, *The Crossing of the Ways: William Faulkner, the South, and the Modern World* (New Brunswick: Rutgers University Press, 1989), 30.

10. *Lion in the Garden*, 253.

11. Ibid., 180.

12. Joseph Blotner, *Faulkner: A Biography*, 2 vols. (New York: Random House, 1974), 2:1305.

13. *Lion in the Garden*, 248.

14. Arthur Symons, *The Symbolist Movement in Literature* (New York: Haskell House, 1971), 196. See also my article, "William Faulkner: The Symbolist Connection," *American Literature*, 59 (1987), 389–401.

15. Derrida, *Writing and Difference*, 292.

16. Jacques Derrida, *Margins of Philosophy* (Chicago: University of Chicago Press, 1982), 9.

17. Matthews, 109.

18. Mortimer, 51.

19. Ibid., 51–52.

20. William Faulkner, *Mosquitoes* (New York: Liveright Publishing Corp., 1955), 210.

21. *Lion in the Garden*, 255.

22. William Faulkner, *Absalom, Absalom!* The Corrected Text, ed. Noel Polk (New York: Vintage, 1987), 5.

23. *Absalom, Absalom!* 487.

24. As should be clear by now, I am using the term "metaphysics" in a rather general way, referring to questions of being and ultimate reality. The other terms of my title play with the Derridean concepts of differing, deferring, presence, and absence. In her introduction to *Of Grammatology*, Gayatri Spivak writes that "Derrida uses the word 'metaphysics' very simply as shorthand for any science of presence" (xxi). Consequently, "metaphysics of absence" also functions as a kind of oxymoron, indicative of the paradoxes and tensions that are the subject of this essay.

25. David Minter, *William Faulkner: His Life and Work* (Baltimore: Johns Hopkins University Press, 1980), 121–22.

26. Jacques Lacan, *Ecrits: A Selection*, trans. Alan Sheridan (New York: W. W. Norton and Co., Inc., 1977), 43.

27. Here Lacan's reference to speech as *tessera* seems particularly apt: a *tessera* was a kind of password used in early religions; the fitting together again of two halves of broken pottery signified membership in the community. Ibid., 43; 107 n.12. Note also that Shegog's sermon—and, indeed, Faulkner's overall technique of indirection—is an example of the African-American tradition of Signifying. See Henry Louis Gates, Jr., *The Signifying Monkey: A Theory of Afro-American Literary Criticism* (New York: Oxford University Press, 1988).

28. Roman Jakobson and Morris Halle, *Fundamentals of Language* (The Hague: Mouton and Co., 1956), 76. See also Hayden White, *Tropics of Discourse: Essays in Cultural Criticism* (Baltimore: Johns Hopkins University Press, 1978).

29. Derrida, *Margins*, 9.

30. Jacques Derrida, *Positions*, trans. Alan Bass (Chicago: University of Chicago Press, 1981), 29.

31. Ibid., 19–20.

32. William Faulkner, *The Hamlet* (New York: Vintage, 1956), 165.

33. *Lion in the Garden*, 116.

34. *Faulkner in the University*, 274.

35. *Essays, Speeches, and Public Letters*, ed. James B. Meriwether (New York: Random House, 1965), 120.

Contributors

Doreen Fowler is associate professor of English and codirector of the annual Faulkner and Yoknapatawpha Conference at the University of Mississippi. Coeditor of the conference volumes since 1979, she is the author of *Faulkner's Changing Vision: From Outrage to Affirmation* (1983) and has published articles in *American Literature, Journal of Modern Literature, Studies in American Fiction,* and others. Currently she is working on another book-length study of Faulkner.

Giles Gunn has taught at many universities, including the University of Chicago, the University of North Carolina at Chapel Hill, the College of William and Mary, and the University of Florida at Gainesville. Currently he is professor of English at the University of California, Santa Barbara. An expert in the interplay of religion and literature, he is the author of numerous articles and several books, including *F. O. Matthiessen: The Critical Achievement* (1975), *The Interpretation of Otherness: Literature, Religion, and the American Imagination* (1979), and *The Culture of Criticism and the Criticism of Culture* (1987). Among the works he has edited are *Literature and Religion,* (1971), *The Bible and American Arts and Letters* (1983), and *Church, State, and American Culture* (1985).

Evans Harrington earned M.A. and Ph.D. degrees from the University of Mississippi, where he has taught since 1955 and directed the Faulkner and Yoknapatawpha Conference since its inception in 1974. His publications include four novels, thirteen short stories, and numerous articles and book reviews in scholarly journals. Also, he is the author of the script for the documentary film *Faulkner's Mississippi: Land into Legend;* wrote the book and lyrics for *The Battle of Harrykin Creek,* a musical comedy based on a Faulkner short story; and has selected and arranged passages for dramatic readings called *Voices from Yoknapatawpha*. Professor Harrington has served three terms as president of the Southern Literary Festival Association and was in charge of the organization's programs in 1965, 1978, and 1987.

Virginia V. Hlavsa, who received a Ph.D. degree from New York State University at Stony Brook, has published essays on Faulkner in *American Literature, Bulletin of Research in the Humanities*, and *Faulkner and Humor: Faulkner and Yoknapatawpha, 1984*. Her essay "The Mirror, the Lamp, and the Bed: Faulkner and the Modernists" was reprinted in the Duke University Press publication on *William Faulkner: The Best from "American Literature."* Her book *Faulkner and the Thoroughly Modern Novel* has just been released by the University Press of Virginia. Currently, she is editing a special issue of *Women's Studies* on Faulkner and Women/Women and Faulkner.

Alfred Kazin is one of America's most influential literary critics. Since reviewing *The Unvanquished* in 1938 and *The Wild Palms* in 1939, he has written about William Faulkner in such works as *On Native Grounds: An Interpretation of Modern Prose Literature* (1942), *The Inmost Leaf: A Selection of Essays* (1955), *Bright Book of Life: American Novelists and Storytellers from Hemingway to Mailer* (1973), *A Writer's America: Landscape in Literature* (1988), and *The Almighty Has His Own Purposes* (forthcoming). In addition to writing and editing a long list of publications, he has lectured throughout the world and has taught at numerous institutions, including the New School for Social Research, Smith and Amherst Colleges, Harvard, Notre Dame, Cornell, Berkeley, and the State University of New York at Stony Brook. He is currently Distinguished Professor of English Emeritus, Hunter College and Graduate Center of the City University of New York.

Richard H. King has been a reader in American Studies at the University of Nottingham since 1983 and was a visiting professor at the University of Mississippi during the 1989–90 academic year. A specialist in American thought and culture, he is the author of *The*

Party of Eros: Radical Social Thought and the Realm of Freedom (1972) and *A Southern Renaissance: The Cultural Awakening of the American South, 1930–1955* (1980).

William D. Lindsey chairs the theology department at Belmont Abbey College in North Carolina. His advanced degrees include a Ph.D. in theology from Toronto School of Theology and an M.A. in English from Tulane University. In the spring of 1989 he was a research fellow at the Center for the Humanities at Oregon State University. He is the author of *Praying in a Strange Land: Praying and Acting with the Poor* and has published essays and reviews in *American Journal of Theology and Philosophy, Toronto Journal of Theology, Studies in Religion, Journal of the American Academy of Religion,* and others.

Alexander J. Marshall, III is an assistant professor of English at Randolph-Macon College. His article "William Faulkner: The Symbolist Connection" was reprinted in *On William Faulkner: The Best from "American Literature."*

Glenn Meeter is a professor of English at Northern Illinois University. A talented fiction writer, he has published a novel, *Letters to Barbara* (1981), and his short stories have appeared in *Atlantic Monthly, Redbook, Chicago Review,* among others, and have been reprinted in such collections as *Touchstones* and *Innovative Fiction.* His publications also include *Bernard Malamud and Philip Roth* (1968), a monograph in the Contemporary Writers in Christian Perspective series, and *Faith and Fiction: The Modern Short Story* (1979), edited with Robert Detweiler.

Charles Reagan Wilson is an associate professor of history and Southern Studies at the University of Mississippi. A specialist in religious and cultural history, he is the author of *Baptized in Blood: The Religion of the Lost Cause, 1865–1920* (1980), editor of *Religion in the South* (1985), and coeditor of *Perspectives on the American South: An Annual Review of Society, Politics, and Culture* (1985—) and the *Encyclopedia of Southern Culture* (1989). Among his other publications are five entries in the *Encyclopedia of Southern Religion* (1984), "The Death of Bear Bryant:

Myth and Ritual in the Modern South" (*South Atlantic Quarterly,* Summer 1987), and "God's Project: The Southern Civil Religion, 1920–1980," in *Revisioning America: Religion and the Life of the Nation* (forthcoming).

Index